Under the Bramble Arch

UNDER the BRAMBLE ARCH

*A Folk Grimoire of
Wayside Plant Lore
and Practicum*

Corinne Boyer

Under the Bramble Arch © 2019 by Corinne Boyer. All rights reserved. No part of this book may be used or reproduced in any manner whatsoever, including Internet usage, without written permission from Llewellyn Publications, except in the case of brief quotations embodied in critical articles and reviews.

First North American Edition, 2020
Second Printing, 2020
ISBN 978-0-7387-6587-7

Originally published by Troy Books Inc. 2019
ISBN 978-1-909602-35-9

Llewellyn Publications is a registered trademark of Llewellyn Worldwide Ltd.

Cataloging-in-Publication Programme data is on file with the British National Bibliography.

Llewellyn Worldwide Ltd. does not participate in, endorse, or have any authority or responsibility concerning private business transactions between our authors and the public.

All mail addressed to the author is forwarded but the publisher cannot, unless specifically instructed by the author, give out an address or phone number.

Any Internet references contained in this work are current at publication time, but the publisher cannot guarantee that a specific location will continue to be maintained. Please refer to the publisher's website for links to authors' websites and other sources.

Llewellyn Publications
A Division of Llewellyn Worldwide Ltd. 2143 Wooddale Drive
Woodbury, MN 55125-2989 www.llewellyn.com

Printed in the United States of America

Disclaimer

The content of this book is based on historical information along with the author's own experience. As such, any medicinal or ritual use of the plants involved is the sole responsibility and choice of the reader. It is their responsibility to be educated on proper plant identification, harvesting and recommended dosages, which is beyond the scope of this book. The author and publisher therefore take no responsibility, legal or otherwise, for any misuse of the plants that comes as a result of poor judgement or misinformation by the reader.

Illustration and Photo Credit Information
All photos taken by Claude Mahmood
Self Heal Illustration by Jessica Herrera, 2018
All other illustrations are taken from the Handbook of Plant and Floral Ornament – Selected from the Herbals of the Sixteenth Century, by Richard G. Hatton, Dover Publications, 1960 (1909). Used with permission.
This work is dedicated to all of the ancestors who toiled and worked with the plants to continue the traditions and pass them on to the future generations. To all that was lost, and to all that remains.

Contents

Introduction	*13*
Autumn's Blood and Earth	*16*
Blackberry	*19*
Bittersweet Nightshade	*31*
Thistle/Teasel	*37*
Mullein	*49*
Tansy	*59*
The Witches Mirror of Midwinter	*67*
English Ivy	*69*
Mistletoe	*81*
Broom	*93*
Burdock	*101*
Dock	*109*
Charms of a Faerie Wyfe	*117*
Violet	*121*
Dandelion	*131*
Plantain	*141*
Stinging Nettle	*149*
Clover	*163*
Midsummer Offerings	*172*
Rose	*175*
Mugwort	*191*
Yarrow	*201*
Self Heal	*213*
St. John's wort	*219*
Appendices	
A: The Home Apothecary	*231*
B: Water Extracts – Infusions and Decoctions	*233*
C: Poultices and Compresses	*237*
D: Folk Tinctures	*240*
E: Infused Honey	*243*
F: Infused Vinegars and Oxymels	*246*
Bibliography	*248*
About the Author	*251*
Index	*252*

Specific Recipes and Charms within the Book, created by the Author:

Blackberry Queen Elixir	28
A Baneful Blackberry Charm	29
A Witches Rope	35
Charmed Thistle Garland Against the Nightmare	46
Making Hag Tapers	55
A Wicked Water of Defense	64
A Protective Amulet for the Womb	65
Love Powder	78
Mistletoe Spirit Powder for Scrying	91
Home and Hearth Sweeping Tool	99
Autumn Roots Oxymel for Building the Blood	107
Dock Root Syrup	117
Mineral Elixir	116
Violet Infused Honey	128
Violet Elixir for Grief and Courage	129
Dandelion Wine	138
Dark Hollow Tea	139
Emerald Healing Salve	149
A Nettle Charm for Safe Passage	159
Nettle Banishing box	160
Red Clover Syrup	170
Trinity Protection Charm	171
Rose Elixir	188
Rose Wine	188
Blood of the Rose Magical Ink	189
Scrying in the Mugwort Cauldron	199
Mugwort Orange Elixir	198
Dreaming Salve	210
Witches Winter Brandy	211
Forest Tonic Tea	217
Soothing Flowers Ointment	217
St. Johns Wort Infused Oil	229
Midsummer Oracle Garland	229

Photoplates
between pages 136-137

1. *Author in Autumn Garden*
2. *Bittersweet on Ram Skull*
3. *Blackberry in Flowers*
4. *Blackberry Medcines*
5. *Broadleaf Plantain*
6. *Broom and Birch Sweeping Tools*
7. *Burdock Bouquet*
8. *Dandelion Root Love Charm*
9. *Dock Root Medicine*
10. *Dock Seeds with Spiders Web*
11. *Four Leaf Clover in Locket*
12. *Graveyard Ivy Charms*
13. *Graveyard Mistletoe Altar*
14. *Graveyard Mistletoe in Berry*
15. *Hag Tapper*
16. *Love Powder*
17. *Making Rose Infused Honey*
18. *Midsummer Oracle Garland*
19. *Mullien in Flower*
20. *Nettle Banishing Box*
21. *Purple Violet*
22. *Rose Beads*
23. *Rose Ink*
24. *Scrying in the Mugwort Well*
25. *Self Heal*
26. *St Johns Wort Oil and Iron*
27. *Stinging Nettles Hanging*
28. *Tansy Horseshoe Charm*
29. *Teasel Spindle*
30. *Thistle Garland*
31. *St. Johns Wort in Mortar* 32.
33. *White Violets*
34. *Witches Rope*
35. *Yarrow Infused Wine*

All photographs taken by Claude Mahmood

Acknowledgements

Many thanks to my family and students for their unending support in my work. It is a blessing to share with you all every week. I wish to thank as always my teachers: Carol Trasatto, Joyce Netishen, Bob 'Sandman' Coalson and Johannes Gårdbäck. You all have inspired me more than words can say. A huge thank you goes out to Claude Mahmood for his amazing support, creative eye and tolerance for my need of particulars! I am grateful to Troy Books for their patience and support with this book – I am honored indeed to bring this work into the world with their assistance.

Without the plants and the spirits that are watching and warding, this work would not have been possible. Greatest heartfelt thanks to the invisible realms, for the energy to dream and put into action all that has inspired my heart. To the rustic beauty of the wayside plants, I am forever in debt.

*The virtue of herbs is great, but they must be gathered at night,
and laid in the hand of a dead man to hold.
There are herbs that produce love, and herbs that produce sterility;
but only the fairy doctor knows the secrets of their power, and he
will reveal this knowledge to no man unless to an adept.
The wise women learn the mystic powers from the fairies, but how
they pay for this knowledge none dare to tell.*

Legends, Charms and Superstitions of Ireland, Lady Wilde, 1887.

INTRODUCTION

The realm of the wayside is one of humble utility and careless beauty. This particular landscape often includes a wildness that cannot be tamed and yet there is a human element and influence upon the land as well. Places abandoned, forgotten, and cast aside by humans hold a secret power. The plants that grow and thrive on roadsides, next to graveyards, in wild patches outside of housing developments, near decaying structures or in places disturbed and left are hardy and exist outside of domestic control. Not of the garden, not of the pristine wilderness, the wayside is indeed a liminal edge. The vitality found in such places is Other and onto its own.

Plants of the wayside are often the ones that have been with humans for a very long time and have traveled with them as well. Many of these Genera are native to entire Northern continents, or all temperate continents. On the farmstead of old and with folks whom have walked the agricultural year, these plants have existed and evolved through time. As with all plants, there is an invisible shroud of dynamic power that surrounds these robust and resilient wanderers. The uses material, medicinal and magical have imprinted the plants energy and can be touched and felt just under the surfaces of perception, if one takes the time and care.

Many of the plants chosen for this book are considered to be invasive or are thought of as a nuisance by common folk and even plant folk alike. If we consider that plant intelligence is far more clever than the human mind can imagine, then we can trust that the plants themselves are here in abundance for reasons unknown to us. All reference points are null in terms of understanding the larger patterns of the evolution of landscapes. We are indeed in times of great destruction, pollution, and environmental collapse in comparison to all centuries that have past before now. Losing the diversity of species is the way of it, but is it truly for not? Some plants, such as Scotch Broom and Clover fix nitrogen in the soil with their root nodules after heavy machinery has destroyed the land and English Ivy is thought to be most prevalent in places where air pollution is great. Many of these plants offer abundant medicine for common ailments where populations of humans are high. If only people knew how to use the readily available weedy plants instead of spray them with poisons and discard them as garbage.

As much as I am a lover of gardens and the intimacy that comes with cultivating plants, in truth the flora that exists in the wayside and the forest has always had my heart. The accessibility and wildness therein is not only refreshing and inspiring in the constant face of human control and dominance, but there is a power unmatched in the wild places existing in tandem with the human footprint. These plants belong to no one but are a gift to everyone. The old medicine ways and home-crafted magics are there for the gathering basket in need.

This is the companion volume to my previous *Under the Witching Tree* also published by Troy Books in 2017. The plants chosen are some of the most helpful and haunting plants of the wayside, ones that I could never be without and ones that I work most closely with. It is my hope that both the folklore and personal information provided inspires one to investigate the wild and weedy edges and forgotten places nearby, to find the treasure chest of green magic and medicine awaiting them there. While I do not provide information for properly identifying the plants, as this is widely available elsewhere, my goal is to shed light on the little-known uses of these plants from times past and how they can still be used today.

More than ever before, we as humans need to value the verdant world and get our hands dirty in the harvesting and application of this necessary pastime. My advice is to

Introduction

seek out the plant lovers in one's area and study with them directly; we learn best from seeing, sensing and interacting with the plants throughout the seasons. We remember when a person can show us a wild rose so that we can softly touch large thorns, smell the perfumed blossoms, and see the both vibrant and fading pink on stem, flower and leaf vein. All humans are hard-wired to learn plants, it is for our survival and has always been so.

In keeping with my previous volume of tree lore, there are seasonal poems throughout the text and the plants are organized by season. This is done to provide a roadmap of sorts for contemplation of the plants throughout the year, rather than for a plain functional purpose. Learning the ways of plants takes time, it is helpful to approach them seasonally for many reasons. During the deep winter when the plants are at rest, one can focus more on apothecary and magical work that can be a challenge during the busy times of summer and harvest season. The ongoing cycles of the year ebb and flow with opportunity for different angles and aspects of herbcraft, all valuable to the wanderer of the wild places. The appendices in the back of the book aim to provide more details about simple yet effective medicine making and the home apothecary.

To watch a plants yearly cycle is to behold a mirror of what is also happening in our animal bodies and psyches. The endless creative life and fading death pattern repeats itself throughout the light and dark moons, though not as outwardly obvious to busy minds and hands. The graceful plants of old carry hidden instructions on how to exist with more harmony, nuance and wildness. May we learn from them and take heart – for within everything seen there are many layers unseen. It is from this place of mystery that lies behind the visible where meaning is best perceived.

Corinne Boyer
Maple Mist Wood of Western Washington
All Hallow's Day 2018

Under the Bramble Arch

Autumn's Blood and Earth

Crescent Horseshoe, tell me my future
A ring of blood and earth
Of ash and roses
Of black scented beads from Lady Fate's hand
Walking backwards I spy the carrion crow

Golden sheen comes from Her seeing eye
Stores of rusty oil and Thorns
We tempt Fate and then wait
Within a magical circle, boundaries
Both discussed and invisible

Truth is blood spilled and toil exerted
Dreams vanish like smoke on the water
Bound to me, black claw and garnet dust
Bound to me, the soil of my ancestors
It flows through my veins as milk offerings

Are given back to the earth, to the wise stone
That was born before time was invented
Now ancient whisperings are sung in hushed tones
Where silken braids and feathers once stood
Remember what you asked for

Her altar of red and black medicines
Haunt the hedges, the gateway of bramble arches
Secreted from beyond the talking mind
With treasures dried and kept,
Crafted and tooled with a dead hand

No sleep for tonight, your animal will find you
Scarlet string of black feathers
To send up prayers of acrid smoke
Her tattered velvet cloak
Trails mud on roads less traveled

Introduction

Where fruit becomes wine
In the damp of the cellar
Red liquid traded between mouths
And crossed fingers, the candle burns low
At the meeting and parting of ways

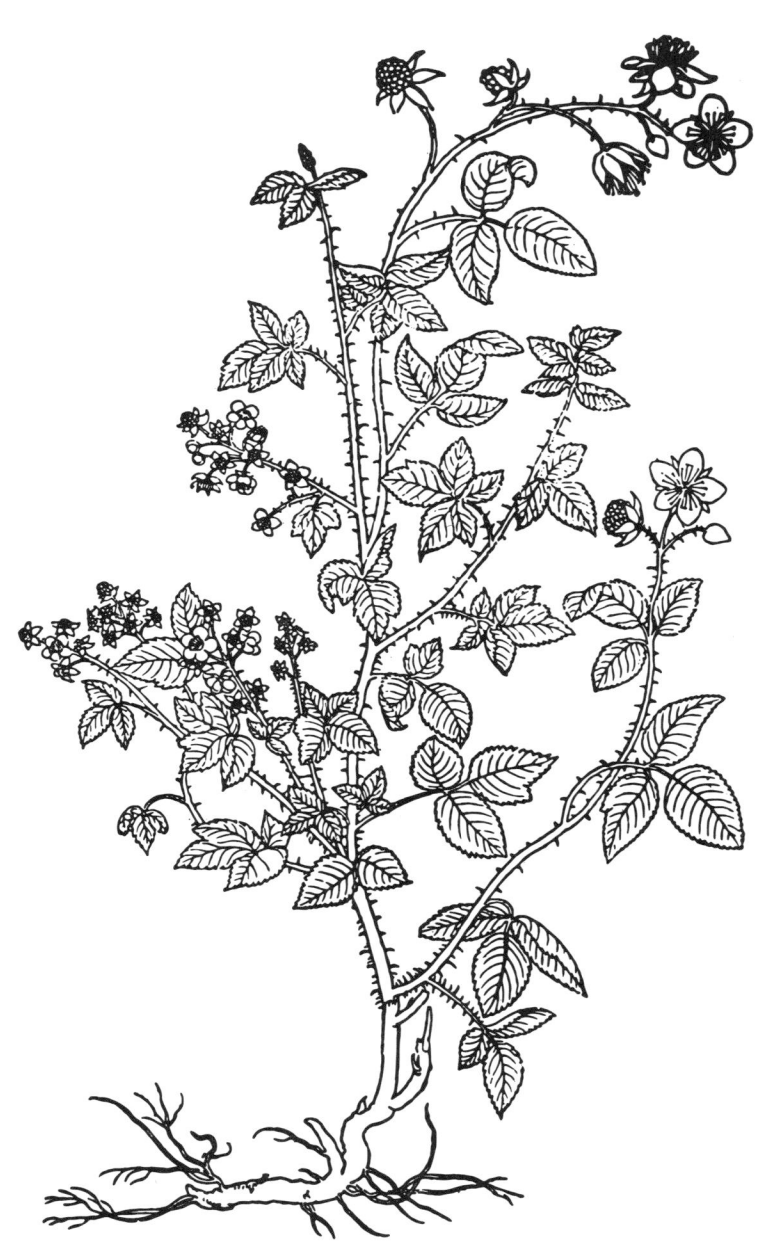

BLACKBERRY
Rubus spp.

Lady blackberry of the wild edges brings a power dark and defensive to the rustic practitioner. Her magics are shadowed in the between places, the disturbed grounds, the uncanny edges of the land. Blackberry briars form thorny tunnels, the purple tinged sharp canes protecting hidden creatures and sheltering many birds. This plant is not ruled by humans, it exists onto its own, forming ill-omened thickets of food and medicine, as well as arches for those seeking to preform various folk rites under its shade.

The *Rubus* genus has hundreds of species within it and belongs to the rose family, *Roseaceae*. Blackberry flowers themselves look like miniature white or pinkish roses, depending on the species. Generally the European blackberry most referenced is *R.fruticosus*. This genus also includes raspberries, blackcaps, salmonberries, thimble berries and many other different aggregate berries. The Latin name *Rubus* has its root meaning in the color red. Some older common names for blackberry included: Black Longberry, Bumble-Kite, Brummel, Scaldhead, Blackbides, Blackbutters and Fingerberry. An old European name for blackberry is simply 'Bramble' and this is still commonly used today. The word bramble is thought to come from Old English *Brymble* meaning 'prickly'. 'Bramble Apple' is another name for a blackberry.

There are many European superstitions that surround picking the berries themselves. Generally it was thought unlucky to harvest the berries after Michaelmas day, September 29th or after old Michaelmas day October 11th, depending on the location. To eat blackberries on this day was believed to bring death to the person before the year was out. Even though the berries are beginning to rot after this time and are unfit to eat, it was believed that they were connected to the Devil, witches and faeries after a certain point. One belief tells that the Devil placed his cloven hoof on the blackberries after September 29, and that it was he who colored the berries black. From Scotland, a belief told that the Devil covered the brambles with his cloak after this time. The Devil was known to spit on them or even possess the berries after these particular dates, some lore tells after November first. It was believed that blackberries became poisonous in October. To stop harvesting became like an offering to the Devil, so that he may have his share. Blackberries were called 'Devils Grapes' from the Balkans, as folklore tells that he tried to grow grapes and ended up with the thorny blackberry instead. The belief that the Devil was connected to blackberries comes from a story about how when he was expelled from heaven, he fell into a blackberry patch on his way to hell.

In some parts of England, witches were known to ruin the late harvest of blackberries, or in Ireland a bogey called a *pooka* did – related to faerie spirits. From Brittany, it was the faeries as well that blighted the late harvest of the berries. Blackberries in general were feared in parts of Europe. They were a taboo food in old Celtic countries. In some parts of Wales, they were unlucky to eat. Some lore tells that blackberry thorns were used to crown Christ and the berries represented his blood.

Despite all of this, the blackberry has been enjoyed as a food source by many European cultures and featured in recipes during the harvest timeframe, from August through the end of September. From Scotland comes a use of the blackberry during the harvest feast of St. Michael, September 29. A cake was made that included blackberries, bilberries, cranberries, caraway seeds and wild honey. It was baked on a fire of blessed woods including rowan, oak and bramble briars.

The time that the blackberry flowers bloomed in May was sometimes called 'Blackberry Winter', as a cold snap was known to occur then. This sounds similar to 'Blackthorn Winter', referring to the same phenomenon when the blackthorn tree bloomed in March. During the time when the blackberries ripen, cats were supposed to have problems and not do well from Devon. Kittens born during this time were supposedly small and weak and more mischievous and unruly than normal. Chickens as well had problems during the blackberry's fruiting season (could this be their natural molting time anyway?). It was thought that a blackberry cut would not heal until the plant that caused the cut was hacked down and burned. Another belief along similar lines tells that a blackberry stain could not be washed out until blackberry season was over.

Symbolically, blackberry stood for remorse. Shakespeare attributed blackberries with worthlessness and lowliness because of the way that they grow. To dream of passing through a blackberry patch meant one was in some sort of trouble. To dream of picking blackberries told of an upcoming illness. To be pricked by them in a dream tells that secret enemies will harm your friends. If they actually draw blood in a dream, it is a bad sign of poverty and difficulties to come. If one passes unhurt though blackberries in a dream however it is a sign of triumph over one's enemies and challenges.

A 'briar' is a name for any thorny plant vine in particular blackberry or dog rose, *Rosa canina*. A blackberry briar that had rooted in two spots on the ground and formed a hoop, was used in folk magic of different sorts usually featuring in transference magic. If a person went under the briar and gave himself to the Devil, he was thought to have good luck in card playing and gambling. From Ireland if one wanted to invoke evil spirits, one was to go under the bramble arch on All Hallows Eve to make the invocation. Other beliefs stated that to go under a blackberry briar would bring the person good health and extra strength. Some magical cures were to bring a child that suffered with rickets or that was slow to walk through a briar three times to help the problem, done three Fridays in a row from a Welsh custom. Creeping under a blackberry briar was also supposed to cure whooping cough especially if done nine times. A rhyme of sorts could be repeated: *'Under the briar and over the briar, I wish to leave the chin cough here.'* Other ailments could be cured as well by this method – boils, hernia, blackheads, jaundice…. Sometimes the charm would only work if each rooted part of the bramble grew on two different men's lands. An offering of bread and butter was often left under the arch, sounding much like a Faerie offering. Even animals were made to pass under this magical arch, for the healing of lameness and other problems.

Some protective beliefs prevailed with this ill-favored plant. Blackberries were at times planted or placed on graves, to keep the dead from walking or to keep grazing animals off of them. A wreath made of blackberry brambles could be hung on the barn or house to protect from witches or evil spirits, hoping to catch the spirit as it passed through – a spirit trap of sorts. Sometimes instead of a rowan wand, a bramble wand was placed in a milking pail to protect the milk. Fumigating the bridal chamber with dried blackberry canes was a protective measure to guard against the ill wish upon the new couple. Though attaching a piece of bramble to a cow's tail on May Eve sounds like a protective practice, in parts of Ireland it was thought to be a sign of bewitchment instead, the cane placed there by a spiteful neighbor. In East Anglian magic a spirit flail was made from blackberry canes. Nine thorny canes were cut in the springtime, usually an ell in length (a measurement from one's elbow to the tip of one's middle finger). They were then bound at one end (leather works best) and used to remove unwanted spirits from a place by way of sweeping magic. One would hold the blackberry flail in the left hand and make a sweeping motion nine times in the other direction to rid of malevolent spirits.

Some magical uses for blackberry leaves included this charm for a burn from Cornwall, England: Nine leaves were moistened with spring water or water from a Holy Well, and laid on the part troubled. As this poultice was applied, these words were spoken nine times. *'There came three angels out of the West. One brought fire and two brought frost; Out fire, in frost; In the name of the Father, Son and Holy Ghost.'*

If a woman wanted her hair to grow longer, she could perform this simple charm. By cutting the tips of her hair and sprinkling them on the new growth of blackberries, her hair would grow by imitative magic. She must be careful therefore to make sure no one cuts the bush down, as her hair would also receive the same effect.

An ancient Anglo-Saxon magical charm for blackberry goes thus: *'against any evil rune (witchcraft) and for one full of elvish tricks (enchantment), Take Bramble apple, pound and sift them, put them in a pouch, lay them under the alter and sing nine masses over them. Then put this dust into milk, drip holy water three times upon it, and drink every three hours'*.

From traditional Balkans magic, the blackberry was known to house female supernatural spirits and Faeries. Its briars were used in folk magic for transferring diseases, similar to above. The blackberry root kept in the home was and is a protective amulet for bringing good fortune and prosperity to the dwelling. To hurt an enemy, a rustic spell involved one catching a frog. The unfortunate frog was cut in two and each half was tied to a separate blackberry cane. Then when the enemy passed by the bush, the one casting the spell was to recite *'Shrivel like the blackberry, hang yourself like the frog'*. A powerful curse would be in effect, to be sure.

A few folk divinations follow. To have prophetic dreams on All Hallows Eve, a girl could search for a blackberry briar grown into a hoop, crawl through it three times in the name of the Devil, and cut it in silence taking a piece home to sleep with it under her pillow. In Ireland, if a man crawled under a blackberry arch he would see the shadow of the woman he was to marry. Interestingly if a girl was walking with her boyfriend and her dress got caught and ripped on a bramble it foretold his loyalty to her. A good crop of blackberries foretold a good fishing season in particular for herring, from Cornwall. Blackberry is ruled by Venus according to the astrologers of the past.

Folk Medicine

Older medicinal uses for blackberry were many. Bramble tips were used for bronchitis in Somerset, applied by peeling the young shoots and nibbling on them as a cough was coming on. In Scotland they were used for asthma. Blackberry vinegar was used medicinally in Lincolnshire for sore throats and coughs. Blackberry jam and the young tips decocted with honey were both older sore throat remedies. Chewing the young tips was thought to help with ulcers of the mouth and gums. Indeed, the young peeled tips are astringent and taste of rose strongly, depending on the species. In Devon England, the leaf tea was taken as a general tonic.

Blackberry leaves were chewed to help with toothache, and the root bark and leaves were decocted for diarrhea and dysentery. The unripe green berries could also be decocted for diarrhea and stomach troubles. Blackberry was used to help alleviate heartburn in the past attributed to 'choler', meaning anger. The tips were chewed for this. Norway folk medicine used blackberry for scurvy and 'melancholy' diseases. The Naturalist Pliny, from around 2000 years ago, recommended a decoction of the flowers and berries in wine to be taken for kidney stones. The berries themselves have long been known to help with anemia. The roots were decocted in Balkans and taken for skin diseases. Blackberry also had connections with women's medicine and has been used for menstruation, conception and childbirth for many years. The leaves are similar to red raspberry leaves and were used as a pregnancy tonic. Here are a few old recipes that involve blackberry for its healing effects on the digestive tract.

Old Remedy for Cholera

2 quarts blackberry juice, 1 pound sugar, ½ oz. nutmeg, ½ oz allspice, boil all together, stand until cold, add ¼ pint

brandy and 1 tsp to 1-2 wineglasses full a day – from 1787, a handwritten recipe.

For Diseases of the Bowels 🌸

Make a syrup of 8 oz. blackberry root, 4 oz. bayberry root, 2 oz. cranesbill, 1 oz. myrrh, 2 oz. cinnamon, ½ oz. fennel seeds, 1 oz. cloves, all steeped in 6 quarts of water for 8 hours at a low simmer until reduced by half. Strain to 2 pints and add 1 pound sugar and 1 pint French brandy

In Dorset an ointment was made from bramble tips and primroses to help with spots and pimples on the face. The leaves infused in olive oil made healing oil for the skin, a remedy for wounds. A very old remedy comes from some of the early literature from the twelfth century – laying blackberry leaves on the breast would help with heart trouble. Greek writers from Classical times believed that blackberry could help with venomous bites. Fresh leaves warmed over a fire and then applied to the skin for wounds was a Romany remedy. A wash made from the leaves was a remedy for sore eyes. Even cancers have been treated with a blackberry poultice, though the part used was not specified. I imagine it to be the leaves. Hildegard von Bingen used bramble powder topically for worms, applied to the infested wound.

The Native Americans had extensive medicinal uses for different blackberry species as well. Many of them were similar to the European uses above. There is a Coast Salish Legend that tells about how the trailing blackberries *Rubus ursinus* came to be. A woman was chased up a tree by her jealous husband and her blood that was shed from above became the blackberry. The Native Americans generally used the leaves, root and whole vine of the local trailing blackberry *R.ursinus* internally for stomach upsets, diarrhea, and as a gastrointestinal aid. The Hesquiat tribe used a decoction from the entire vine for an overall sick feeling. The Kwaliutl tribe made a compound decoction of the vine and roots for vomiting and for spitting blood. Topically, blackberry also had its uses as well. A wash was made from the leaves for wounds, mouth irritations and genital sores.

Personal Practices

Blackberry is a plant that can be used in defensive magic of all sorts. The canes harvested on a full moon and tied with waxed linen into the shape of a pentagram can be hung inside or outside of the home to keep away evil influences. It will shrink a bit, so care is needed to tie it tightly. A small equal armed cross can be made from the blackberry canes and tied with black thread and hung in the windows for the same. Large thorns can be gathered very carefully and dried in the autumn time and kept in glass vials, to be placed in protective pouches when needed, similar to dog rose thorns, which are easier to remove. When tied into a spirit flail, as mentioned previously, the canes can be used to remove ghosts and negative energy from a place. A decoction made with the old brown canes and their sharp thorns, can be used as a wash to clean tools, stones, and any working space needing to rid of stagnant darkness.

The live thorny arches can not only be used to call spirits for healing and for divinations, they can be used in birthing rites where one is bringing a spirit into an object, such as with a house doll or fetish. Done by candle light on the full moon, or better yet in the moonlight itself this a powerful way to invoke the spirit, passing the object under the bramble arch, usually nine times. Crawling under the arch oneself can be done as a cleansing procedure, where the thorns act to catch any darkness or poison affecting the person involved.

The beautiful flowers, if harvested on the full moon and dried, can be used in love magic where one is desiring to draw love to oneself, but is in need of protection as well, possibly from a past tragedy. These dried flowers can be used in fumigations, along with Everlasting *Anaphalis spp.*, dog rose petals *Rosa spp*, and moon daisy *Chrysanthemum leucanthemum* for women's rites during the late summer full moon helpful for healing, bringing fertility and protecting pregnancy. A pouch of these herbs would be an appropriate gift for one whom had miscarried, had an abortion, or hysterectomy.

The whole plant of blackberry is considered cooling, astringent and tonifying. The leaves can be harvested in early May or late April, usually before the plant is in full flower. Remember that the leaves need to be completely dried when used, not wilted. Apparently the *Rubus* genus leaves become temporarily toxic during the drying process due to the presence of some cyanide type compounds. After drying the leaves need to be garbled and put away with clean leather gloves, as they are often slightly thorny.

An infusion of dried leaves is delicious even by itself. Blackberry leaf tea is a digestive tonic for folks that suffer from chronic digestive irritations. When combined with equal parts stinging nettle leaf, it makes a gentle cleansing tea that is supportive during the seasonal changes that often bring fatigue. The leaves are wonderful for women's health issues in general, added to tea blends, such as for painful menstruation and heavy flow. The leaves are also of value in smoking blends – they are spectacular for flavor. They are helpful in a hair rinse for irritated scalp and dandruff. Decocted for a short time, they make a cooling wound wash. The young shoots of blackberry when peeled often taste of rose, they are refreshing and astringent and make a delightful trail nibble in the spring.

The root of blackberry is a supreme astringent, called for when there is any inflammation or irritation of either the GI tract or the skin. The tincture of the fresh root bark is used for travelers' diarrhea and loose bowels, and a decoction of the dried bark can be used for the same. A strong decoction when mixed with salt can be used as a helpful sore throat gargle and for any infection in the mouth and gums. Without the addition of the salt it is a helpful wound wash, even stronger than the leaf wash. It can be taken internally or used externally for bleeding. The dried root bark added along with other roots and cinnamon makes a lovely blood cleansing tea, good for building the blood during the autumn months. The roots can be dug with appropriate offerings made during the late autumn months, the older plants boasting incredible rose-colored root bark covered with a soft black outer layer. The bark is tough and dry just like its medicine, and needs to be washed and stripped off with a knife immediately before more drying takes place. The stripped bark can be dried in open baskets for a few weeks, and then stored. Older larger roots can be carved into pipes.

The berries are spectacular in flavoring syrups, vinegars, oxymels, elixirs, and wines for their nutritional and tonic properties. Besides the many culinary delights that are gifted from berries, they are also helpful for digestive upsets and complaints. Prepared with some warming spices, they are particularly delicious. They are nutritive and full of antioxidants, as any dark colored berry will be. Blackberry wine drunk warm is a lovely tonic on a winter night and as the berries are often free for the picking, there is no end to the creations that can be made by them. Add the syrup to tincture formulas for the digestive system, giving them another layer of flavor and medicine. Also add the syrup to iron tonics for anemia. Make blackberry vinegar or oxymel for a sore throat gargle, use diluted. Make a cordial for sipping on during the winter months, and for infusing with other roots or spices. The gentle yet helpful medicine of the berries adds so much to the winter pantry, capturing the abundance of deep purple potions in the larder.

Many thanks to this wild and unruly dark Queen of the wayside – her black and red medicines in glass, in iron, in leather, so helpful and healing if one is careful of her sharp thorns. As with many defensive plants, there is a great power being protected, if one cares to find it. May we remember to visit her sanctuary regularly, adoring her flowers as the bees do, and seeking out the spirit powers that reside under her thorny corridors.

Blackberry Queen Elixir

On an August or September full moon, fill a quart jar 1/2 full of fresh or dethawed blackberries – be careful about adding too much juice. Add ¼ cup of dried blackberry leaves crumbled, 2 Tablespoons dried root bark, 1 Tablespoon of dried flowers and 3 small pieces of the thorny stem. Add brandy until the jar is ¾ full, then add blackberry flower honey to fill up the remaining quarter. Leave about 1 inch of shaking room. Shake daily for a full moon cycle and on the next full moon, strain into dark glass bottles. Store in a dark cupboard, it will get better with age. This amazing cordial makes an excellent digestive tonic, good for strengthening the system. It is wonderful for anemia and for strengthening the womb. It can also be taken when protection is needed, during vulnerable times. This elixir can be consumed in small sips, three times per day, as needed.

A Baneful Blackberry Charm

To protect one from physical or verbal attack, this charm employs the defensive and sharp nature of the bramble. Have at the ready some dirt from the malefactor's footprint. Gather 13 thorny fresh stalks, about a foot in length. If time allows, do this during the waning moon, while it is old. Go to some spot long abandoned and out of the way and dig a hole in the earth roughly one-foot-deep by two feet wide. Line the earthen hole with the vertical stalks, proportionally arranged, and make a small fire in the center, from alder wood, oak wood and extra dried bramble stalks if available. Once burning, sprinkle the footprint dirt onto the fire, while reciting this simple charm for a total of nine times:

> *'The Old One I summon upon (name), to pierce the violent hand, to bury the violent words, to burn the violent heart.*
> *May there be no rest to (his/her) suffering until the violence departs.'*

Then bury the living fire and fill the hole with the nearby earth. Have the one whom is in need of protection urinate then upon the buried charm, and finally spit thrice upon it. It is thus complete and will work its protective influence to stop all violent actions against the one afflicted.

BITTERSWEET NIGHTSHADE
Solanum dulcamara

Trailing vine of the disturbed and abandoned places, the bittersweet nightshade is like the wild and younger sister to the Beautiful Lady in Black, *Aptropa belladonna*. This rustic vine is often overlooked, however still has a place in the glass bottles of apotropaic herbs in the locked cupboard. A plant of the witch's basket, gathered in secret, she has protective medicine for the humble folk and the practitioner alike.

Bittersweet nightshade is a plant native to Eurasia that has been introduced to the US, now considered an invasive weed in the Great Lakes Region. It is in the nightshade family, *Solanaceae*. The common name of 'bittersweet' comes from the observance of the red berries themselves having the strange property of first tasting bitter, then fading to sweet-these berries are toxic however to consume, so we can leave that observation in the depths of folk memory. This same phenomenon was attributed to the leaves and stems by some early writers and herbalists, which was a low dose botanical medicine. Bittersweet nightshade had the common names of Woody Nightshade, Felonwort, Solanum, Solsequim (Old English), Alprauke (German meaning – 'elfwort'), Poison Berry, Mad Dogs Berries (Scotland), Amaradulcis (old herbal name), Poison Flower, Shooting Star, Blue Bindweed, Climbing Nightshade, Scarlett Berry, Shady Night, Snake Flower and Witch Flower. A name from Sweden translates to 'Troll Berries'. So many common names tell us that this was a widespread plant. This is the most common nightshade in both Britain and is also widespread in the US. This nightshade is poisonous but considered less so than Deadly Nightshade *Atropa belladonna*.

Some magical lore about the bittersweet nightshade is to be found. A protective practice from Lincolnshire wound collars around pigs to cure them from being overlooked or ill wished. From other parts of Britain comes the use of combining the flowering vines with holly leaves, made into a protective garland for horses if they were hag ridden. A quote from English natural philosopher John Aubrey, from the seventeenth century goes: *A receipt to cure a horse of being Hag-Ridden – take Bittersweet and Holly. Twist them together, and hang it about the horse's neck like a garland; it will certainly cure him'*. Culpepper also stated that it was 'excellent to remove *witchcraft from men and beasts'*. From Norway comes the practice of mixing bittersweet nightshade with the heath spotted orchid *Dactyloriza maculata* and adding unspecified tree sap (likely spruce *Picea spp.*) to protect people and animals from demonic forces. Sometimes *Daphne mezareum* or Mezeron was added as well, a magically protective plant native to Scandinavia and Russia.

This plant was used for destruction and cursing in Sweden, if one was hit in the head with this plant it was supposed to bring death to them. From the Scottish Highlands bittersweet nightshade was known as an evil witch plant that could even give one rheumatism if it was touched. Interestingly in other places, it was used as a cure for this very ailment. Garlands of it were worn to cure vertigo and dizziness, from Ireland. Folk magical practices with bittersweet included tying a collar of it around a baby as a preventative for convulsions, which were thought to be caused by Faeries or supernatural creatures. It was also used as a sympathetic cure in the same form for teething babies, a wreath made to fit around the neck. Bittersweet nightshade is ruled by Mercury or Saturn, according to astrologers of old.

Folk Medicine 🌸

Bittersweet nightshade was applied in Anglo-Saxon medicine for various skin ailments, externally. One receipt goes: *For a swelling, take this wort, which is named solatrum, and by another name solsequa, pounded and mingled with oil, lay it thereto, it will do good*. Local Scottish folk medicine used the juice of the crushed twigs externally to treat painful bruises, scrofula (glandular swellings), and ulcers. From Sweden comes a recipe for treating the pain of gout – the ripe berries were mixed and boiled with hops to apply as a poultice (Thank you to Johannes Björn Gårdbäck for this transmission).

As its common name Felonwort tells, it was used for felons, which were also known as 'whitlows'. These are infected and very painful abscesses located on the fingertip. Often unheard of in the modern world, felons were common when people worked outside in the cold with their hands for much of the year. The berries of bittersweet were rubbed onto the part affected, to help ease the infection. Chilblains could be treated in the same way, these being areas of the hands and feet that were swollen and red, due to exposure of harsh weather. Country people would sometimes preserve the berries somehow in bottles for their use during the winter months. Some country people swore that the best way to apply the berries were with the addition of 'rusty bacon', the soothing pig fat acting to hold on the juiced berry on like a bandage. The bright scarlet berries were also used to remove warts, applied externally. The berries infused in lard made into an ointment was an old remedy for piles (hemorrhoids) from Ozark American folk medicine.

Sometimes bittersweet was used internally. I do **not** recommend this, unless you are working with a qualified herbalist who understands low-dose botanicals. The parts used were the stems and leaves. One old English recipe tells to steep the leaves and tender branches of bittersweet in three pints of white wine, the mixture being covered and set on a low fire to steep for twelve hours. The resulting infused wine was to be drunk in quarter pint dosages, in both the morning and evening, for obstructions of the liver, spleen, gallbladder, for dropsy and for breathing troubles. One recipe recommends the dried leaves infused in milk. Bittersweet was an old cure for leprosy, cancer and tumors. On the Isle of Man, bittersweet was boiled in beer and taken as a tonic to treat inward bruising. Bittersweet was a sedative and taken to ease pain, this is no surprise as a nightshade, the family name *Solanaceae* meaning 'to give solace'. In Scottish folk medicine, it was taken internally for rheumatism, fever, catarrh, whopping cough, asthma and jaundice.

Personal Practices

This nightshade of the wayside can be found with its 'witch flowers', climbing abandoned rubble or small trees in its path. It also can be found in hedgerows. It goes on to produce berries in a cluster that ripen at separate intervals, ranging from green, orange and scarlet when fully ripe, reminding one of an eerie rainbow. The handsome dark stems hold the scarlet berries long into the winter months. While I have no internal suggestions or use for this plant, there are a handful of magical ones. The flowering vine can be harvested and wound in a circle to hang up for protection from evil forces, it also can be dried and cut to provide material for amulet bags to protect one in need, in particular while traveling to new places. The tiny beautiful dried flowers can be added to dreaming pillows or bottles.

If gathered from a graveyard (not while flowering), the leaves can be included in divination powders, when fully dried and crushed. Other plants such as marigold flower *Calendula off.* and cottonwood leaf *Populus trichocarpa* can be added as well, sprinkled on the surface of water on auspicious eves of the year, at twilight time for scrying. If the flowers are made into a night essence on the night before the dark moon, the liquid can be dropped on ones pillow for evoking prophetic dreams. The vines are appropriate for binding magic of all sorts, especially if harvested during the dark moon. Bury your bound object in the earth surrounded by bittersweet cords.

Many thanks to this climbing nightshade, a pretty Lady with delicate star flowers and strong magic, berries to feed the chthonic snakes under the hedgerow. May her ways of dreaming bring insight into the black mirror on nights evoked between worlds, may her circlet protect those in need, be they daring enough to find her in the abandoned places during the witching time of the moon.

A Witches Rope

Make this charm as a protective amulet, to hang near the chimney of the home, against fire or dark witches. It can also be used against nightmares and bad dreams, hung above the bed. Before the snow and rains arrive in early autumn on a full moon, gather the longest vine of bittersweet nightshade, and also honeysuckle *Lonicera periclymenum* vine and ivy vine *Hedera helix*. Bind the top of the three vines together with a scrap of red cloth. Anoint each of the vines with one drop of your own blood, or the blood of the person to be protected, who is to be present. Work in silence. Braid the 'rope' while chanting this simple rhyme, over and over:

Woven braid, red, and black, Evil depart, protect the heart.

When finished, tie into a circlet with the scarlet cloth. Animal bones of one's liking can be threaded upon it, larger vertebrae are good. The poisonous nature of the berries red that are produced by these vines, will protect the one whoms blood is stained upon the cords, as will the braid itself.

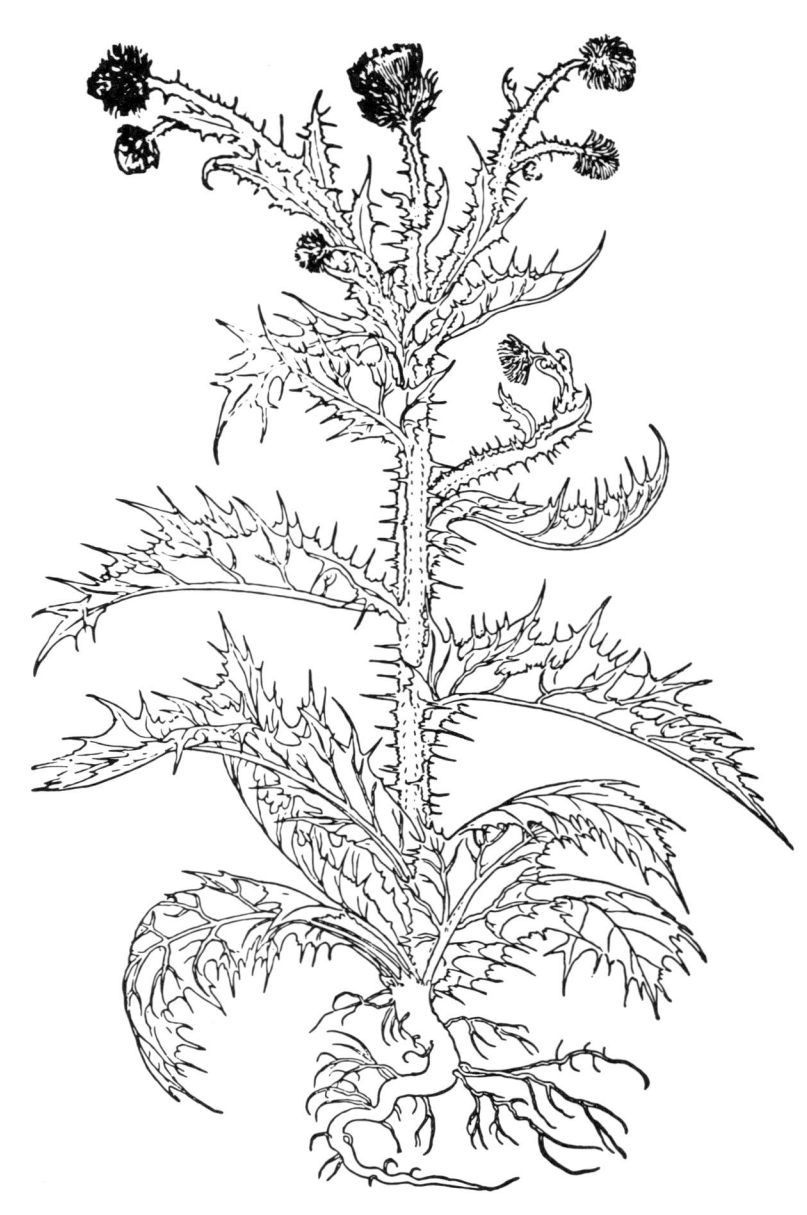

THISTLE
Various Genus and Species

Thistles have long been associated with archaic magical powers, the protective spiny sharp leaves turning fawny during the autumn months, the soft silver silk an offering for bleeding wounds and rustic pillows. They have been said to dwell near the habitats of witches, by the rustic tumbledown cottage on the edge of town. The witch of yesteryear surely used this wayside beauty for magic and healing, so available and accessible on nearly any piece of abandoned or disturbed ground. The thistle makes a stately presence with its gorgeous purple sweet-scented flower heads, adored by bees and butterflies alike. For the ancient healer it was gathered and revered, its uses surrounded by the lore of old.

The thistle plant contains various genus and species, including Scotch Thistle *Onopordum acanthium*, Blessed Thistle *Carduus benedictus*, Milk Thistle *Silybum marianum*, and *Carlina spp.*. Thistles belong to the aster family, *Asteraceae*. There were of course many common names for the different varieties, which I will not confuse you with here. Teasel *Dipsacus spp* is a gorgeous member of the thistle tribe, with a special section below. All of these prickly and spiny plants have a surprising amount of folk magical and medicinal use, little considered in modern herbalism.

There are a few stories that tell us about the thistle being a protective plant. From a Greek myth, the Earth created the thistle from the grief of lost love after the poetic shepherd Daphnis died. From another tale thistle is well known as a national emblem for Scotland because of the commonly circulated but debated story about how it saved the country from a Viking attack. The story tells that the Vikings had to pass through a field of thistle during a secret night time attack, and one of the warriors stepped on a plant and let out a loud yelp. That alerted the Scots to the approaching enemies and gave them enough time to secure an eventual victory thus saving their lands.

This German story teaches about the protective nature of the thistle as well. A merchant traveling through lonely lands forgot to wear his thistle for protection. He got robbed by a jealous peasant, who murdered him out of envy. As the merchant was dying, he invoked a curse of the thistle and threatened the murderer with the thistles betrayal. From then on, the man was haunted by his evil deeds and could not even spend the money and goods he had stolen. He avoided thistles in the nearby fields, and finally confessed to his crime. He was hanged and in Mecklenburg at the murder scene grew a thistle that was shaped like a man. In the ending of another version, there grows a thistle every day at noon at the place where the murder occurred. It grows heads and hands like a human and one time a shepherd passed over the exact spot and he was paralyzed, his staff turning instantly to tinder.

Thistle features specifically in protective folk magic, understandably with its defensive nature and expression. It was unlucky to tread over thistle or step on them. Apuleius wrote of carrying the wild thistle as an amulet to 'avert all ills', from almost two thousand years ago. An Estonian practice was to place cut thistle plants on grain that had begun to ripen in the field, to protect it from evil spirits that might spoil the harvest.

Thistle stalks were used magically for protection, cut on the Eve of St. George, April 22. This was thought to come originally from a Romany custom, often performed by old women. They were harvested before sunset and hung on the doors of cow sheds to protect livestock. These thistle stalks were also placed within protective garlands and hung around the necks of cattle. One older story tells about a man who did not have faith in the power of the thistle.

He began having problems with witches stealing the milk from his cows, they did not produce and were dry upon the morning milking. He wanted to find out the thief and so hid in the barn to see. Around eleven o'clock a large milk pail came into the barn moving on its own accord and went to each cow to gather the milk. When the farmer kicked the bucket over it transformed into a huge toad and he fled to his house in refuge. The following week happened to be St. George's Day and he hung thistle stalks on the barn door. His milk supply greatly increased after doing so and he kept up the practice every year from then on.

An exotic Medieval love potion that came to Europe from Persia included Italian thistle, cloves, laurel seeds *Laurus nobilis*, and sparrow wort (likely *Thymelaea hirsute*), mixed in pigeon broth and drunk. A magical cure from East Prussia involved thistle, for an animal with an open wound. One was to gather four heads of the purple thistle blooms before sunrise and place them in a circle facing each of the four directions then placing a stone in the middle-a sympathetic blood staunching rite I suppose. A Polish cure for 'elf-lock' which is similar to elf-shot or troll-shot, was to burn thistle seeds. Anglo-Saxons carried wood thistle as an amulet against any evil encounters especially effective if harvested while the moon was in Capricorn as the sun rose.

Holy thistle *Carduus benedictus* was used magically in Medieval times. If carried in a red bag and replaced every seven days, it was known to bring good luck. The herb was also used to call spirits. It was to be decocted in water and as the steam rose up, the person looking to receive messages from spirits was to lay near it. It was known to cure all poisons; the leaf, juice and seed infused in water. Foretelling thistle *Carlina vulgaris* was used in Scandinavian folk magic to draw strength and power from another. It was carried in the hand to draw energy from someone while thinking of them in the same moment. The person doing this would gain strength as the other one would lose it. To grow the carline thistle for matters of love magic (unspecified) it was recommended to take soil from a rose garden when the roses were in full bloom, mix this with the semen of a black stallion, and plant the thistle at midnight on a new moon in this fertile soil. If watered with the urine of a white mare, the next new moon the plant could be uprooted, cooked and eaten. One wonders if it was a thistle that was transplanted or a seed that would then sprout over the month to be consumed.

There was in times past a Welsh practice of 'casting scorn' upon the graves of old spinsters and bachelors. People would plant thistles, stinging nettles and poison plants such as henbane upon certain graves. Was this then a way to protect the living from the dead arising, in particular if they were believed to be a witch? It was thought by some that thistles were weeds belonging to Satan. Another name for thistle was 'Devil's Grain'. From Essex comes the belief that the tallest thistle in a group was known as the 'Devil's Thistle' and therefore under protection by Him. This thistle stalk could be used as a walking stick by a wizard or witch, affording the same protective properties to the one bearing it.

Even with their association with the Devil, thistles were protective and thought to be good to plant near the home. This is because they had long time associations with Thor and Mother Mary both beneficial and powerful allies. The flowers of thistle were believed in Nordic culture to come from lightning, another association with Thor. They could protect from lightning if hung in a building. In witchcraft from the Balkans, the silver thistle *Carlina acaulis* is still carried as an amulet against slander and it is also hung in the home to protect it from evil. If placed on an altar, the thistle flower is said to draw protective Faerie spirits to the home. They then are able to act as a guardian of the dwelling. In Russia, the thistle (and burdock *Arctium spp.*) was known as Devil Alarmer or alternately, Devil Conqueror. It was used to protect from demons and witches, protect livestock and cure illness. One rather harsh use to rid of epilepsy was to draw a circle around the one suffering using a thistle, and them beat him mercilessly with it.

Thistle

There were some love divinations associated with thistle. One placed a thistle head at each of the four corners under one's pillow, naming each one after a different suitor. In the morning, the head that grew a new shoot indicated the person's future spouse. Another one tells to pick thistle heads just before they burst into bloom, put them in a dark place and name each one after a potential suiter. The first one to bloom would indicate the future spouse. To dream of thistles was thought to be a good omen overall. If thistle down was to blow into one's window, it was considered a sign of good news to come.

Thistles are a natural weather oracle, they close up before rainfall. It was told that if the thistle down was floating through the air without any sign of wind, it was a sign of rain to come. Thistle is ruled by Mars, on account of its sharp and bitter nature, though some astrologers of the past designated it to Saturn.

Folk Medicine

Thistle juice was applied to bald patches to bring on new hair growth. Thistle down was used by poor folks in the past to stuff mattresses and pillows, along with wormwood and chamomile to keep away fleas and bedbugs. Anglo-Saxons used wood thistle *Carduum siluaticum* for stomach pains by taking the tender leaves and shoots, making a tea of it, and 'sweetening' it with vinegar to drink. This makes sense as all thistles are considered to be strong bitters.

The Scotch thistle *Onopordum acanthium* was used as a Romany folk remedy for cancer. It was also drank as a tea in the Scottish Highlands for depression, I assume the leaves were used. Bitter actions are associated with liver stimulation, which is indeed helpful for states of depression.

Blessed thistle *Carduus benedictus* was used for treating many ailments, including pleurisy, infected wounds, mad dog bites, fever, colds, stomach afflictions, to increase breast milk supply and for the plague. Irish folk medicine used the leaves boiled in milk for an asthma cure, also used for whooping cough. In American folk medicine, it was taken as a syrup to help stimulate the appetite. Hildegard von Bingen believed thistle to be born from the sweat of the earth, which in turn produced 'twisted herbs'. She used 'Lady Thistle' for a stich in the heart or pain in any part of the body, taken and boiled with a little sage.

Milk thistle *Silybum marianum* was also called Marian thistle, as it was believed the characteristic white veins on the leaves were from Mother Mary's milk that stained them when she nursed baby Jesus. It also was used to increase breast milk supply because of this signature. Nowadays we know of its liver protecting properties that are associated with taking the seeds.

TEASEL

Dipsacus *spp*

This plant is one of my all-time favorite wayside weeds. It is so tall and striking, with its strange cupped leaves and claw like flower heads. They dry to a lovely brown, with tiny lavender blooms surrounding the protected barb like head. A lovely Anglo-Saxon name for this plant was Wolf's Comb. Others include Venus's Basin, Venus's Bath, Our Ladies Basin, Shepard's Yard, some Latin names translated to mean 'the Bath of Venus' or 'the Lips of Venus'. The Latin *Dipsacus* comes from the Greek *Dipsao*, meaning 'to thirst'. My own imagination calls this plant the Devil's Spindle.

Dew or water gathered from the teasel plants cupped leaves was used for sore eyes and inflammations of the eyes since Anglo-Saxon times. Other uses for the magical teasel liquid was as a beauty treatment, for removing warts and freckles. The little maggots found in the seed head were even used in folk medicine and accredited with magical powers to cure ague. If they were worn in a cloth bag as an amulet, they were told to help with the fever. If the heads were cut open and an odd number of the little worms were counted, it was kept as an amulet for a charm to keep away sickness. Teasel is ruled by Venus, according to astrologers of the past.

In Wales, teasel was used somehow to protect from witches. Wild teasel *Dipsacus silvesteris* is still used in the Balkans to protect against vampires. It is placed on the front door and above the windows of a dwelling to keep them from entering. Wild teasel was used in the Book of Secrets, by Albertus Magnus. It was tempered with mandrake juice (the part not specified) and given to an animal, to become pregnant and bring forth a baby. This baby animal would have a tooth that if taken and dipped in meat or drink, could be given to promote peace among warriors to begin in battle. Valerian juice was given afterwards – quite a strange use, all in all!

Teasel roots were boiled to make a poultice for abscesses and as a wart treatment. A poultice of the crushed plant was laid on the shaven head to calm frenzies, from a fifteenth century receipt. The dried plant was used in women's medicine to help prevent excessive discharge (possibly indicating an approaching infection) and heavy menstruation.

There were a number of Anglo-Saxon receipts (recipes) that included teasel. One for 'dimness of the eyes' calls for infusing the lower part of wolf's comb (the leaves and stems) in honey for three days, draining off the honey, pounding the stem, and straining the liquid through a flax colored cloth into the eyes. In general teasel root was recommended for liver sickness, dropsy, difficulty urinating, internal worms, and poisons. For worms, one was to take the powder or juice of the root and put it in wine in which pennyroyal *Mentha pulegium* had been boiled, taken then as a drink. Teasel was used along with a list of magically employed herbs for a drink to be taken against all enemies (evil) temptations. It was placed under an altar with the other fresh herbs, nine masses sung over it, then scraped into Holy water. A cupful was given to the person that needed aid, having fasted overnight. The remaining water was placed into the persons food as well.

Personal Practices

The thistle and teasel plants have long held my adoration, their beauty is unlike any other. They have powerful magic hiding beneath spines and prickles. Thistles spiny leaves can be used in banishing powders once dried. If harvested on the waning moon nearest to the dark moon, they are particularly helpful. Use a left hand motion to powder them in a mortar and pestle. Mixed with other protective or baneful herbs, or used alone, the powder can be sprinkled in the footsteps of one whom's attention or affection is unwanted. Or in their pathway. A wash made by boiling green thistle leaves, wormwood *Artemisia absinthium*, rue *Ruta graveolens*, blackthorn fruits or thorns *Prunus spinosa* and salt is helpful for washing tools to protect them from being seen, found or stolen. This wash can also be used to cleanse a room where any unfortunate situation has occurred, by washing the walls and floors with the solution.

Harvest the old plants in the autumn time for the most protective work; seed heads, sharp yellowing leaves, roots and all. Hang in bundles above the entrances of the home to protect from the evil dead or haunting, though expect a bit of a mess from the silver seed down. Bury whole plants near the threshold as well. Once dried, the entire plant can be crushed and saved for protective amulets, powders and whatnot. Thistle is very effective against unwanted entities, especially when combined with St. john's wort *Hypericum perforatum*. Burn the whole plant in the woodstove or fire place to protect the home from storms, most helpful if done while a storm is happening.

The seed and down can be gathered separately and saved for use in protective pouches worn about a person to protect specifically from haunting and psychic attack. If the thistle heads are cut off in perfect flower and floated in water under the full moon's light for a few hours, this essence can be used to bath one suffering from major depression. It can be then poured into their bath, flowers and all with candles burning. Carry a pressed flower head (which will start to go to seed during the drying process) against depression.

The teasel plant can be harvested during the autumn months to hang in the home for protection and beauty. The head or wolf's comb can be used as a spirit trap, placed within the corners of a room or home, also on any altar space to occupy spirits. While still fresh, wind some white thread about the head. There are many seeds inside the head to keep the spirit occupied. The teasel stalk and flower head can be used like a wand for blessing or protective magic. It can also be hung during Lammas Tide, fastened to the dwelling with a piece of white silk.

Many thanks to the protective plants of the disturbed edge, that carry healing waters and baneful spines both. One can imagine lightning striking the earth, and a crop of thistles coming up in the same spot the flowers an Otherworldly color of purple. In iron cauldrons, in white silk, in boiled milk, these wild botanicals work wonders. In pouches, laid on altars, many thanks to the Faerie silk and enchanted spindles of old.

Charmed Thistle Garland Against the Nightmare

When dreams are haunted and sleep is disturbed, employ the thistles power to bring peace and rest. During the flowering time of the plant on a full moon, gather thirteen heads in perfect bloom. Offerings for the plant can be milk or honey in return for its assistance, poured at the root. If possible, sit outside in the moonlight to work the charm. Otherwise being in a candlelit chamber should suffice. Dried heads can be used for other times of the year, but care should be taken to get them early in their opening, rather than later, as the seed down will spill everywhere if done too late.

Have at the ready a spool of thick white thread, a large needle, scissors and a hag stone. Tie a loop at one end of the thread and simply thread the thistle heads, carefully from bottom to top. You will want to use leather gloves for this as they are sharp. Tie the hag stone to the end of the garland, completing its construction. Make it into a circle if so desired. Now fumigate it with St. Johns Wort *Hypericum perforatum* and frankincense. Speak these words over it thrice:

Holy Flower of wandering spirits,
Bitter root of silver fire —
Catch the moon upon your nectar
Hold the Shade on gleaming spire.

Protect the sleeping one encircled,
By way of enchanted power
Restore the dreamer and the dream,
The slumber and the darkened bower.

After these words are spoken and the charm fumigated, it can be hung near the bedstead of the one suffering. The thistle heads will likely burst open with silver fluff depending on their stage of harvest but the charm should stay intact, this being part of the protection offered from such a plant that holds the virtue of lightning.

MULLEIN
Verbascum Thapsus

The witches candle burns brightly to light the dark trail into the hedgerow, tall and stately mullein is a beacon in the night. This beautiful rustic taper graces the wayside and roadside, loving disturbed ground and full sun. The golden flowers have a long season of beautifying the garden and meadow edge. Their perfume is only available at certain hours. Brown withered stalks persist through the winter, reminding one of Faerie candles left long after a season of feasting and dancing. Many tiny seeds are shaken by the wind, waiting for the rain to tamp them, and for the sunlight to crack them open. This entire plant provides much for the rustic apothecary, every part being useful and wholesome. It is a companion on the path, offering much protection and medicine to those in need.

Mullein is in the figwort family *Scrophulariaceae* and is originally native to Eurasia. Some common names for this plant were Mary's Candle, Torches, Velvet Dock, Our Ladies Candle, Blanket Herb, Feltwort, Candle Wick Plant, Candelaria (Roman), Beggars Blanket, Torch Weed, Sheppard's Staff, Ladies Foxglove, Hag's Taper, Hedge Taper, Heavenly Fire (German), Kings Candle (German), Aarons Rod, St. Peter's Staff, Bullocks Lungwort, Poor Man's Blanket, Adam's Flannel, and Hare's Beard. Mullein leaves were rubbed on the cheeks to bring color to them, hence the common name 'Quakers Rouge'. With so many common names, we see that this wayside torch was indeed widespread.

According to some sources, the name 'Hags Taper' did not mean 'witches candle', but hedge taper. The flower stalks were dipped in animal fat and burned at country gatherings and at funerals. Also known as 'candlewick plant' the leaves were used as primitive wicks in fat lamps. The flower heads dipped in tallow were used in Europe in some parts as a torch to frighten away witches, though some lore tells that these countryside tapers were burned at the witches Sabbat, lighting the night for the Devil's dance round the fire and used for light as witches cast their spells. It was said during Victorian times by folklorist Richard Folkard that the 'mullein was formerly employed by wizards and witches in their incantations'. Indeed, we find that mullein is ruled by Saturn, according to astrologers of the past. From Medieval magic mullein leaf was used as an incense in black magic rituals and sprinkled on food for love magic. In Southern American Hoodoo folk magic, the leaf is used as a substitute for or adjunct to grave dust.

Mullein was also thought to be protective of evil powers. Some lore tells that it would repel evil witches and enchantments. From the Anglo-Saxons comes this bit of lore about mullein (which they called 'Feldwort') relating to Greek mythology: *Of Feldwort it is said that Mercurius gave this wort to Ulixes the Cheiftain, when he came to Circe, and after that he dreaded none of her witchcraft... If one weareth with him one twig of this wort, he will not be terrified with any awe, nor will a wild beast hurt him, or any evil come near.'*

Kept in the home, mullein was known to protect one from witchcraft. In Ireland, the leaves were placed under the butter churn to restore the milk from being enchanted and stolen by witches. From Poitou France, there was a custom of passing mullein flower stalks and walnuts across the flames of the protective bonfire made on Midsummer's (St. John's) Eve. These walnuts were used to cure toothache somehow and the mullein was used to protect cattle from illness and dark sorcery likely hung as an amulet. A British practice was to gather a mullein stalk when the sun was in Virgo and the moon was in Aries, thus offering protection from illness to the one whom carried it.

During the Middle Ages, it was said that Mother Mary went through the land to bless the mullein during

Mullein

late summer time when the harvest had begun. If she touched the sick with mullein, they would be healed. One old saying was '*Our beloved Lady goes through the land, and she carries mullein in her hand*'. This lore speaks even more to the protective properties of this common yet magical plant. From Germany's Rhineland, mullein was included in the herbs that were annually consecrated. Similarly from Southern Germany mullein is still placed in the center of the bouquet to be blessed on Assumption Day, a Catholic practice. This bouquet is saved and kept, hung in the home to protect the family from disaster for the following year. If livestock are faced with any ailments or problems, the dried mullein flowers can be taken from the stalk and incorporated into their feed to help restore them. Also, the preserved flowers can be thrown on the hearth fire during a storm to protect the home from damage.

There were some love divinations associated with mullein from early American times. After naming someone if you twisted the flower stalk off of the plant and it continued to live, then it was a sure sign that the one named loved you. By counting the shoots that grew up, you could tell the number of children that you would have. Another related charm was to point the stalk either towards the sun or towards the desired persons home while it was still attached to the plant. If it grew straight again, the person loved you.

Mullein leaves were worn as a charm to ensure conception. Contradicting this, seventeenth century herbalist John Gerard wrote that wearing mullein in the shoe would 'bring down in maidens their desired sickness', which meant to bring on menstruation. He also wrote that carrying the leaf on a person would help prevent epileptic fits.

Mullein acted as a rustic weather prognosticator – if there were flowers low on the stalk, early snows were to be expected. However, a stalk with blooms mostly located at the top of the stalk indicated a long winter with heavy snow later in the season. German fisherman used the seed magically to enchant a fishing pond or hole. They would sprinkle the seed on the waters and then return the following day to catch fish in plenty, thanks to mulleins supposed powers to stupefy and numb the fish into their submission.

Folk Medicine 🌿

One of the first written herbals by Dioscorides *De Materia Medica* from roughly 2000 years ago mentions mullein for lung complaints. Mullein has been used for every known lung complaint, including croup, bronchitis, bleeding lungs, pneumonia, consumption, asthma, coughs and catarrh. Mullein leaves were boiled in vinegar and applied as a poultice to the throat and chest for soreness and coughs and after applied, a few cups of peppermint tea could be then drank to prevent infection. One old recipe calls for boiling the leaves in milk and then straining to drink warm twice per day for afflictions of the lungs in particular for tuberculosis. Mullein leaves were smoked by the Amish in North America for the relief of asthma attacks. The flowers were also used in tea for chest complaints, as was the root for colds and coughs. From South Carolina folk medicine comes the use of mullein leaves mixed with basil leaves and pine needles in a tea for colds and fever. An infusion of the flowers acted as a sedative, to promote sleep. Hildegard von Bingen believed that mullein was good for weak and sad hearts and would make one happy.

Other uses included sitting over the smoke from the leaves for piles (hemorrhoids) and using the juice of the leaves and flowers for warts. The flowers were and still are used in earache remedies made into a solar infused olive oil. I have been told the old original recipe called for the flowers to be put in a bottle, stopped closed, left for a time and the resulting putrid liquid dropped in the ears for relief. The fresh flowers infused in lard were rubbed around the ear and lymph area for pain. This resulting salve was also used to rub on hemorrhoids, frost bite, bee stings and bruises. Distilled mullein flower water was used topically for ringworm and burns.

A wash made from the whole plant including the roots was applied to bruises, inflammations, wounds, and injuries. The leaves boiled in vinegar were also applied to bruises, swellings and sprains among the folk of the Ozark mountains. A mullein leaf roasted between two dock leaves *Rumex spp.* and moistened with spittle was used as a poultice for boils in Ulster, Ireland. From Ireland also comes the use of washing the body with water in which the leaves were decocted, for pain and rheumatism. The leaves were used as a poultice for beestings, running sores, gout and goiter in historical British folk medicine. The leaves and flowers of mullein were also used as a hair rinse, particularly for light hair.

In Colonial American folk medicine, mullein leaf was used in rheumatism by either applying a compress made with the tea to the affected area, or by decocting the root and mixing with whiskey. In Alabama the sugared root was eaten in small amounts, or a tea made from it was drank for the croup. Mullein was also used to treat bed wetting (a few drops of the flower infused olive oil taken internally before bed), sore feet (wearing the leaves in shoes), diarrhea (tea made of the leaves), flu and hay fever in North American folk medicine. Though not native to North America, the Native Americans adopted many uses of the plant as well, including for teething, fevers, rheumatism, and respiratory troubles of all sorts. The dried leaves were a classic ingredient in smoking mixtures as this is another way for the medicine to reach the lungs. Because it is astringent, mullein leaf tea was used for loose bowels, with a decoction prepared with milk recommended.

Personal Practices

Mullein is truly a wild plant in that it seems to do better without the interference from humans, often eluding them. In my experience intentionally planting it results in the seeds germinating in some other intended place, at an unexpected time of year. I have seen this over and over again – mullein follows no rules of order nor human imposed structure. During the late summer and autumn months, natures candle is breathtaking and certainly attracts spirits of the deceased. I have found that the plant is helpful as a funerary taper and amulet to carry while traveling to a funeral or cemetery. It has helped me with grief in this way, easing the pain of loss.

This certainly is a plant of light and illumination. It lights the darkened pathway across the hedge and wild edge. The infused flower oil can be applied to the third eye as a way to illuminate dark situations and dreams. The hag taper itself can be used to illuminate nighttime rites and ceremonies, as described below. Harvest the root of a plant in its first autumn for spirit counsel and hang up to protect the home.

Mullein is a biennial, which means that it makes its basal rosette of leaves during the first season, it grows and makes its flower stalk and seed head during the second season. It dies after the second year when it finishes dropping its many seeds. For medicinal use, there is hardly a better plant for the afflictions of the lungs. The leaves can be harvested selectively during the plants first summer, and then again during late spring and early summer of its following year. Great care must be taken to not mistake mullein for the deadly foxglove *Digitalis purpurea*, as they look very similar to the untrained eye. Be absolutely sure of its identification before harvesting the leaves.

The mullein leaves dried make an excellent simple infusion, particularly delicious with the addition of milk and honey. It is a very comforting tea in its own right, but is applicable for lung troubles whether at the beginning of a cough, during an acute sickness, or during the healing that comes afterwards. Combined with horsetail *Equisetum arvense*, it makes a tonic for asthma, alternating also with plantain leaf *Plantago spp.* and Stinging Nettles *Urtica dioica*. It is a helpful addition to any hay fever/allergy blend as well.

The flowers can be harvested as they come on, dried and added to teas made with the leaves for additional assistance. An infused oil can be made by slowly adding the flowers to a jar of olive oil, kept in a spot that gets partial sun exposure for a month or more, careful to shake every day. As the flowers do not come on all at once, it takes a few weeks during late summer to accumulate enough to make a potent oil. Once finished the oil is strained and then kept for later use. It is helpful for earaches and pain, a small vial warmed in a glass of hot water, then a few drops placed in both ears and cotton used to hold the liquid in. Also use the oil to gently massage around the ear and lymph area. This is helpful for adults and children alike. Some recipes call for mullein flower along with garlic bulb and willow bark added for additional antimicrobial and pain relieving properties.

The leaves can be used as a base in smoking blends, combined with other fragrant and woody additions. Good advice to heed to is to not smoke during a sickness unless you are already a smoker. As a smoke for ceremony and prayer, mullein leaf can be up to half of the mixture. It needs to be broken down with the hands significantly before smoking, as with all herbal blends.

Many thanks to the Wild Candle of hag and hedge, of blessed crone and the Lady of the land. May you stumble upon her abundant medicines, so bright and warm for the damp and dark times of life. May the witches taper burn long into the night.

Making Hag Tapers

Harvest the mullein seed heads in late summer after flowering, but before the rains have truly arrived. This is best done with offerings near a full moon. Make sure to cut them low enough to have a good strong handle that is part of the stem itself. Also be sure to leave some of the seed stalks for their own purposes on the land, though once it is in disturbed soil, there is no getting rid of it! In baskets spread wax paper, lay the seed heads to dry for a full month. During this time they will open their seed pods and let out many tiny seeds – collect these in wax paper and replant in disturbed edges in the fall, be sure to tamp down to help with germination. Once the seed heads are totally dried and empty of their precious contents, making the hag tapers can begin.

You will need home rendered beef or lamb tallow (see the appendices of *Under the Witching Tree* for details on how to render fat at home). Some people use beeswax, though I have not tried it. The tallow needs to be melted and painted on with a paint brush fit for the job. Do this while laying the stalks on wax paper, to catch any mess. Rotate the stalks to cover every inch of the flower head itself a number of times, repeating the application of the tallow. Then let dry and harden and dry before use. Some folks use a mixture of softer lard and harder tallow, but beware of applying too much fat, as it can drip off while aflame being a hazard to the one holding the torch and also being a fire hazard if used indoors. They will smoke and smell intensely, so outdoor use is recommended.

To use, have a candle ready and take the tip of the hag taper to it, holding at an angle. It may take a minute to light but persist – it will alight. Once it has, it will burn brightly and effortlessly staying alit and making a perfect torch for the rustic ritual. It may go out if enough fat was not applied. Do beware of dripping fat from the parts where the tallow collected. These tapers will burn for a long time, depending on how long the stalk is. For holders place the stalks in a sturdy pot of earth. They can be extinguished carefully in a pan of ashes and saved for later use. I have tried just burning the dried seed head without the addition of the tallow, but it just smokes and barley lights. The tallow is truly needed to have a bright and long lasting flame – it is beyond lovely to behold during night time gatherings.

Just to mention – tallow used alone without any other wax makes spectacular taper candles when poured in a mold, with wicks attached. Contrary to popular belief, they do not smoke or smell at all but are very fragile and need to be stored in a taper candle box away from the heat of a woodstove or furnace. They do tend to drip and burn faster than harder wax but make exceptional candles for special indoor occasions where old world ambiance is desired.

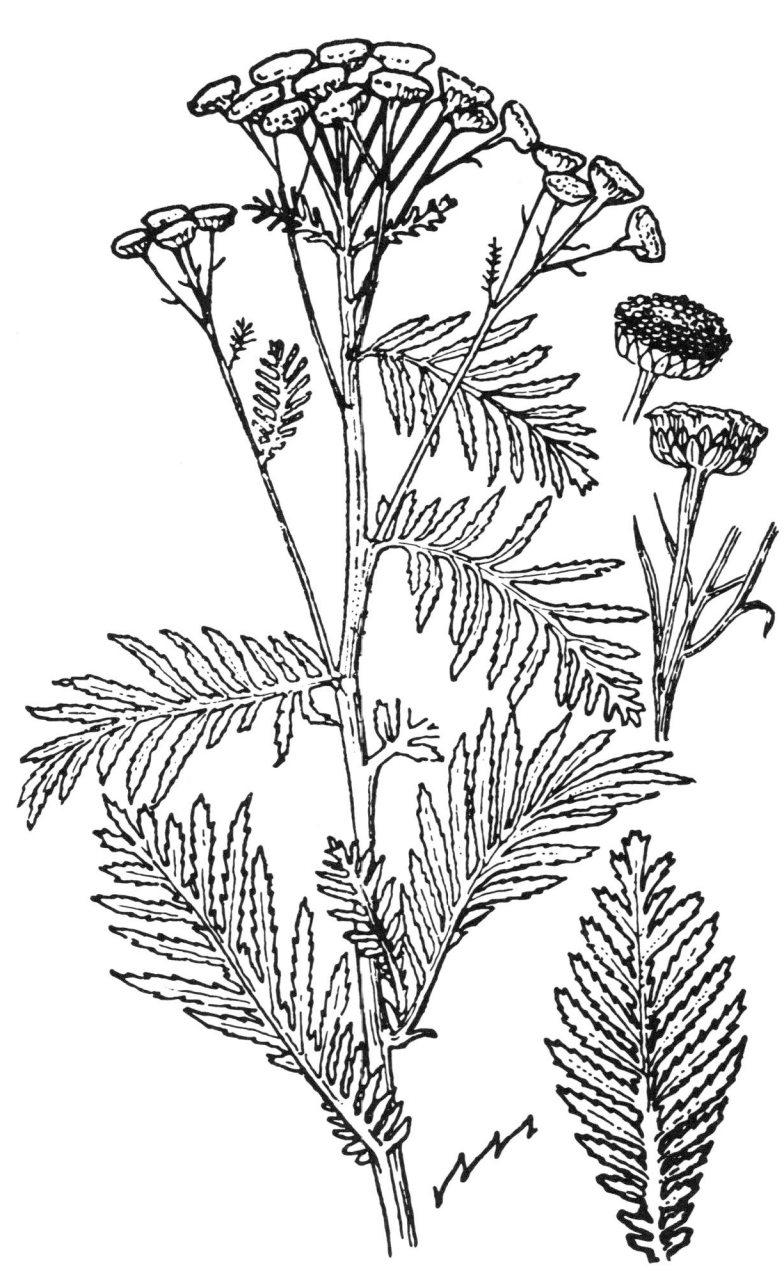

TANSY
Tanacetum vulgare

The aromatic true tansy can be found nowadays on roadsides and in patches of disturbed ground in full sun. The flowers, also known as 'brass buttons' are bright yellow small disk like in clusters, an elegant top to handsome finely divided dark green leaves. The leaves are incredibly fragrant when bruised – they smell of camphor and vanilla strongly. This potent wayside plant offers its regal and timeless perfume to cauldron fumigations and scented waters. Mostly despised during modern times, yesteryears apothecary would not be complete without this late summer beauty tucked away in a darkened jar.

Tansy is in the Asteraceae family, sharing its genus *Tanacetum* with both feverfew *T. parthenium* and costmary *T. balsamita*. It is native to temperate Eurasia. This perennial plant spreads by underground running rhizomes and spreading thick stems. An important identification feature is the flowers that are without petals, and the strongly pleasant smell of the crushed leaves. If the small yellow flowers have many petals, then the plant could be tansy ragwort *Senecio jacobea* or St. Jonhs wort *Hypericum perforatum*. Older names for true tansy included Bitter Buttons, Cow Bitter, Helde (Old English),

The Medieval Greek name for tansy *athanaton* translates into 'Immortal, Deathless'. Another old name for it was *anthanasia*. Coffins were packed with tansy to preserve the dead and the body could even be washed with an infusion for a similar purpose. An older belief from Maryland was that one should never sow tansy seed or there would be a death in the family. An adage from Fenland UK tells that where there were wild rabbits, there was sure to be tansy growing near – relating the plant to fertility for which it had some medicinal use. Wearing a sprig of tansy inside one's boot was a charm to protect from ague. In parts of Italy, it was a custom to give wild tansy stalks to those who were disliked as an insult. Tansy is ruled by Venus and was valued and grown in many cottage gardens in times past, though it is regarded as a weed by many today.

Hanging tansy in the home was a German practice to protect against 'magical monsters'. The herb was burned as an incense as well because of its aromatic nature. Tansy was included in a sacred bundle of nine herbs gathered on Lughnasa along with others for protection. The other herbs included yarrow, dill, calendula, valerian, sage, mugwort, arnica and loveage. These herbs were to be harvested by a woman unclothed, an hour before sunrise and picked without the use of any iron. They could be preserved for burning as a protective incense during the darkest nights of the year, placed in the coffins of the deceased, or used for health and fertility in the coming year.

Tansy is still used in a defensive practice from the Balkan region. When a witch feels like she is under threat, a kettle of water is placed on the fire; when it begins to boil she adds tansy to the pot, then letting it come to a rolling boil. She then takes the pot of hot liquid and herbs and goes to the front door of the home. She pours the contents over the threshold while speaking once simply: '*I don't track, I give it back*'. If a sizzling sound occurs, it is a sign that the magic has been reversed. Tansy is also worn as an amulet for protection from the same from the Balkans.

Folk Medicine

Tansy has natural insecticide properties because of its aromatic oils. The plant was a favorite strewing herb of the past and used to discourage vermin, fleas and moths. In Ireland it was grown around cattle barns and houses to keep away flies. It was used to keep flies off of raw meat by rubbing the meat with the fresh leaves, also it was rubbed on dogs to discourage fleas. Bundles of tansy and elder leaves were hung in the windows to keep flies at bay. Tansy was included in straw bedding as a bed bug deterrent. An old prescription for curing thread worms from the early 1900s: *'Boil the flowers or foliage of tansy weed and drink the infusion. The dose-a wineglassful each morning'*. Wearing an amulet of tansy around the neck was thought to discourage worms.

Tansy was used externally as a hot compress for gout and sprains. An ointment was made by infusing the whole fresh plant in warm butter, then straining it out and using it for an all-purpose wound salve. Also an infused oil was made from the flowers and used to treat rheumatism. An infused vinegar with tansy flowers was used to take the soreness out of a dog bite, and also to relieve a toothache when used as a gargle. A wash made with tansy leaves and salt water was used to bath painful joints in Ireland. It was a varicose vein remedy – applied as a compress or poultice to large knotted varicosities. Juliet de Baircli Levy recommended it externally for tumors, toothaches, bruises, earaches and for all swellings. The tansy plant was soaked in buttermilk or white wine and used as a wash to make the complexion fair.

One Anglo-Saxon leechdom used tansy along with other herbs in a magical cure 'against every evil'. It instructs to take equal amounts of tansy leaf, sage leaf, rue leaf, fennel leaf, chervil leaf, cleavers, peach leaves and red willow leaves. All of these were pounded and steeped in water or clear ale, then strained off. The resulting liquid was to be sweetened with honey and drunk, particularly before being bled. It was also recommended to take a bath before a hot fire and drip the liquid on every limb for its healing virtue.

Tansy was a loved herb of the English Romany and used internally **in small amounts** (it can be toxic if taken in too large of a dose – care and caution is advised, read below) as a general digestive tonic, nervine, to expel worms, for jaundice, nausea, failing appetite, for kidney ailments, to strengthen veins and for heart troubles. Tansy was combined with calendula in an infusion for bronchitis and taken for colds and fevers. An old recipe for bitters from American folk medicine includes tansy, chamomile, centaury, orange peel, and wormwood, covered in brandy to steep. Tansy was used as a cure for gout, one remedy called for the root to be preserved in honey and taken; another

American recipe for severe stomach pain reads: *'For violent pains in the stomach and even for the gout – A handful of garden tansy boiled in a quart of strong Mountain Wine – strain it off, to a person in a violent pain, give a small tea cup full'* – taken from Southern Folk Medicine 1750-1820, Kay K. Moss.

Tansy was also used as a woman's herb for painful periods, to induce abortion and interestingly for fertility. It was actually in formulas to help prevent miscarriage, from the time of Culpepper and quite possibly before. Although the information sounds contradictory, the power of plants is in the dose and frequency taken. One recipe recommends the bruised root applied to the navel for miscarriage prevention. From my great, great grandmothers handwritten receipts that I am blessed enough to have access to comes this bit of use for women's troubles: *'For painful menstruation, crush tansy and drink the water off of it.'* I take this to mean, crush the plant and place it in a glass of water and sip for dysmenorrhea. One must be careful of taking too much of this plant. Because of the high aromatic oils tansy is an antispasmodic in small doses such as this, and in that way would act to quell heavy cramps and therefore possible miscarriage as well. However, this particular method is not recommended! I would personally try crampbark *Viburnum opulus* under the care of a qualified midwife.

Hildegard von Bingen recommended tansy in small amounts internally for coughs, catarrh, and heaviness in the stomach from eating. Her advice for using tansy for obstructed menstruation is brilliant; make a warm steam with tansy, feverfew and mullein to soften the skin, flesh and womb, done by sitting over the hot tea in a sauna. For detailed instructions, see *Hildegard von Bingen's Physica*, translated by Priscilla Throop, Healing Arts Press, 1998, p.58.

This plant is considered toxic to take internally by many modern herbalists. Many of the poisonings from tansy have occurred because of women trying to induce abortion and taking the tincture or essential oil internally and even the tea in large amounts, sometimes with deadly results and/ or irreversible kidney damage. Internal use should be very

Tansy

limited and only used by one who is comfortable with this plant and has an understanding of dosage.

That said, tansy was used as a bitter herb in culinary dishes in small amounts and put in Easter puddings during Medieval times. One recipe of ingredients included scrambled eggs with cream, the juice of wheat grass, tansy, violet leaves, strawberry leaves, spinach, English walnut buds and then sprinkled with nutmeg, cinnamon, sugar and breadcrumbs to be baked. Tansy leaf was also used to flavor a sausage made from sheep's blood and milk in Ireland. The Danish used tansy as a flavoring substitute for the more expensive nutmeg and cinnamon.

Personal Practices

Tansy is a powerful and protective plant, I have always been drawn to include it in protective powders and formulas, in particular against hauntings and the dead. The everlasting quality of the plant lends itself to be dried in beautiful bundles when harvested in late summer, these bundles can be hung over doorways and windows to protect the home from misfortune. It keeps away that which you do not want and so can be added to other charms for the purposes of repelling. The dried crushed plant sprinkled with salt around the perimeter of the home is a good cleansing practice. The dried leaves and flowers can be added to any smudge blend for the same, taking advantage of the purification that smoke and fire offer. A charm can be made by utilizing the protective horseshoe, black horsehair, red thread and the tansy flower – all for domestic peace and productive affairs within the home.

Tansy has very strong and woody stems that can be used defensively as well. Cut during autumn time when they are fully developed for the year, they can be dried and saved, then applied as needed. Cut them at an angle to make them sharp on both ends. They can be used to encircle one in need of protection during a ritual, where they are stabbed into the earth surrounding the one in need. Similarly, they can be used to mark the corners of a home for the same purpose. If a woman is dealing with advances from an unwanted lover/ suitor, tansy is a plant to consider. Have the woman bath in water where a few cups of the fragrant tea has been added after any negative interaction, and make a small equal armed cross with the sharpened tansy stalks tied with black thread. Place this in a pouch of doubled yellow silk and add some ritually harvested grave earth, salt and the crushed tansy flowers. This can be hung above the woman's bed for protection or worn upon her when she is out in the world. Also a strong tea made from the whole plant can be brushed on door locks with a rag from the inside, to keep away intruders.

This plant does seem to have an affinity for women in a physical way as well. Bathing the feet and carrying as an amulet can help with heavy menstruation and cramping. Also, a hot compress applied to the womb area is good. Tansy can be harvested in full flower in late summer on the full moon and hung to dry. When stripping the leaves from the stalks, do use leather gloves. The oils in this plant are very strong.

I use tansy primarily externally. It is helpful added to sinus steams, made into a hair rinse for lice prevention, and scattered as a strewing herb for ants, mice and fleas. It makes a flavorful wild seasoning in small amounts – it is good in eggs and on meat. A few of the fresh crushed leaves rubbed on the arms and shoulders, though not the face, make a quick insect rub while wandering the wild edges.

This ancient herb has a place yet on the herbalist's apothecary shelf, as both defensive medicine and great cleanser, as yellow flower bitter and protective smoke. May we remember the value of common herbs in plain sight – regal golden flower heads shining brightly in the meadow sun. Many thanks to the aromatic feathery leaves and immortal flowers of this graceful herb of woman's womb and autumnal bouquets.

A Wicked Water of Defense

This wash can be employed for many uses. Made on the day before the dark moon, it has magnetic and defensive virtues, helpful for a variety of situations. Make a strong tea from dried tansy leaf and flower, dried thistle leaves, dried stinging nettle leaves and 13 thorns from the dog rose, *Rosa canina*, harvested with blood offerings. Ideally boil this mixture in an iron cauldron on an open fire outdoors. Add a good measure of salt, a few pinches of soot, and three crow feathers. When boiling and all mixed together, stir the pot in circles to the left with a sharpened tansy stalk, say these words thrice over the brew:

> *The Bitter flowers, the thistles scorn, the stinging dust, the sharpest thorn,*
> *By black moon water, by reddened fire, by cauldron iron, by corvid dire,*
> *I stir the brew, against the sun, to trap and bind, which has ill done,*
> *To blast with steam, the brew of strife, for cunning crow, escape the knife.*

Let the brew then be taken off the fire to set. Once cool, transfer to an earthenware flask, laying the feathers to dry. Hang these inside near the chimney of the home, or near the heat source. Use the liquid to cleanse tainted items, to anoint a place of dwelling that is cursed, to sprinkle on a person for the same, to flood the footstep of an enemy, to wash a threshold that has been broken into, to pour onto cursed ground, or any other situation needing defense and reconciliation of dark deeds. It will keep in the fridge for a time, if enough salt was added initially. The tansy will also help preserve the wash.

A Protective Amulet for the Womb

For a woman whom has miscarried, had an abortion, or given birth, this charm can be made to bring protection to the opened and vulnerable womb. For forty days after these events, a woman is not only physically vulnerable and in need of deep nourishment and rest, but she is spiritually vulnerable to all sorts of vampires, attacks, illness of the Evil Eye and whatnot. So is the precious wee one. It is a time to have protective measures in place and be very wary of the energy of those around her, as well as the places she visits. No graveyards, hospitals (if possible), haunted trees, draining or demanding people or large crowds. Certainly no jealous relatives or acquaintances.

Have tansy that was harvested in full flower on the full moon, likely in the month of August. Then when needed, make this charm ideally on another night before the full moon. By candlelight, take a small handful of the leaf and flower combined and mix to a powder in a mortar and pestle. This will be difficult if the herb is not completely dry, in which case finish drying in a low oven careful not to burn. To this powder, add some of the woman's womb blood, and the tincture of amber to make a paste. Her blood can be added by soaking a cloth that is stained and squeezing it out, if needed. The amber tincture needs to be made in advance (make this with very small crumbles of amber, in brandy, near a heat source. Stir daily for a month or more, most if it will dissolve) The paste should be pressed into a largish and strong walled snail shell, that spiraled creature of fertility, love and good fortune. Set this on a scrap of red velvet and speak these words:

> *By blood of seed, and waters red,*
> *By moon of silver, and darkling thread,*
> *The golden dust and drop do heal,*
> *To stitch the womb, the scar, to seal,*
> *A spiral circled protects the soul,*
> *Enclosed with care, defend the whole.*

Any extra paste must be buried carefully under an apple tree, not merely discarded. Lay the charm to dry for three days in a protected spot, and then enclose in the red velvet, along with 3 whole dried rosehips. As you sew this shut, repeat the charmed words. Give to her to carry with her and sleep with under her pillow for forty days. Then it is to be saved in a dark drawer indefinitely, not to be discarded or lost. This charm can be thereafter used for heavy monthly bleeding and all other troubles of the womb, carried with during times of need.

The Witches Mirror of Midwinter

Many long years ago, a small fire was lit,
Tended gracefully with shaking hands
Tiny moths, they still arrive,
On Feast Days of the Black Moods
Witching roots and Rocking chairs

If only she would appear, as young and as beautiful
Butterflies poison the vine, you are One Other
The last to see the stars, the last one
Who walks round mulberry stained rags
And our hands, they toil, they remember

This is no illusion — the velvet coverlet, the leaded mirror,
The winding stair — the animals indeed speak at midnight.
But of all visions that are burned and recorded
Those crystalline moments remain, those jewels,
That take root under blood and under water

Wooden tower crackling, open grave
Spellbound, I align stars with powders
Dreams refuse me, last one standing
Sees ghosts that tells future or past
Globe of glass is circling fast

My Sister, my Mother, my Daughter
Three sheets to the wind, my heart, my skin
One bitter draught deserves another
The dark moon is lonely, is deep
Like magnet darkling, and midnight sleep

ENGLISH IVY
Hedera helix

Lady Ivy is a forest loving vine, twisted and elegant in her dominance. As time allows, her pervasive nature accommodates ruins so haunted. She is a regular sight upon old buildings, sprawling through cemeteries, her gorgeous leaves of emerald geometric perfection clinging to the old stones, devouring them. Her dull black berries that arrive after the white waxy flowers conjure up the name of 'owl berries', as she has been associated with this magical bird of ill omen. It is no surprise that ivy holds folklore of a dark and magical nature, along with oracular powers. She also offers rustic healing applications for the wayside crone or wizard, such a powerful wort is she.

Ivy is in the *Araliaceae* family, there are three subspecies and over thirty cultivars. It is native to most of Europe as well as western Asia. The Latin name *Hedera* is a generalized word for 'Ivy', and the epithet helix comes from a Greek word meaning 'to twist and turn'. Ivy which is sometimes known as 'English Ivy' is considered invasive by many states in the US, however I have read that it has an affinity to places where there is significant air pollution. I challenge the concept of 'invasive species' in most but not all cases, and believe that the plants have a deeper intelligence at work than humans are keen to acknowledge.

There was an Irish legend known as *Suibhne Geilt* or 'Mad Sweeny', where a King was driven mad by a curse and sought refuge by living in the wild forests. He described many plants, including ivy, saying *O ivy, little ivy, Thou art familiar in the dusky wood*. He ate the berries which are toxic to regular humans and valued the ivy for the shelter it provided to him. He claimed to live alone in the 'top' of the ivy, stating *A proud ivy bush which grows through a twisted tree, If I were right at its summit, I would fear to come out.* In Northern mythology ivy was dedicated to Thor because of its black berries, which were said to be an offering for his messenger elf according to folklorist Richard Folkard.

There was a certain darkness associated with ivy quite possibly because of her associations with death, graveyards and ruins. In Cornwall if you wanted to dream of the Devil, you would pin four ivy leaves to the corners of your pillow. In early American folklore, ivy was unlucky to give as a gift in Maine and Massachusetts because it could bring death to a family. A Somerset belief was that to pick an ivy leaf off of a church wall, one would develop sickness. To fall asleep under a large ivy vine climbing a tree was told to bring death to the one in slumber. Ivy's black berries were sometimes used in cursing rituals in the British Isles. It is no surprise that ivy is ruled by Saturn, according to astrologers of old. Ivy was a burial plant due to its evergreen nature and was associated with immortality. It was believed that if ivy grew profusely from a grave, that the one died had suffered from secret lovesickness in particular for a woman. If the ivy withered and died from a gravesite however, it was a sign that the soul of the deceased was uneasy in the Otherworld, according to an American belief.

Ivy was an unlucky plant to bring indoors or to be grown indoors, lest misfortune and death shall befall the dwellers therein. Some lore specified that it should only be used as a decoration on outside doors or porches, from England. It was also very unlucky for a gardener to plant it as it was a graveyard vine. In American superstition, to give ivy could break up a friendship. In some parts of England it was even forbidden as a Christmas decoration, though in many places it had a history of being paired with Holly for Midwinter traditions. Holly was known to be the Master of the house and ivy the Mistress, thus holly being masculine and ivy being feminine. Ivy was supposedly a female plant coming from beliefs from medieval times, due to its dark and vining nature and black berries. *Ivy is soft and meek of speech* was an old saying. There is an English Yuletide Carol called 'The Holly and the Ivy' that tells of this. In a Guernsey belief it was unlucky to bring ivy in the house before Christmas Eve, especially if it would touch the fireplace mantle. Then it would surely bring bad luck to the women folk of the home. In olden times in many parts of England the specific time for bringing in the Christmas greenery was generally on December 24, all of the decorations besides mistletoe being removed by Epiphany.

Ivy featured in many folk divinations, some related to love, others to health or death. A British yuletide divination was to put an ivy leaf in a bowl full of water, cover it, and leave it for 12 nights – the twelve days of Christmas being an auspicious time for foretelling and contacting spirits. This was done on New Year's Eve during later times. It could foretell the health of the person it was named after, depending on where or if black spots developed on the leaf. If no spots developed, it was a sign of perfect health for the year to come. If spots did show up on the leaf, they would correspond to a certain part of the body, to tell where disease would develop. If the developed spot was shaped like a coffin, it indicated death. Sometimes each of the family members would name a leaf after themselves and watch to see their fate for the coming year in this manner. Ivy was used along with holly in an Irish love divination on New Year's Eve. Ivy and holly leaves were placed under one's pillow, and the following simple charm was spoken to bring dreams of a future mate: *Oh ivy green and holly red, tell me tell me whom I shall wed.*

A bunch of ivy kept inside the home would also tell the future for the person whom picked it; if it flourished long life and happiness were expected, if it withered however it was an omen of early death. In Normandy the leaves were used to help one find out which saints to pray to. A number of ivy leaves were put in holy water, each one named after a saint. The first one to turn yellow would indicate the saint that one would need to pray to.

Because of its intense clinging nature ivy has been used in love magic in times past, being a symbol of love, fidelity and friendship. Country names for this plant were 'bindwood' and 'love stone'. Ivy was used in marriage divinations, some were as simple as if a girl placed an ivy leaf in her pocket, the next man that she met would be her future husband. An old charm from Dunbartonshire was for a young maid to take an ivy leaf that was growing on a church, place it under her blouse and whisper this rhyme: *Ivy, Ivy, I love you. In my bosom put you. The first young man who speaks to me, My future husband he will be.*

Ivy featured in a number of British love divinations to be performed on the night of All Hallows Eve. Here is a charm that includes the simple instructions: *Nine ivy leaves I place under my head, To dream of the living and not of the dead, To dream of the man that I am going to wed, And to see him tonight at the foot of my bed.* In a Welsh All Hallows Eve divination, a rounded ivy leaf was picked to represent a woman and a pointed ivy leaf was picked to represent the man. These leaves were placed together in a fire and if they jumped towards each other, it was a sign of true love; if they jumped apart, it foretold future relationship trouble. An English love divination for a man to bring about prophetic dreams of his future wife was to gather ten ivy leaves, throw one away and sleep with the nine remaining leaves under his pillow.

In the Balkans small ivy wood cups were made and if a woman refused to drink out of the cup, it was a sure sign that she was a witch. Another Balkan charm for finding out a witch was to encircle a full church on Christmas night with a white thread and bury it under the threshold of church, along with a little spoon made from ivy wood. This way no witch could leave the church, she would be trapped inside. A German belief was that one who wore a garland of ivy would have the ability to see and recognize witches.

A Medieval German curse to 'burn' a witch, or to cause a witch pain and suffering goes thus. One was to take butter

English Ivy

and heat it in an iron pan, adding to it ivy leaves (or mistletoe leaves *Viscum album*) to fry in the butter, along with three coffin nails. This mixture was then taken and left in a place of darkness, where no sunlight or moonlight could shine upon it. If done, the witch would be sick with pock marks and burns all over her body for half a year.

There were a few Scandinavian folk uses for ivy that come from a Swedish Black Book known as *The Black Book*, translated by *Fredrik Eytzinger*, in *Salomonic* Magical Arts (Three Hands Press). One was to find out if a woman was carrying a boy or girl child. A root of ivy was to be dug and placed somehow on the woman's head, without her knowing. One assumes it was a small piece. If she then spoke a man's name first the child was a boy, or if she spoke a woman's name first it was a girl that she carried.

In some places in Europe such as in the Scottish Highlands, ivy was seen as protective. There was a custom of hanging it over the stable door to keep the cattle protected from witchcraft and disease. A Highland charm to bring about more milk from the dairy cows was to pluck an ivy leaf and speak these words: *I will pluck the tree entwining ivy, as Mary plucked with her one hand.* In another practice to protect milk from being bewitched ivy, honeysuckle *Lonicera periclymenum* and rowan *Sorbus acuparia* twigs were woven together in a wreath and placed under the milk vessels. In some parts bramble canes were substituted for the honeysuckle. The same wreath could be hung above the threshold of the cow shed to protect the animals as well. In Germany when first driving animals out to their summer pastures, the cows were given wreaths of ivy to wear for protection.

A general British belief was that ivy growing on a house would protect the inhabitants from witchcraft and misfortune and a Welsh belief indicated that monetary loss was expected if ivy started to wither or fall away from the walls on the home. A Herefordshire belief was that if the ivy growing on a house died, it foretold the death of the family within. In the Balkans, ivy was used to protect against demons and thought to be protective of children. It was also used in love magic. Ivy in general was protective of women and to gather a leaf leftover from church decorations would promote the birth of twins. It was thought that dreaming of ivy was a good omen and that it meant 'your friendships are true'. Friendship was sometimes symbolized by a fallen tree covered in the ivy vine, meaning 'Nothing can part us'. It is interesting to note the contradictions within the beliefs held in different areas.

This emerald vine was associated with wine taverns. It was thought that the cooling nature of ivy compared to the heat of the grapevine, would help counteract drunkenness. There was a saying in Somerset: *Put a trail of Ivy across a drunkards path and he will become a sober citizen.* Wearing a crown of Ivy leaves was supposed to prevent a hangover. Bacchus, the Roman God of Wine himself was crowned with a ring of ivy leaves. Pliny wrote that the berries taken in wine would prevent intoxication. A cup of ivy wood was known to separate wine from water with the wine seeping out of the cup and the water remaining, because of the antipathy between them.

There were a few folk magical cures for ivy. An interesting French custom was to make an ivy root necklace for a teething baby. An odd number of roots had to be used for the charm to work. Ivy wood cups were used to deliver milk to children with whooping cough and were supposed to help cure it, more effectual when cut at a secret phase of the moon and planetary hour. These ivy cups were also used to help with the cramp. An Irish practice for cattle with sore eyes was to hang an ivy leaf above the fireplace; as it withered, the soreness would disappear. Though one wonders about the possible missing information here, where the transference magic came from. Ivy that was growing on a hawthorn tree or hedge was specifically used for eye disease as well.

From Ross-shire Scotland comes the custom of maidens collecting the leaves of ivy that had dew on them on May morning, without the use of any steel. This was done to bring luck for the following year. An Essex transference wart charm was to prick a hole in an ivy leaf, one hole for each wart, then impale the leaf on a thorn hedge. As the leaf withered away, so would the warts. A Scottish cure for consumption was to cut ivy vines and keep them for an entire year, then passing a person with consumption underneath them as needed. It likely that more details have been lost over time, as with much lore that was passed orally and held in secret throughout the ages.

Folk Medicine

There are a surprising amount of medicinal uses for ivy, though it was known to be moderately toxic. Older folk uses of ivy in Europe include its external use as an infused vinegar or bruised leaf poultice for corns, skin disease in general, carbuncles, boils, ringworm, eczema, warts and burns. One Welsh remedy for corns involved making a poultice with boiled ivy leaves, kept on for five days. Ivy leaves cooked in lard until the lard turned green was an old remedy for burns, known to help with scarring. A Scottish remedy for burns was to pound ivy leaves in olive oil, and then use this on the burned part, covering it with brown paper. A Romany eczema cure to help cool the skin was to gather fresh ivy leaves, boil them in water and leave them for a whole day, then apply the liquid to the place grieved. An Irish cure for a boil was to apply a heated ivy leaf, one side of the leaf used for drawing and the other side of the leaf used for healing. Hildegard von Bingen recommended using it saturated in deer fat and applied externally for jaundice; the jaundice was thought to pass into the ivy leaves and leave a yellow mark on the skin, essentially transference magic at work.

Ivy was taken in small doses internally for adult mumps and other glandular disorders, to help bring forth retained afterbirth or stillbirth (the berries), as an emmenagogue, for fevers, to cure stomach pains and against all infectious diseases including the plague. The toxic ivy berries were eaten in midland counties of Ireland to cure aches and pains, but one wonders at the dose. Ivy was also considered a remedy for coughs, bronchitis and colds, with the juice of the leaves being snuffed up the nose for the latter. None of these internal uses are recommended however, without more knowledge of the dosage from a skilled herbalist.

An infused vinegar from the berries was held hot in the mouth for toothache, then spat out when it had cooled. A cure for stuttering from Devon used an ivy leaf wash applied to the throat. A wash from the leaf infusion was used for sore eyes and today the homeopathic medicine is used to treat cataracts. A wreath of Ivy leaves could be worn to help keep hair from falling out, or to make it grow back again. The leaves were also put on children's heads for eczema and sewn into caps for children that had sores or rashes on their heads. Ivy was used as a lice treatment, which makes sense, based on its moderate toxicity.

In Anglo-Saxon medicine, ivy leaves were gathered at harvest time, shredded small, and dried to keep for later use. They were combined with cinquefoil *Potentilla spp.*, earth gall questionably *Erythreae* or *Gentiana*, adderwort *Polygonum bistorta*, and ladderwort *Polemonium caeruleum* for gout, boiled in ale. Ivy leaves that were harvested from a stone, along with yarrow leaf *Achilliea millefolium*, woodbine or honeysuckle leaf *Lonicera periclymenum*, cowslip flower *Primula veris* and primrose Primula vulgaris, were pounded together and used in a steam for inflammations by applying to a hot stone in a trough and adding water to make a steam for the person afflicted. Ivy was used for water sickness (likely edema), by crushing twenty seeds, infusing them in wine, and three draught's drank for seven days. Another Anglo-Saxon remedy was to boil ivy shoots in butter and use the grease for sunburn.

It is known that grazing animals eat ivy, especially goats and are often thought to be healthier because of it. The herbalist Juliette de Bairacli Levy believed that giving ivy greens at certain times kept cows, sheep and goats healthy.

However, do not drink the milk from an animal fed on ivy. An old saying tells that if sick sheep will not eat ivy leaves, they will die.

Personal Practices 🌺

Though I do not use ivy for medicine, I do value it in magical applications. It is a helpful and powerful addition to any love magic, but one must be careful. Gather these leaves only from where they sprawl on the ground, rather than from where they dominate a tree or building. A recipe for love powder follows. Harvested on May Eve, the leaves are particularly powerful, as are the flowers used for purposes of enchantment. They can be hidden under one's pillow or carried with, dried in a little vial for such purposes. Ivy wood taken from larger vines can be cut into small rounds, sanded by hand and carried as a 'love stone' to draw love to one. The flowers can be infused in oil on a full moon, to then be used for the same purpose, by applying lightly to the table, hearth and bedstead.

For protective purposes, the vines can be braided with other protective plants to make a witches rope, see 'Bittersweet Nightshade'. These strong withies can be made use of in any binding ritual, used to keep dark powers in check. This would be especially effective if done with graveyard ivy vines. Ivy is appropriate for the decoration of ancestor altars in the autumn months, and can be used for foretelling as the lore reveals, particularly powerful in dreaming applications by placing under the pillow. Ivy has a connection to the land of the dead and can be put into conjuration powders for Otherworld communications.

Burning the dried leaves in a sacred fire around Midwinter time is both protective and oracular, and a small outdoor fire made from ivy wood and leaves can be made for fire scrying and visioning. The ashes saved from such a fire can be kept in a pouch for the coming year, incorporated into protective powders. Often ivy wood and leaves can be obtained from saving large old forest trees from her embrace, a worthy pursuit. Some people make baskets from the vines here in the Pacific northwest, where ivy can be a problem in the natural landscapes. The crushed leaves have such a fresh green invigorating smell, ivy is powerful in her ways of magic to be sure.

> *Many thanks to the dark green enchantress of the forgotten lands, her verdant fingers entwined with wood and stone, her fruit feeding ghosts and owl shadows. May we remember her connection to the Other world and seek her out during the winter and autumn months, during the dark half of the year, for her immortal green magics.*

Love Powder

Harvest ivy leaves on an autumn full moon, dry and save these. Ideally, this powder should be made on a Friday, just before a full moon. After nightfall by the light of a candle, grind these to a powder in a mortar, using a clockwise motion, one at a time: Ivy leaves, pink yarrow flowers, hawthorn flowers, vervain leaves, moss roses, dragons blood resin and cane sugar. Combine in a copper dish. Over the powder breathe and kiss, speaking these words three times:

> *By Venus night and copper ore,*
> *This powder to excite the heart,*
> *By cryptic vine and flower lore,*
> *The Old Ones breath upon my Arte*
>
> *By sweetest perfume, by moonlight,*
> *This powder of beauty to entice,*
> *By prophetic dreams at midnight,*
> *With fire and blood, I bless it thrice.*

Let the powder then sit in the copper dish, if it can be placed in the moons light for the night, all the better. Then store in glass, out of the light, with a raw garnet piece. This powder can be used in many ways relating to love magic.

English Ivy

It can be carried with in a red pouch, along with certain inscribed words and symbols to attract love, also paired with a lodestone anointed in one's own blood for the same. It can be sprinkled around the perimeter of a home to draw love there. It can be scattered upon water for scrying under a full moon, when seeking information pertaining to matters of love. It can be sprinkled around a dwelling or a bed to bring harmony and amorous affections to a troubled partnership. It can be burned at midnight to help bring visions of ones future mate or sprinkled under the pillow to bring dreams of the same. Also, it can be incorporated into other love charms as needed.

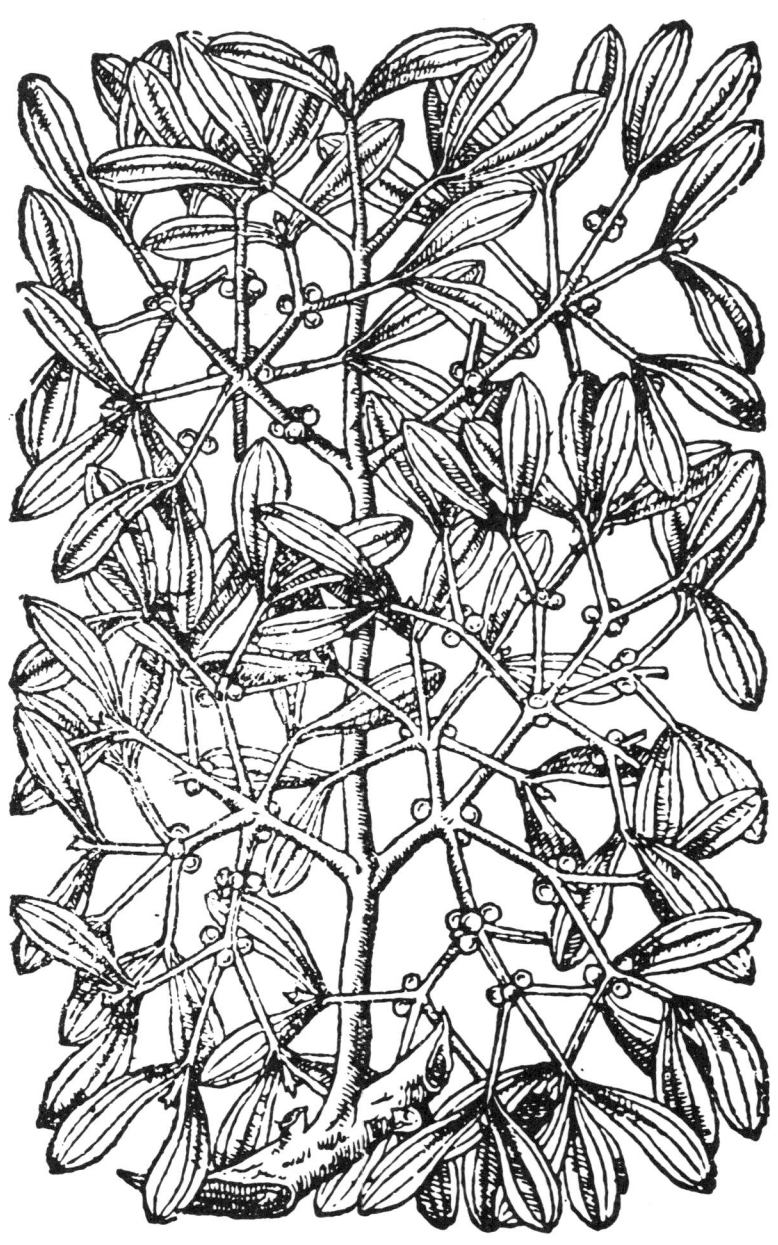

MISTLETOE
Viscum album

Neither plant nor shrub, this beauty was revered for its liminal nature, bearing leaves and fruit during the cold time when its host was bare. The mistletoe plant has long been associated with supernatural powers and healing abilities. The ghostly translucent white berries are indeed Otherworldly and conjure up a sense of magical smoke encapsulated in a ghostly fruit. They also remind one of the luminous semen of the Gods being offered to the Holy altar of the darkest winter shadows, their association with fertility is plain. Perhaps no other plant has created such a reputation for magical powers, save the Mandragora, and the lore presented here is a testament to this.

Older names for mistletoe included All-heal, Thors Broom, Thunder broom, Witches broom, Witch Nest, Crackling, Birdlime, Kiss and Go, Churchman's Greetings, Wintergreen and Winter Green Wood. A few Welsh names translate to mean *Pren Awyr* Merry Tree, *Pren Uchelvar* Tree of the High Summit or *Pren Puraur* Tree of Pure Knowledge. Mistletoe typically grows on oak, poplar, apple and pear trees, and occasionally hawthorn. It is native to Europe and southwestern Asia. It grows most commonly in the southwest of UK, apparently it did not originally grow in Ireland, though it has naturalized there over the years. The American species that I am most familiar with is *Phoradendron leucarpum* and grows on oak trees throughout Oregon and California, though there are numerous other species. Mistletoe is in the *Viscaceae* family, having seven genera total. The common name mistletoe comes from the Old English *mistiltan*, resulting from mistil meaning 'different' and tan meaning 'twig'.

Mistletoe was dedicated to Freya in Norse Mythology, after Loki used it to harm her son Baldur. After Baldur was restored to life, the mistletoe was placed under special protection from Freya, and ever after brought only good fortune and love to those whom hung it in their homes. One legend tells that mistletoe was created by the falling tears of Venus, after being unintentionally wounded from one of Cupids arrows.

Mistletoe was believed to be the most holy plant of the Druids according to Pliny from nearly two thousand years ago. It grew on their sacred oak trees. Roman poet Ovid also tells of the Druids singing under the mistletoe. The 'Golden Bough' refers to this plant, as it turns gold according to first Virgil, then Frazer. There are written records of it being harvested with the classic golden sickle, knife or 'upright hatchets of brass'. Other accounts tell of two bulls being sacrificed under the oak tree from where the mistletoe grew, and then a white cloth being laid out for the mistletoe to fall upon, lest it should touch the ground directly and lose its powers – according to Pliny. This sacred harvest would then be distributed to the people, the magical plants being used then for repelling evil spirits, witchcraft, for protection, and for amulet magic in many matters of health. One belief told that when the oak lost its leaves, the spirit of mistletoe then went into the oak tree. Lore of old also tells that if no mistletoe could be found growing on oak trees, it was a sign that great dangers were at hand.

This strange parasitic plant was connected with birds and there was a belief that it could not sprout unless the seed had been passed through a bird. This association with birds may have come from its manner of growing up in trees, nearest the sky. Mistletoe was dedicated to Thor/Donar, the rainmaking thunder god of vegetation, it was sacred to both the Teutonic peoples and the Celts. At Gristhorpe, near Scarborough in England, a bronze age burial site was found to have mistletoe included within it. A man's skeleton was within an oak coffin covered itself in oak branches, and inside with the bones was a brass dagger and a large amount of mistletoe.

In European folklore the mistletoe stood for immortality, helping to ward off death, being indestructible by both fire and water. It was also considered to be the embodiment of lightning and symbolized a sign of peace. It has long associations with Christmas time because of its uncanny white berries that flourish during that time of year, along with its evergreen nature. It was thought to be unlucky if cut at any other time of year besides on midnight of Christmas Eve, when the branch from last year's harvest would in turn be burnt. A bunch could be saved and used as a fumigation under the following years Christmas pudding or worn around the neck to repel witches, according to Worcestershire lore. It was important to not harvest the whole plant, always leaving some behind. It could be adorned with ribbons, nuts and with apples in the spirit of ornamentation. The mistletoe was left to hang all year, never removed with other Christmas decorations. It would lend its magical and protective virtue over the household for the coming seasons. Though this practice was condemned by the church in some parts, the tradition of hanging the mistletoe persisted into modern times. Even in parts of the UK where it did not grow, such as the Lincolnshire marsh lands, another evergreen acted in its place and function. Its representation during Yuletide therefor was essential, for the magic that it offered the peasant householders. A Welsh custom tells to obtain some mistletoe from the church Christmas decorations and place it in the home to bring good luck to its possessor for the following year.

A 'witches chain' could be made during the time of Midwinter, by threading holly berries, juniper berries and mistletoe berries on a thread and attaching an acorn on the ends. From old lore this was traditionally made by three younger women at a witch's cottage, the older witch woman instructing them. It was bound to a log and burned in a fire ritual in a particular way. When the acorns were finally consumed by the flames, each girl would see a glimpse of her future husband, or else if spinsterhood was her fate she would see the shape of a coffin instead.

Mistletoe was believed to be an antidote to all poisons since ancient times. It also had associations with fertility. With thick evergreen leaves, mate and dense, the clear white berries that emerge in November and December were symbolic of drops of semen from the cosmic bull that impregnated the earth goddess. Hence the tradition of kissing under the mistletoe being connected to fertility magic. One practice told that after each kiss under the mistletoe, the man would remove a berry. When all of the berries were removed, the tradition of kissing under it was over for that year. From an American superstition, if a woman refused a kiss under the mistletoe, she risked dying unmarried. And a maiden that married without ever being kissed under the mistletoe, was said to remain childless. Hanging mistletoe in full berry over the bed was supposed to bring conception of a child. Wearing mistletoe around the neck was thought to bring fertility and placing it in a bride's bouquet would ensure a good marriage. A Welsh custom tells that if an unmarried woman put a sprig of mistletoe from the parish church under her pillow, it would reveal dreams of her future husband.

A love spell involving mistletoe follows. A maiden desiring to attract the love of another retires to her chamber and locks the door. She brings with her one berry and one leaf of mistletoe, plucked from the mistletoe under which she had been saluted. The berry was to be swallowed and the leaf pricked with a pin, to inscribe the initials of the one whom her heart loved best. The leaf was then to be sewn into her underclothes and worn closest to her heart.

A love potion concerning mistletoe comes down to us from Aristotle. A powder is made from the leaves of mistletoe, vervain *Verbena officinalis*, and elecampane *Inula helenium* (the part not specified). This powder was used to arouse the passions and acted as an aphrodisiac when sprinkled into the food of the one desired.

Mistletoe

There were love divination games for mistletoe, such as gathering mistletoe leaves on the eve of St Johns before it fruited, and sleeping with them under one's pillow to reveal dreams of true love. A mistletoe potion could be made to procure such prophetic dreams – nine fresh berries were used, and steeped in a mixture of equal parts wine, beer, vinegar and honey. These little fermented 'pills' were taken on an empty stomach before going to bed, to cause dreams of one's future mate – a slightly toxic formula I would assume. To be most effective this was to be done just before midnight on Christmas Eve, or during the new moon. From Kentucky a love divination involved naming the leaves of mistletoe after a boy and a girl. These leaves were placed on a hot stove and if they jumped towards each other it was a good omen of love to come. From Alabama and Kentucky, mistletoe could be hung over a door by a man and the first maiden to walk through the door would be his future wife. Another old divination along similar lines tells to draw a circle in front of a fire, take two mistletoe leaves and name one after yourself placing it within the circle. Name the other after your intended sweetheart and place it outside of the circle. If a bond of marriage is to be formed, the outer leaf will jump into the circle, thus revealing that fate.

Mistletoe was associated with good luck in general for keeping cattle or for a fertile fruit producing orchard. Given in a tea, it was supposed to cure all animals of barrenness. In Wales it was believed that 'no mistletoe, no luck', and a branch was placed beside the first cow that had calved after the first hour of the new year had passed. In order to harvest it, a stone had to be thrown to get it to fall or in later times a shotguns blast. From American folklore, the plant could never touch the ground or be harvested by human hands. In Germany it was used somehow to protect cattle and also as a hunting charm. In Sweden, it was hung in farmhouses for protective purposes as well. Cutting down a tree that bared the magical mistletoe would certainly bring bad luck to the one doing so. Interestingly in Devonshire it was an unlucky plant, and not allowed to grow in orchards. From the same county possibly because of its strong fertility associations, if mistletoe was planted and it grew, one's daughters would never marry.

Mistletoe was known to help the wearer of it become invisible, to help open focus, and to help find hidden treasure. It had the magical ability to open locks ascribed to it. From Austrian lore hanging a branch above the bedstead would protect against the nightmare. A divining rod was cut from mistletoe in Swedish tradition, done so on Midsummers Eve. This was used to find hidden treasure. Certain families were connected to ancient oak trees, and the mistletoe that grew on these trees was also regarded as magical for these particular families.

From the works of Albertus Magnus comes a use to 'loosen bonds', believed to utilize the herb mistletoe. One was to go to a wood and find where the magpie had her nest of babies. One must then climb the tree and bind the hole of the nest with something unspecified. The magpie was told to then go a bring an herb (mistletoe) and put it to the binding in order to break it. Once broken the herb would fall out of the tree, and if one had carefully placed a cloth on the ground below, the herb could be collected and preserved for the same use that the magpie employed it for. A brilliant example, all in all.

A famous oak in Scotland grew mistletoe and it was harvested by a member of the Hays family of Errol on All Hallows Eve with a new knife after circling the tree sunwise three times. A secret spell was spoken and the plant that was harvested after this folk rite was then used to protect infants by attaching a sprig to the cradle. This was done to prevent the baby from being changed in to an 'Elf-bairn' by the Faeries. Of this same tree, it was told that when the root finally perished (it has since done so), that grass would grow from the hearth of Errol and a raven would sit in the falcon's nest – a prophesy of doom to say the least.

To hang mistletoe around the neck would protect children from against witchcraft and the Devil, an English practice. In

Devon the plant would protect the home from being struck by lightning. If by chance mistletoe was found growing on an ash or hazel tree, under the roots of the tree would be a snake with a magical jewel in its head – according to Welsh folklore. Or treasure was to be found under the roots. Another Welsh tradition was to stuff a bunch of mistletoe up the chimney for the summer months, helping to keep the evil spirits away.

Mistletoe was used to assist in spirit communications in times past. From Greek mythology a mistletoe wand was used to help Persephone open the gates of the Underworld. From Holstein, UK, mistletoe was known as a 'spectre's wand', as the one holding it was known to see and communicate with ghosts. It would compel them to speak. In Germany if one took a sprig of mistletoe into an old house, spirits would appear and could be forced to answer questions. Wearing a small bag around the neck would repel evil spirits and keep one safe from dark witchcraft, from UK. From Alabama folks placed mistletoe seeds above the doors to repel evil spirits. According to astrologers of old, mistletoe is a plant dedicated to the sun.

From Morayshire Scotland, during the full moon in March green branches of the magical mistletoe were cut. These were woven into a circular wreath and kept for the rest of the year, to help with curing many diseases. The wreath could be passed up and down the body for this. Mistletoe growing on an oak was known as a panacea, having the ability to 'heal-all'. Southern American folk magic tells that African American women would use mistletoe as an amulet, hung around the neck for drying up milk during the weaning process.

Folk Medicine

The Berries of mistletoe are known to be toxic and the leaves are considered to be a low-dose botanical and generally consumed under the care of a qualified herbalist. The powder was given to women who could not conceive – an old Druid remedy, and a decoction was prescribed for barrenness. One assumes the leaf was used in these accounts, taken in small doses. From Brittany it had the ability to cure fevers. From Sweden mistletoe was used for epilepsy and as an antidote to all poisons. Mistletoe from a hawthorn tree was used as a cure for dropsy and if it was soaked in mare's milk, this milk could then be given to children for coughing fits. The Welsh Physicians of Myddfai used the leaf for jaundice. Jaundice was also cured in Normandy by placing the berries of the plant in a male babies urine, and then laying it on the patients head with a secret incantation. The powder of mistletoe gathered from an oak tree was an old cure for epilepsy

In fact, mistletoe was known as a cure for epilepsy throughout different cultures. One folk cure was to take powdered mistletoe the dosage being as much as would fit on a six pence, to be consumed in the morning with beer or black cherry water for a number of days nearest the full moon. For the same complaint rings of the plant were worn on the fingers in Sweden. Even chaplets hung around the bed were said to be effective from Normandy or necklaces made from it. Combined with peony root, it was worn as an amulet by infants for fits, from Sussex. Hawthorn mistletoe was used specifically for epilepsy in Herefordshire.

It has been known since ancient times to have a beneficial effect on the heart, one record from Inverness Shire in Scotland where a woman used the leaves to treat palpitations. It was used for calming the nerves, an Irish cure from Meath and Cavan. From Cork and Limerick, it was recorded as being used for epilepsy and hysteria. Used for tumors, the juice of the leaves was applied. In North America, mistletoe tea as given to women where menstruation was stagnant due to a cold condition. The juice of the bruised leaves was used as drops for the ear but the intention here is unclear, whether for alleviating pain or for hearing purposes. It was a cure for measles from Somerset, in particular if gathered from a hawthorn tree. In Essex a mistletoe leaf soaked in milk was eaten as a preventative for having a stroke. Another old use was the berries used for the stich in the side, or for sudden pain. On a veterinary note, the plant was given to cows and sheep after giving birth in Herefordshire.

From ancient Anglo-Saxon medicine the plant was used for headache, soreness and swelling of the eyes and for pain in the kidneys. In one receipt for a headache, mistletoe was pounded with rose juice, or myrtle, and then vinegar, being bound to the face. For eye soreness mistletoe was crushed with wine and then applied. For kidney pain it was combined somehow with pomegranate rind.

From North American folk medicine, *Viscum album* was used similarly, though not a native plant. It is unclear whether this was from the imported plant, or the local genus *Phorodendron*. There are folk records of it being used as an infusion for high blood pressure, for dizziness and for hives. The leaves were chewed or worn in one's hat for treating headaches. An infusion made from the berries was an epilepsy treatment, or the leaves could be worn as an amulet to prevent the same.

There were some medicinal and magical uses of the local mistletoe species in different Native tribes as well. The oak mistletoe that I am most familiar with *P. leucarpum* was made into a sort of a wash to bath the head for headache, from the Cherokee tribe. From the same tribe, it was dried and pulverized, taken for epilepsy and fits in particular if gathered from oak trees. It was used as a woman's medicine in an unspecified way for pregnant women. And it was taken after 4 days of vomiting from lovesickness, a magical use. The Creek tribe used the leaves and branches somehow for lung and pulmonary troubles and the Mendocino tribe used it as an abortifacient, and toothache remedy. The Seminole tribe steamed the branches and leaves, rubbing them on the body for soreness and deer sickness, which manifested as numb painful joints and limbs. The same tribe used it for ill babies, though the application is not specified. It was also taken as an emetic for ceremonial purposes.

Personal Use

While I have not used mistletoe internally or medicinally, I certainly have been blessed to have access to some *Phorodendron* for magical use. Either the European or the American species can be used interchangeably for magical purposes, in my opinion as I have used both. Gather while in full berry during the dark month of December on a full moon closest to Christmas Eve. For fertility, hang the plant in full berry with a green ribbon on the bed stand for a simple amulet. I have received *Viscum album* from England that was harvested from an old apple tree that fell, and I do tend to reserve its use for the more protective and apotropaic uses, just a personal preference I suppose.

This magical and strange plant offers something very uncanny and Otherworldly to the magical apothecary. Its use in spirit conjuring is unmatched, and its one plant that is both protective and conductive in that regard. If one is lucky enough to find it growing in a grave yard upon an old oak tree in the winter months, this mistletoe wood can be used to make a wand for calling and directing ghosts. The leaves taken can be used in protective powders or pouches, in particular from dark and malign spirits rather than just generalized protection. Try the leaves in an oracular powder to be sprinkled on water for scrying on the nights of the year where the veil is thinnest, a simple recipe is provided below.

With mistletoe being connected to the Yuletide holiday, hanging up the mistletoe with the other Midwinter evergreens is an essential aspect of bringing the immortal and long lived magical wildness indoors, blessing the dwelling with such potency and honoring the darkness. As tradition has it the mistletoe is to be left up after all other greens are removed for the remainder of the year. When I have gotten the chance to harvest the plant myself for any purpose, I have done so without the use of any metal and make certain that the plant does not touch the ground.

Many thanks to the golden green mistletoe, thriving and fruiting when all else is dead. May its power bring truth and opening to visions perceived and may its beauty grace the Yuletide table and hearth. A beckoner of ghosts and a force of fire, this uncommon walker between worlds touches the stars and is blessed by birdwings, from beyond the veil.

Mistletoe Spirit Powder for Scrying

Gather graveyard mistletoe leaves on a full moon, in the dark months, dry them and reduce them to a powder in a heavy mortar and pestle. Combine them in a vessel with equal parts of dried and sifted grave earth and store until needed.

For cauldron scrying, gather well water or water from a spring. Pour it into the cauldron and wait until it settles. Once it has, sprinkle a bit of the powder on the surface. It is helpful to have the lighting in the room just right – enough to allow for distortion in the water, but not too much to fix the shapes there. Before beginning, call in the powers of both the Dead and the mistletoe plant to help open the Third Eye to assist with seeing what is normally unseen. Then allow your eyes to relax and a trance like state to fall upon you, until visions are acquired. It is a process that can take some practice and be frustrating to beginners who are often desirous of instant results. But remember as with anything, the more time that is spent exercising that muscle so to speak, the more clear things will become. With practice, a sharper level of discernment will be refined, this being just as helpful as the visions that are produced and the interpretation of them. Burning a bit of yarrow *Achillea millefolium* is helpful if one is communicating with spirits of the Dead, as is using yarrow tea in the cauldron in place of the well water.

BROOM
Cytisus scoparious

Evergreen broom with her long and slender stems growing in dense clusters is a classic plant of the wayside. Verdant through the winter months in places with a mild climate, Scotch broom explodes with deep golden bonnets of flowers in mid-spring. Gracing a thicket of Scotch broom in glowing bloom is almost painful for the eyes to behold, so bright and intense are the flowers against the handsome emerald stems.

Though many plants and trees were used to make besoms in times past, Scotch broom more commonly called just 'broom', is very effective and it is clear as to why its common name tells of its function. I have been blessed to acquire a locally made besom made from a cedar handle and a bundle of broom. When used for the mundane purpose of sweeping the cottage floor, it is very effective indeed, with a charming creaking noise that comes from the sweeping motion itself. Butchers broom *Ruscus aculeatus* is sometimes found scattered throughout the lore, however when just the entry of 'Broom' is found, it is Scotch broom that is being referenced at least in my research.

Appearing in the places where heavy machinery has devastated the soil and native habitat, Scotch broom grows and helps to heal the earth with nitrogen fixing roots, as do many of the plants in the *Fabaceae* or legume family. Many folks do not know that this plant is beneficial, as it is a despised invasive plant in the Pacific Northwest. She often grows on hillsides, assisting in preventing erosion and mending the soil. After local trees of the area return and get larger, Scotch broom eventually gets crowded out and dies back. Sadly, it is environments such as our native prairies that are most effected by her invasive nature. If practices such as controlled burnings were still utilized, this would not be such a problem.

Broom is a perennial native to western and central Europe. Common names of broom included Basam, Bizzom, Bisom, Brum, Browme, Golden Chain, Cat's Peas and Green Broom. Its Latin species name also indicates its use as a broom, the Latin *scoparius* comes from *scopa* meaning 'besom'. In England Scotch broom was believed to be a favorite plant of the witches. As this plant makes the classic besom of the rustic county home it was associated with assisting the witches flight to the great Sabbat along with pitchforks, animals, eggshells, ragwort and straw to name a few other potential vehicles.

Broom played a part in a magical formula from the Welsh tale of the Mabinogion, to make the Lady Blodeuedd. The magicians Math and Gwydion made a wife for the hero Lleu: *'(from) the flowers of the oak, the flowers of the broom and the flowers of the meadowsweet, and from those they conjured up the fairest and most beautiful maiden that anyone had ever seen.'*

Broom had some protective properties surrounding it, as many yellow flowered plants do. There was a formula from Tyrol, to enable one to see witches. A bundle of broom, rue *Ruta graveolens*, agrimony *Agrimonia eupatoria*, maidenhair Adiantum spp., and ground Ivy *Glechoma hederacae*, was carried and one would have the power then to distinguish witches. This bundle if laid over the threshold would also prevent witches from entering the home. From the western Balkans, broom was used as a strong protection from hostile enemies however the way it was used is not specified.

In other protective lore, to burn it was a charm to keep witches away from Italy. To ride a broom around a field on Good Friday was a way to prevent moles from disturbing the grounds, a peasant Bohemian practice. From East Prussia riding a broom was known to prevent fevers though in what context, it is not clear. If cattle were driven over a broom placed within the threshold of the barn, it was believed to keep them safe from possession of evil spirits for the entire year in particular if the brooms were made during the 12 days of Christmas. Using a spray of the golden flowers was a traditional decoration for the Whitsuntide festivals, though it is surprising that the flowers would still be on in early June or the seventh Sunday after Easter. If the flowers were heavy on the plant, it meant the grain harvest would be plentiful that season from Scotland.

There is an interesting old recipe for making yeast using broom that was recorded from a Scottish witch: *'Take an oaken bough in the summer, or in winter a Broom bush, put either of them into the yest that workes, and let it imbibe as much as it will, so hang it up and keep it for your use. When you use it, put a little of this to a little wort, about two quarts, bloud warm.'* Hildegard von Bingen from the twelfth century had a recipe for countering the effects of the magical mandrake that included broom. One was to harvest seven shoots of broom, the roots and leaves of one cranesbill plant *Geranium spp.*, and two mallows *Malva spp.* If these were all pounded together using the middle finger only and made into a paste, this could be spread on a cloth and held to the body to take away the power of the mandrake.

From Guernsey there comes an example of amulet magic that is quite impressive, involving broom. This was to be hung around one's neck and worn against the power of dark witches. One was to take nine bits of green broom and two sprigs of the same to fashion a cross from, nine morsels of elder (*Sambucus nigra*), nine leaves of betony (*Stachys officinalis*), nine of agrimoony (*Agrimonia eupatoia*), a little bay salt, sal ammoniac, new wax, barley, leaven, camphor and quick silver, which was enclosed in cobblers wax. These were put all in a new linen cloth and sewn shut. A powerful formula, no doubt.

A German charm for healing an amputated limb involved broom. The charmer would take a broom twig and press it together with the wound. Then the broom twig was taken along with the bloody linen, and it was brought to a dry place with these words spoken over it: *The wounds of our Lord Christ, they are not bound: But these wounds, they are bound, in the name of the Father, the Son and the Holy Ghost, Amen!*

Dreaming of this plant meant an increase in the family, as brooms in general were often associated with marriages and fertility. The golden flowers were sometimes used in rustic bridal bouquets in the springtime. In some parts they were strewn along with other flowers for the wedding processions as this quote tells: 'The wheaten ear was scatter'd near the porch, The green bloom blossom'd strew'd the way to church'. If a woman put a besom outside of her home, it was an indication that she was searching for a new husband. In the language of the flowers broom symbolized humility and the plant is ruled by Mars according to astrologers of old.

Broom had its ill-omened associations as well. There was a rhyme that told *If you sweep the house with blossomed broom in May, you sweep the head of the house away.* This indicates that the blooms were not to be brought inside in particular during May, which was considered on the British Isles to be an unlucky month. To do so was to bring death to the family. If the flowers were picked in general, it was believed the mother or father of the house would die. One possible reason for its unlucky lore goes back to a story that tells of the broom plant and the cracking sound of its ripe black seed pods. It almost gave away the hiding place of Mary and Joseph as they fled to Egypt. The noise from the plant threatened to reveal their whereabouts to the soldiers of Herod, the tale tells.

In Wales it was used as a charm, a swath waved over a restless person to cause sleep. Sprinkling the flowers in a circle on a hillside would cause people to sleep as well. From an ancient Scottish ballad we learn:

Then out it speaks an auld witch wife,
Sat in the bower aboon
'O ye shall gang to Broomfield hills,
Walk nine times round and round,
Down below a bonny burn bank,
Ye find your love sleeping sound
Ye'll pu' the bloom frae off the broom,
Strew't at his head and feet,
And aye the thicker that ye do strew,
The sounder he will sleep.'

It seems in this instance to be used in some sort of love magic, though there is no doubt some things are missing from the traditional formula. Understandably broom flowers were a symbol of humility, likely because it was used as a necessary domestic tool. In addition to being used for a besom, the flowers and whole plant were used as a dye plant for fiber, for making baskets with, and the plant itself was used as a rustic thatch for animal sheds and small shelters.

Folk Medicine

There were some folk medicinal uses for broom, though it is known as a low dose botanical in modern times. Dosage is essential to avoid toxicity. One must be careful to make sure that Spanish broom is avoided, *Spartium junceum*, though this plant is more commonly found in Southern Europe. Broom tops were used for dropsy and as a heart remedy as it was a diuretic. In Norfolk an infusion of the flowers, stem and root was used to cure jaundice. It was known to bring on labor and promote fast child birth. A few sprigs boiled in water was taken as a Romany kidney tonic, the dosage being one wineglassful in the morning. From Staffordshire in the last 100 years comes a rheumatism recipe using broom. The sprigs were collected, cut up and dried and then made into tea for the complaint.

It was an antidote to many poisons and was used topically as well. A wash from the tops made from the tea was an Irish remedy for abscesses and soaking the feet in the same was a cure for dropsy. The flowers were made into an ointment and applied for gout. It was known to staunch bleeding and a magical cure from Scotland was to wrap a stem around the neck to stop a nosebleed. A Cornish remedy for rheumatic pains was to use the golden flowers in a bath. An old recipe for killing lice included the juice of broom mixed with radish oil, applied topically to the scalp.

Personal Practices

Broom is a constant companion in the Pacific Northwest areas of disturbed ground. Its vibrant green stems, golden flowers and black seed pods make it a striking bush, in the patches and dense clusters as it prefers to grow. I don't use it medicinally or internally, though I do have an old recipe for Scotch broom blossom wine that I want to try. In my experience this plant is a wonderful one to include in any domestic magical work. It can be incorporated into charms for hearth and home, the stems wrap and bundle nicely with other plants. The yellow flowers can be harvested and dried for use in sleeping and dream pillows, but also for protective purposes. Many yellow flowered plants had the ability to keep away dark witches in lore from times past. Such an illuminating quality these flowers indeed possess. They can be used in sprinkling powders or herb mixtures for the protection of dwellings and animal shelters, as well as worn in a pouch on a person for the same.

A besom made from this plant can be used for home protection, if placed stems upright just inside the front door. Importantly this besom can be used ritually. It is a satisfying experience to open and close a circle byway of sweeping. I find that sweeping in general is my most preferred household chore, it is relaxing to the mind and body. A besom can be swept around the perimeter of the home or a room, during house cleansings in a sunwise direction. Traditionally, brooms were used in marriages, therefor in rustic ceremonies the couple can jump over the broom together similar to jumping over the fire to bless the union. A besom is a lovely gift for a newly wedded couple, a blessing not only for their marriage but for their home. I have met numerous witches who keep one broom for magical work and one for actual sweeping of the floors, a good practice in general.

> *Many thanks to the golden Witches Broom, gathered during the dark 12 days to sweep protections into the home and hearth. May her dried bonnet shaped blooms bring peace and ease to dreams and the matron's bedstead. By night flight, might circles be cast and then closed again, by the creaking besom of the crone's ride.*

Home and Hearth Sweeping Tool

Harvest Scotch broom stems with offerings of milk and honey near Beltane Eve. Some of the flowers should be gone now and there will be green pods turning black, depending on your climate. If the pods are ripe when you harvest it is fine, but you will likely have to deal with a bit of a mess with the seeds and pods shedding themselves from the stems. You can also harvest during the twelve days of Christmas, another powerful time of year. This way there are no flowers/seedpods to worry about, though the plants are beautiful to behold in both flower and seed.

Hang them to partially dry for about 5 days. Then cut them to a similar length and bind them with some natural twine tightly to make a hand broom of sorts. One can attach a hag stone, rowan berries, a feather or three of a domestic bird, or any sort of additional charms to it so long as it does not make it overly cumbersome to use. I like one that is about two feet long. This needs to be dried out for a few weeks or so, though it can be used fresh. It will shrink when dried so if the bindings were not tight, one may have to retighten them.

This small broom can be used specifically to sweep and cleanse the hearth area, and if kept in the vicinity of the house spirit, all the better. Even this smaller besom can be used to sweep open ritual circles, with one hunched over just as a crone might be – humility indeed. Stood next to the cauldron it is symbolic of not only simple and once common domestic tools, but of the witch's tools as well. It can be used to sweep bad energy out of the house, after a quarrel has occurred there. Ordinary objects used for magic often have some of the most incredible applications and lore. This sweeping tool can be burned in an outdoor fire as a ritual offering, it is quite flammable material however, take care. Eventually it will need to be made anew, as the lower stems will begin to break off and become brittle.

BURDOCK
Arctium lappa/minus

Burdock is a strikingly beautiful plant that grows on the edges of disturbed ground loving part or full sun. This plant has been used extensively in folk medicine for ages, with all parts being helpful for a spectrum of maladies. She looks like a thistle but upon closer inspection, is completely soft lacking the spines and prickles of her more protective sisters. However, the burdocks large brown burrs attach themselves to every animal or human passing by, and though not sharp or painful they are a tiresome ornament to remove especially if they have begun to decompose during the winter months. urdocks lovely purple flower heads are very thistle like attracting bees with their sweetness. While there is not a great deal of magic or occult lore associated with burdock, interestingly many of the uses are amuletic in nature. There are however many folk medicinal applications of note.

Great burdock is *A.lappa* and lesser burdock is *A.minus*. The Latin name *Arctium* has roots in the Greek word *Arctos*, meaning 'bear'. This connection to the bear is thought to be from the brown furry burrs. *Lappa* apparently comes from the Celtic word *llap*, meaning 'hand', though some sources suggest it refers to the burrs as well. Other common names for burdock included: Billy Buttons (Cornish), Herrif (Old English), Beggars Buttons, Clotburr, Happy Major, Gypsy Rhubarb, Touch-Me-Not, Sweethearts, Great Bur, Cockle Buttons, Love Leaves, Lappa, Stick Tight, Burr Seed, Hare Burr, Turkey-Burr, and Snakes Rhubarb. These many common names indicate the widespread nature of this plant. Burdock is native to Europe, now introduced and considered an invasive weed in some parts of the US and Australia. It is in the Asteraceae or sunflower family.

Burdock was gathered during Midsummer time to hang and protect the home from lightning storms and evil giants. Like thistle, it was sacred to Thor and therefore a lightning plant. It was hung up around the doors of a dwelling to protect it from evil forces entering. It was also braided into the tails of cows to protect them from bewitchment. One rustic charm for getting rid of threadworm in cows was to hold a bundle of burdock in one hand, and a stone in the other – the stone was to represent Thor's hammer. These words were repeated: *Burdock leaf, I strangle you, burdock leaf you shall not go*, 'till the cow lets the threadworm go. In Russia similar to thistle, burdock had the name of Devil Alarmer, or Devil Conqueror. It was hung up for the protection of buildings, animals and homes.

As found with plantain *Plantago major* and mugwort *Artemisia vulgaris*, a magical coal could be dug from under the burdock on Midsummer's Eve. This was to be gathered at either midnight or noon and worn as an amulet for protection during the following year. Sometimes it was gathered for a particular illness. Some scholars speculate that this black 'coal' was just a portion of rotten root, but folks within living memory still believe it to be a magical offering from the plant only available at this powerful time of year.

Burdock

The burrs of the burdock themselves have much whimsical lore associated with them. One Cornish belief was that piskies (little Folk) were known to amuse themselves after nightfall by riding their Faerie colts around and either braiding their manes, or tangling them with the burrs of burdock. An old custom in some parts of Britain was for a man to dress up as the 'Burry Man', on the second Friday in August. This is where a suit was cleverly fashioned out of the burdocks many burrs and then worn by a masked man through the town, along with a procession of followers. Flowers were also used to decorate him. Money and gifts are given, later to be divided between the parade's party. It is speculated that this custom which occurred around harvest time, was similar in origins to the 'Jack in the Green' processions of May Day. The Burry Man is less known about however and is not recorded before the mid nineteenth century.

To have burdock burrs stick to your clothing was a bad omen in some parts, foretelling difficulty in a favorite undertaking. Another bit of lore tells that if you have burrs stuck to your clothing after a walk, to then throw them into the fire. If the flame is clear, it tells that the next fortnight (two weeks) will be lucky for any endeavor.

Burdock had some historical uses in love magic another common name for it being Loves Leaves, for the heart shaped soft leaf tinged with pink near the stems. A reason for this use certainly comes from the clinging nature of the burrs. A common childhood love divination game that many remember was to throw a burr at the back of one's crush; if it stuck to them, it was a sign of their returned affections and if not, it told of love not reciprocated. Another version of this was for a girl to pick a burr and name it after her lover. Then it was to be thrown against her skirt by another girl; if it stuck, it was a sign he was faithful. In Balkan folk magic, burdock is used in love magic and to bring couples together. According to astrologers of old burdock is ruled by Venus, which makes sense with these considerations.

In American folk magic from Arkansas, burdock roots were threaded onto a necklace and worn against enchantment and bewitchment. An Albanian use from the Balkans employed burdock leaves in an exorcism rite. It was believed that a person could become possessed by evil forest spirits, and that a priest would be needed to exorcise them if this was the case. This could be done by a ceremony that used bread soaked in wine, the whole placed on broad burdock leaves. One wonders at the details of the ceremony, which are sadly to remain a mystery for lack of information.

Folk Medicine

Burdock has much interesting folk medicine ascribed to it, throughout many cultures due to its widespread distribution. A Romany remedy for rheumatism was to take an infusion of the crushed leaves, flowers or seeds (most preferred). They carried small bags of the seeds as an amulet against the same. An early American folk remedy combined burdock root, dandelion root *Taraxacum officinalis*, and Virginia snakeroot *Aristolochia serpentaria* as one formula for rheumatic pains.

In general, burdock was known as a blood purifier and indeed this is still how it is used by herbalists today. The roots specifically were used for this. From Middle Age medicine, burdock was used as a cure for kidney/urinary complaints and gallstones. An old remedy for lung complaints calls for the roots preserved in sugar, also this was a remedy for gout. Burdock roots were strung onto necklaces and worn by babies for teething pain, these necklaces were known as 'anodyne necklaces'. An interesting use from John Gerard was to take the peeled raw or boiled stalks in broth as an aphrodisiac – another connection to matters of love. One old recipe called for burdock root to be decocted in wine and drunk for wheezing of the lungs and shortness of breath. Another recipe calls for the stamped root added with wine, yolks of eggs, powdered acorns and nutmegs, taken to strengthen the back. An Irish use for burdock was for convulsions and nervousness.

The seeds taken out of the burrs had their own use in folk medicine. They were used for bladder and kidney pain, taken internally as a tea. They were also ground and taken in an infusion for dysentery and neuralgia. The tea made as an infusion was given to teething babies, to help with sleeplessness. One headache recipe involved using the seeds in combination with apple cider, white mustard and horseradish – an infused vinegar to be taken internally, I assume.

The plant was used since olden times for fevers and skin diseases, such as boils, acne and eczema. One of the ways to apply it for a fever was to bind the leaves to the wrists and ankles, with the points directed downward. This was thought to run the fever out of the body. An early American remedy for diarrhea in babies mixed the seeds or crushed roots with yeast, then applied the poultice to the babies' navel. However, care should be taken to be sure the navel had healed after the birth process before applying this remedy.

The large soft leaves of burdock were applied as a poultice for rheumatic pains, swellings, bruises, burns, cuts, boils, sore joints, swollen feet, tumors, infections and open wounds. The juice of the root mixed with salt was a remedy for the pain of snakebite. An Irish remedy for ringworm was to make a poultice of the roots. The leaves boiled in milk made a specific lotion for burns, another old recommendation was crushing the leaves with egg white and applying for the same. A recipe for gout called for the leaves boiled with bran and urine, until the liquid was greatly reduced, and then applying the mash to the painful area.

A shampoo of sorts could be made from the roots (a decoction) and used for dandruff, thinning hair and to promote shiny hair. The leaves were worn in one's hat to prevent getting sunstroke, and also used as a wart remedy by transference magic. They were rubbed on the wart and then buried under a tree, the logic being of course as the leaves rotted in the ground, the warts would disappear.

Burdock had some interesting applications in women's medicine. A seventeenth century use included the leaves being tied to a pregnant woman's belly to help keep the baby in the correct position for birth. They were also used for helping to move the uterus that had prolapsed back to its optimal position, by placing on the top of the head, bottom of the feet or on either side of the navel.

Personal Practices 🌿

The burdock plant is very healing in a medicinal way, and my experience mostly reflects this. Besides using the burrs in love magic as a rustic binding charm, I turn to the root for its incredible blood cleansing abilities. Burdock is a biennial, which means it has a two-year life cycle. The first year, the plants energy goes into making the leaves and establishing the root. The second year, the plants energy goes into making the flower and then the seed, to distribute.

Harvest the roots during the fall or early spring of its first year, before it has gone to flower. After offerings have been made, you can begin the digging process. Start back farther from the plant than you think, it is easy to snap the long thick taproot early on. Digging burdock in stony or compact soil is a chore and takes much effort. But the wild roots are more potent than the store bought ones. Burdock root is sold as a vegetable at natural food stores and used in Japanese cooking, known as 'Gobo'. It is fine to use this, but the wild root is preferred. Likely you will end up breaking the root at some point, so collect from numerous plants, being sure to leave some plants to create their beautiful burrs and seeds. Wash and chop the root to dry or make a folk tincture right away (see Appendices).

I have used burdock to successfully cure acne related to hormone fluctuations, combined with red clover blossom *Trifolium pratense*. The dried root can be decocted for tea and a few cups drunk per day for this, adding the blossoms to steep at the end of the boiling time. The root decoction is also helpful as a hair rinse for dandruff. Burdocks mineral rich and cooling root is considered hepatic, alterative and tonic. It can be incorporated into any liver supportive blend or combined with other roots and used to build the blood. I personally find burdock less diuretic than dandelion, though it is still considered a diuretic and used for as a tonic for chronic urinary tract issues. It enhances kidney function as well and is excellent when employed for gout.

Burdock root combined with rosehips in a decoction is especially nice. The dried roots can be roasted and used as a coffee substitute, similar to or along with dandelion root. The fresh roots can be chopped and infused in vinegar along with dock root *Rumex obtusifolius/crispus*, dandelion root *Taraxacum officinalis* and fresh stinging nettles *Urtica dioica* for a tonic drink. See recipe below for a variation.

Many thanks to this healing plant of the disturbed countryside and city scapes, may we notice her during our times of need. When seeking aid to clean up the toxic situation that arises from pollution within our bodies, burdock is an ally to know. With deep brown roots reaching underneath the earths surface, burdock penetrates places unseen and pulls up minerals long hidden, ready to become available in a water elixir once more.

Autumn Roots Oxymel for Building the Blood

Have a clean quart sized French canning jar (this corrodes less than a Mason jar), with an intact seal in place. Harvest, wash and chop (all fresh) one cup of burdock root, one cup of dandelion root *Taraxacum officinalis* and half a cup of dock root *Rumex obtusifolius/crispus*. Place them in the jar. Add half a cup of cleaned and de-seeded rosehips (or one quarter cup dried), the chopped peel of half an orange, and 1-2 Tablespoons of cinnamon chips, to taste. Then fill to three quarters of the jar with apple cider vinegar, topping it off with a quarter honey. Leave an inch or so for stirring room. Stir every day with a chopstick for a month. Then strain and store in dark bottles in a cupboard. Take half a shot glass full, diluted with water if desired, a few times per day to support the liver and build the blood. Excellent taken as a cold and flu preventative as well.

DOCK
Rumex obtusifolius

Dock is one of our most common plants and in many ways, one of the most helpful plants to know. Broad leaf dock *Rumex obtusifolius*, can be found in almost any field, meadow edge, forest edge, and/or disturbed ground at least in the western US. The vibrant green leaves are tinged with deep pink and red, boasting an appearance almost like leathery snake skin. The long seed stalks are topped early in the season with a paper green blush, then deep coral pink, finally ending with a display of dark rusty brown later in the fading days. It wouldn't be autumn time without dock seed heads gracing the roadsides, covered in spider webs.

Dock is in the buckwheat family, *Polygonaceae*, and there are around 200 species in this genus. They have been introduced from Eurasia and are now widespread throughout much of the Northern hemisphere. Other common names for broad leaf dock are Bitter Dock, Red veined Dock and Butter Dock. The later name was given to the plant because in good soil, the leaves grow very large and were used as a natural 'wax paper' to wrap butter in when bringing to market. A few other common names for dock included: Land Robber, Patience, Bitter Patience, Batter Dock, Docken and Donkeys Oats. The genus *Rumex* also includes the common plants garden sorrel *R.acetosa*, sheep sorrel *R.acetosella*, and yellow dock *R.crispus*.

This plant has much more folk medicine historically associated with it, rather than folk magical practices. However there are a few things of interest to mention. There was an Irish practice to tie a dock seed head to a woman's left arm for fertility magic, to keep her from being barren. This was also done in Danish folk magic. This is likely because there are so many seeds that it suggests fertility byway of sympathetic magic, not to mention that almost every seed germinates once fallen from the plant. There was a love divination associated specifically with 'butter dock'. The seeds were to be scattered by a young unmarried woman half an hour before sunrise, on a Friday morning in some lonely place. While she strew the seeds on the ground, she was to repeat this charm, '*I sow, I sow. Then my own dear, Come here, come here, And mow and mow*'. She would then see in a vision her future husband walking toward her with a scythe.

Using a dock leaf to rub on a nettle sting was and still is a British folk remedy. There was a little rhyme to chant when you got stung, '*Nettle out, dock in; Dock remove the nettle sting.*', while rubbing the dock leaf on the affected part. There are different versions of the rhyme depending on where it originated from. A few Irish variants went '*Nettle burnt me and Dock healed me*' and 'Hot, hot nettle and cold, cold dock'. A Cornish version was '*Dock leaf, dock leaf, you go in. Sting nettle, sting nettle, you come out*'. It was traditional in some areas of Britain to spit on the leaf first. In other areas, using the little drop of dew from a newly unfurling dock leaf was the only supposed cure for a nettle sting.

We find that the humble dock features in quite a number of leechdoms from early English Anglo-Saxon magic and medicine. In one charm from *The Leechbook of Bald*, dock was used along with other herbs for helping a patient with 'water elf disease', presumably where a person was essentially ill-wished by a water spirit. Dock was combined with lupin(toxic-not recommended for internal use), yew berries(toxic-not recommended for internal use), helenium (elecampane), marshmallow, elder, pennyroyal, lily, wormwood, dill, fen mint, iris root, comfrey, horehound, thistle, and strawberry leaf. The herbs were chopped up and mixed with both ale and holy water, and this charm was sung three times over the healing potion:

Dock

I have wreathed round the wounds
The best of healing worts,
That the baneful sores may
Neither burn nor burst,
Nor find their way further,
Nor turn foul and fallow,
Nor thump or throb on,
Nor be wicked wounds,
Nor dig deeply down,
But he himself may hold
In a way to heath.
Let it ache thee no more
Than an ear in earth acheth.

The further instructions go: *Sing this many times, that the earth may bear on thee with all her might and main. These charms may one sing over a wound.* One assumes the application of the potion was external.

The seeds of sheep sorrel *R. acetosella* (or possibly garden sorrel *R. acetosa*), were used against elf shot in another leechdom, combined with Scottish wax and the whole blessed by singing twelve masses over it. It was then applied to an animal that had been elf shot, along with Holy water. In another prescription, the whole dock plant, including the roots were placed in a rag and hung around a horse's neck as a magical cure for a cough.

Yet another leechdom is given here: *For an ulcer ... take a handful of springwort, and a handful of waybread, and a handful of maythe, and a handful of the lower part of dock, that which will float, boil in butter, filter the salt and the foam off, add a little English honey, put it over a fire to boil, once it is boiling sing three 'pater noster' over it, take it off again, then sing 'pater noster' nine times onto it, and boil it up thrice, and take it off the boil as often, and cure with it after'* (translation from S. Pollington). This leechdom uses dock root, the springwort likely being Caper Spurge *Euphorbia lathyrix* (known to have a toxic quality to its latex), the waybread being plantain *Plantago major*, and the Maythe being a mystery plant, possibly Roman chamomile *Anthemis nobilis*. These old receipts (an old word for recipe) give us a sense that dock has long been valued as a medicinal plant.

In the language of flowers, dock symbolized patience and shrewdness. The dock plant was mentioned in a phrase in an Irish folktale to portray a moonlit night, the English translation of it being *'The white gelding (the moon) seeking the shade of the dock, and the dock receding from it'*. Dock is ruled by Jupiter, according to astrologers of old.

Folk Medicine

Dock was used extensively in British and Irish domestic folk medicine. Though this information is for broad leaf dock, many sources state that the species *R. obtusifolius* and yellow dock *R. crispus* were not always distinguished in folk record. The plant was used topically and internally. Both the leaves and roots of dock were used as dressings for various wounds, with the roots being cooked, mashed and applied. Burns and scalds were also remedied by using the leaves as a poultice. Another common application was to use the leaves to stop bleeding from a cut. The leaves were soaked in brandy before applying from Essex. An interesting example comes from the *Dictionary of Plant Lore*, by Roy Vickery. This is a firsthand account was taken from an elder from Tiverton, Devon, 1991. *'When I was a child (I am now 91), we lived on the Isle of Man, we were quite hard up and couldn't afford doctors' bills. My father was mowing grass one day and the scythe slipped and cut him very badly on the leg, he daren't stay home from work, so with my mother's help, doctored himself; every day after school I collected large dock leaves, which mother crushed with a rolling pin, then applied leaves straight on the cut which in time healed and caused no further trouble.'*

The leaves were used in first aid for sprains by wrapping the sprained part tightly with them. They were used to draw out boils and to ease rashes. Other topical applications with the leaves included shingles, bee stings, piles, boils, blisters, poison ivy rash, sunburn, chapped skin and bathing cancerous sores with a dock leaf wash. The heated leaves were used as a poultice for headaches in Norfolk and applied for rheumatic pains on the Dorset Somerset borders. The leaves mixed with lard made an ointment for piles, an older term for hemorrhoids. An old Anglo Saxon remedy for genital 'kernel's' which I presume to be warts, was to make a dock leaf plaster by mixing the leaves with grease, wrapping them in a cabbage leaf, warming them in ashes and then applying to the affected part. In the Scottish Highlands a soothing ointment was made from cooking the roots in butter and adding beeswax to firm the mixture up. There was a somewhat magical and medicinal cure involving dock root for resolving a certain kind of sore on the forearm that developed on workers in Ironstone quarries. The dock root was sliced and applied to the sore every three days, until it was cured.

Dock was used internally as well, mainly the root. Here is a rustic remedy from Gabrielle Hatfield's, *Hatfields Herbal*, quoted from F.H., from Bedfordshire in 1985. *'This is a cure for boils, which has proven in my own family. Dig up five dock roots, wash them so that they are very clean, put two cupfuls of clean water in a saucepan, also the five dock roots, and let them boil for thirty minutes. Strain them through fine muslin, and put in a bottle. Drink one teaspoon night and morning.'* There was a Romany cure for a springtime rash made by decocting sliced dock roots in elderberry wine. A cure for shingles comes from Cornwall by mixing the root decoction with bramble (blackberry) juice, drinking some and pouring some on the part afflicted while reciting a magical incantation (unrecorded). In parts of Britain, dock was known as a 'blood cleanser'. The root was also used for jaundice in England and for anemia in the Isle of Man. The Pennsylvanian Dutch decocted the roots and drank them as a tonic for the liver specifically. Many of these older uses point to dock root as having liver supporting capabilities, the main way it is used by modern herbalists today.

The seeds of dock infused in rum were apparently an excellent remedy for coughs, asthma, pleurisy and lung disorders. In Ireland, a decoction of the seeds was drunk for bronchitis and coughs of all kinds. They were also boiled in water and the resulting liquid applied in a compress for drawing pus from an infected boil or wound. Dock leaves were used to clean teeth in times past, by rubbing them with the fresh leaf. Old recipes that I have found include dock roots infused with red wine, licorice and juniper berries taken as a health tonic (France), and dock roots scraped with parsnip roots and boiled in butter used topically for itching (England).

Personal Practices

My magical use with the dock plant has been limited to including the seeds in offerings to appease various nature spirits, for use in general fertility magic and including them in healing charm bags. This plant is so helpful in a physical way, my primary use with it reflects this fact.

The highly scented spicy roots can be harvested with offerings made in the fall, though if needed at other times during the winter, spring and early summer, they are fine to be dug. Ideally any root harvesting happens in the autumn and winter time, when the plants energy is going downward. If the plants have flowered the roots are often tough and woody, but the bright yellow root bark can still be stripped from them. Throughout the growing season, it is helpful to chop off the flower stalk to help the roots be fleshy when harvest time comes, and to prevent the seeds from spreading invasively. However, be sure to leave some plants to seed on the edges of the yard to enjoy in the wayside landscape and keep the plants coming back.

The scent of freshly crushed dock root is so aromatic, spicy, and earthy; almost like ginseng. The roots are a gorgeous yellow, in fact more yellow than 'yellow dock' *Rumex crispus* roots, with which they are interchangeable. Dock root is considered bitter, hepatic, alterative and mildly laxative-aperient. It is excellent in digestive bitters formulas, so helpful for heartburn, sour stomach and bloated feelings after eating strange combinations of food. It is also very helpful for mild constipation that comes with stress or traveling. A favorite decoction in the autumn time is dock root, rosehips and a little cinnamon, all dried. This bitter brew sweetened with a little honey makes for a gently cleansing fall tonic. The syrup made from the fresh roots is fabulous taken straight or added to teas for its ability to decongest and support the liver, used for the above mentioned maladies. The roots contain iron and can also be made into a mineral elixir, used for anemia, see the recipe below.

Dock can be used topically as a fresh leaf poultice for rashes, cuts, beestings and of course nettle stings. The whole fresh plant, roots and all, can be infused in lard and used as a general all-purpose skin healing salve, making a wonderful dark green spicy scented ointment for first aid purposes. An old name for this ointment was 'cancer balm', and it was used for skin cancers as the name suggests.

The *Rumex* leaves are all edible when young. Sheep sorrel is common in fields and is known to children often as 'sour leaves', the small arrow shaped leaves have a distinct likeable lemony flavor. Yellow dock is a dock that is referenced regularly in herbal medicine for its liver supportive, mildly laxative and high iron containing yellow roots. This plant can be found in fields and gardens but is not near as common as broad leaf dock where I live. Yellow dock leaves are longer, with edges that looked wavy, curled and 'crisped', hence the Latin name *R.crispus*. Including broad leaved dock, these three *Rumex* species are true 'wayside' plants, loving disturbed soil and spreading joyfully. Their leaves are edible when young and add a nice green flavor to any spring soup or salad. All three species have been historically eaten in Britain. When cooked, they turn a khaki tan green color, like their relative French or garden sorrel. Just make sure that you don't gorge on any *Rumex* leaf because of their potential to disturb one's mineral balance. Also choose smaller, newer leaves for food use.

Many thanks to the healing balm and bitter brew that comes from the dock plant, so common and yet helpful for the many ailments that occur in the day to day. This underappreciated plant in modern times certainly found itself in the apothecary of the Wise folk of old. Bound roots in grease and rustic leaf bandages, a healer from the dark earth dock remains. Enjoy the yellow and green potions that can be made from this tenacious plant of abundance.

Mineral Elixir

This is a spectacular liquid iron tonic that is helpful after monthly menses and anemia in general. Here is the basic recipe that I have been making and taking for many years – the most helpful remedy for extra energy the week after monthly bleeding. To a wide mouth quart mason jar, add roughly:

½ cup dried dock root **Rumex obtusifolius/crispus**
¾ cup dried nettle leaf, crumbled well *Urtica dioica*
½ cup dried chopped cherries or prunes
1 cup raisins, chopped up
3/4 cup molasses
2 Table spoons of dried or fresh orange peel, chopped (for flavor more than anything)

Cover all of this with a good quality brandy. Shake daily for a month and then strain. If it seems too thick, add a little more brandy. It should taste like a 'cast iron pan', as an anemic friend once remarked when I gave her a dropper full to try without telling her what the dark liquid was. It can be stored at room temperature. I usually take 1-2 droppers full, three times per day, for the week of bleeding. Remember, that if you get a headache while taking this homemade iron supplement, decrease your amount – it is often a sign of taking too much. Make sure not to take store bought supplements at the same time, because of this possibility.

Dock Root Syrup 🌸

Harvest freshly dug dock roots, rinse them well outside and remove the greens. These can be infused in fat for a healing salve, add a chopped root or two as well. Or feed them to the chickens. Chop the roots small, removing any dark or discolored portions. Whatever you have, measure this and add to a heavy bottom saucepan. Roughly double the amount of organic cane sugar, add this as well. Add a shot of water, not any more. The roots themselves will lend water to the whole. Bring the mixture to a boil to dissolve the sugar and turn off. Do not boil hard or overcook, or you will make candy. Let the mixture steep for a few hours in the sugared water. Pour through a sieve to strain, bottle and keep in the fridge.

Take your leftover root pieces, roll in sugar and dry these. The syrup is excellent taken for heartburn, after a heavy meal, for indigestion, constipation, as a tonic for acne and eczema, and as a mild appetite stimulant taken before meals. Do not overuse, because of the oxalic acid – you may be tempted, it is delicious. I take a teaspoon as needed, then wait 15 minutes and take one more. As a tonic, a teaspoon or two can be added to hot water and dissolved, taken each day for a few weeks. The dried root pieces can be used for the same, carried in first aid kits or on trips. A few small pieces can be chewed up as needed. Also, they are excellent for canker sores, thanks to Brenda Hatcher for discovering this.

Charms of a Faerie Wyfe

What can be found, nestled amongst her old robes,
And on wooden altars
Splintered with ancient warp and moonshade
These charms are hushed on the winds,
They are buried in the earth

Under the Bramble Arch

Powders in brown paper, grave dirt, perfumed leaves
And soft amber duff
From the sacred pathways, bring guardians close
Horse tooth and crystal kept
The little Folk do ride and dance on the burial mounds

In the hidden glades, Ghosts and flints
Rowan cross and berry rosary
Keep their arrows at bay
Small cups of purple fringe
To help the woodland elves see in the dark

Seed and egg medicines,
Bring fertility and the spirals of snails
Abundance to the cottage hearth
White silk will wrap the black thorns,
A primrose posy is given for the traveler who walks alone

Hagstones and hawthorn smoke
Release the captives in the mounds
Free from the nightmare
The white horse as she vanishes
Near silver pools and mossy stones

The folksglove bows to the North
White for death, purple for memory
Are the pinpricks felt in the thumbs
Under witches thimbles
Something wicked this way comes
A box of quartz dust and flowers of rue
To bless the new babe, the new life
Shielded from the wights
Widdershuns they circle late
Frolic and prance in the old night

Spirit shades of ancient glade
Hear the footfalls of the Faerie Wyfe

Dock

Who comes with cakes and cream
For the waters blessed and crooked wands
For the muddy quartz unearthed

For the fragrant root dug near the streams
With sharpened deer bone anointed
By red oil of bleeding golden flowers
Passed through the juniper smoke
The amulets made by the Hidden Folk

Cloaked in the tales she goes
To the powers beyond the hedgerows
To the mineral cross and key
To the Easter Eve North running stream
Our Lady the white watcher, from ever land unseen

VIOLET
Viola spp.

Scented springtime violets are one of the special delights of the natural world. This little harbinger of the season's change is the earth mother's flower, an offering after a long winter's nap. They burst forth with tiny bonnet shaped flowers and unfold green heart shaped leaves under the forest canopy or amidst the open plains. Violet has a haunted place in the human heart – it is one of the oldest known and most humble medicinal plant medicines in history. There is something graceful about the violet, something timeless. Visions of an elder crone draped in gray and mud caked robes comes to mind, hunched over collecting the dew covered leaves and flowers that have the very scent of springtime embedded within their medicine.

There are around 100 species of the violet, which is in the violet family, *Violaceae*. They are native to most temperate zones, including Europe, North America and Asia. The violet genus *Viola* is shared with Pansy and Heartsease (or Johnny Jump Up) as *Viola tricolor*, both well-loved and widely known garden plants with medicinal powers as well. Old names for violet from the tenth century and onward translate to: Bonewort, Apple leaf, and Wyolet. The word *Viola* comes from the Latin form of the Greek name *Ione*. This name originates from a Greek legend where the God Jupiter had a beloved dame who was a priestess of his temple. She was named *Io* and when he was caught in a flirtation with her by his jealous wife Juno, he changed her into a white heifer cow. He caused violet flowers to spring from the earth as a sacred food for the heifer and named them after her. An old Greek name for violet is *Ion*, referring also to the nymphs of Ionia – a place that abounded with violets. Violets are sacred to both Jupiter and Venus, according to astrologers of old. There is another legend that tells of violets originally being white. After a petty argument, Venus turned them blue out of spite, because her son cupid adored them so.

Another classical myth involves both pine *Pinus spp.* and violets; Attis, a fertility deity mutilated himself under a pine tree into which his spirit passed. Violets then grew from his blood that was shed. The tree was bled at the vernal(spring) equinox for turpentine. The sacred tree was eventually cut down and adorned with ribbons and carried to a mother goddess's sanctuary, where it was decorated with violets and fleeces. Violets were a symbol of innocence (white ones in particular), faithfulness, beauty and humility. To dream of violets meant 'advancement in life', prosperity and riches to come. Violets were said to have come from the tears that Adam shed, after being banished from the Garden of Eden. As a flower adored by poets, violet is mentioned in many a verse. Here is a quote by Sir Walter Scott, as he crowns violet the Queen of wild flowers: *The Violet in her greenwood bower, Where Birchen boughs with Hazels mingle, May boast itself the fairest flower, In glen, in copse or forest dingle.'*

Here is another gorgeous old-time tribute to violet: "*I must go violetting – it is a necessity – I shall go quite alone with my little basket, twisted like a beehive that I love so well.... I smell them already – their exquisite perfume steams and lingers in this moist heavy air. Through this little gate, and along the green south bank of this green wheat field, and they burst upon me, the lovely violets in tenfold loveliness. The ground is covered with them white and purple, enameling the short dewy grass, looking but more vividly colored under the dull leaden sky*" – Mary Russell Mitford

Violet had associations with death and mourning in Europe. Shakespeare mentions them in this context as one line goes '*The purple Violets and Marigolds, Shall as a carpet hang upon thy grave While summer days do pass.*' This association must have come from earlier times, as the Greeks buried their dead with violets. The color purple was an old mourning and funerary color. Violets were particularly connected to the death of the young. Here is a rhyme from Shelly, an English poet: *'Lillies for a bridal bed, Roses for the matrons head, Violets for a maiden dead.'* It was thought that if both violets and roses bloomed in the autumn time, it foretold an epidemic for the following year. Bringing just a single violet into the house was supposed to bring bad luck to the family living there. In England, violets guarded mourners from poisonous fumes in the cemetery when planted in a graveyard.

The roots of Violet were used in various fumigations from the grimoire tradition for inducing visions, seeing spirits and for prophecy: *A perfume made of hempeseed, of the seeds of fleawort, violett roots and parsley maketh men see things to come and is available for prophsie.* Fleawort being *Plantago psyllium*. Another similar formula to see future events contained linseeds (flax), 'psellium seed' (*Plantago psyllium*), wild violet roots and wild parsley roots, all used as a fumigation as well the difference being the psyllium seeds substituted for the flax seeds in this case.

Romans and Greeks claimed that violets were flowers of love. A wild violet was said to mean 'love in idleness'. Violets were believed to calm anger and help with matters of the heart. Medieval manuscripts tell that their scent alone could calm frenzies. They were a traditional ingredient in love philters. Violets were also used in horse charming, being an ingredient in 'drawing potions' in England. The scent was used specifically to calm horses. Both bride's beds and cradles were historically decorated with violets in Germany. A posy of violets was a traditional gift for Mothering Sunday, three weeks before Easter. A wreath of violets worn around the neck was said to prevent drunkenness and rid of headaches. An old Anglo Saxon list includes violet as an herb to be used against 'wicked spirits'. It was thought that by smelling violets a singer could not use their voice and there were also superstitions that told bringing violet blooms into the house would bring in fleas and vermin.

Folk Medicine 🌸

Violets have a long history of use in both food and medicine. In Medieval times, violet was a salad herb and was eaten with lettuce and onions. They were also cooked as a potherb and served with meat. The flowers were made into a wine, a labor of love indeed. Violets have been used in confectionary for many hundreds of years and I find it true that some sort of sweetener seems to enhance their flavor. Another older way to use violets was to infuse them in raw goat milk – an ancient Celtic beauty treatment for the skin. A violet milk bath for the face as one is surrounded by burning fat lamps and stone walls sounds quite luxurious to modern folks, no doubt.

Older medicinal uses of violet involved inducing sleep. Although their fragrance is fleeting, their scent was thought to bring about sleep and dreams. It is now known that the fragrance of violet contains a chemical that numbs the olfactory sense, so as that the scent becomes only perceivable when you first smell them. There is an old saying *'To smell the smell out of violets'*, which is referring to this exact phenomenon. It is interesting that a flower would give such a remarkable fragrance only to take it away and leave you wanting more, she is a seductive one. In olden times it was thought that too many violets in a room would cause convulsions, probably on account of their strong scent in particular when wilted. Violet flower infused vinegar holds both the color and scent well, at least for a time. An older use of violet infused vinegar was for headaches, applied by being rubbed on the temples.

Both peoples of Europe and North America have used violet leaves and flowers as a tonic for the blood and for cancer, in particular in the last 150 years. The fresh leaves were applied as a poultice for cancerous growths and an infusion of the dried leaves and flowers was taken internally for the same. The roots of violet are purgative and emetic. Violets were used topically for inflammation, such as for bruises, stings and swelling and also as an eyewash for inflamed eyes. An old recipe for using violets topically includes stamping fresh violets along with honey and vinegar and using it as a plaster to heal inflamed boils.

Violet also has a history of use for the lungs and for fevers, thought to be a cooling herb by Medieval practitioners. Violet is soothing and can help coughing fits, bronchitis and asthma. One old piece of lore tells that those who are troubled by the lungs should always wear violets, as they would keep away coughs and keep the lungs strong against 'March Winds'. The leaves were used in North America as a poultice for headaches and a tea from violets was said to cure 'pain in the head' in England.

In Native American medicine, violets had some similar medicinal applications. There are many species that grow on this continent, the ones where I live being *V.glabella* or stream violet and *V.sempervirins*, the evergreen violet. Both are yellow flowered and non-fragrant. Though I cannot find those species in my references for use, a poultice of the leaves of other various species was used by numerous tribes for pain, swelling, sore eyes and lungs. Many tribes used violet in an infusion for colds, cleansing the blood and as a spring tonic. I assume that these uses are for the leaves (how I would use them is similar) rather than the roots, which are emetic. A few tribes used the plant for diseases of the heart, though the way and parts used is unspecified.

Personal Practices

> *The smell of violets, hidden in the green,*
> *Pour'd back into my empty soul and frame*
> *The times when I remember to have been*
> *Joyful and free from blame.*

Tennyson, Dream of Fair Women

Not all violets are fragrant, but I have found the ones that bloom earlier in the season are more likely to be so. The early flowering violets bloom starting in mid February and go until mid March or so. By fragrant, they do indeed possess the classic violet scent – fleeting, sweet, fresh, and floral with soft edges and a mysteriously familiar core perfume. If you cannot smell them directly after picking on a cold spring day, just set them in a small flat basket on your table and wait for a few hours. They will perfume your kitchen once wilted with their incredible scent, almost like fairy powdered sugar. I have found these violets on older homesteads or farms in wooded areas. They come in colors such as indigo purple, dark pink and pure white with little lavender hoods. They are found in patches as a groundcover, under evergreen trees or mixed in grassy areas. They do prefer shade. It is hard to ID their species because violets apparently cross easily. No doubt they are very similar to the true sweet garden violet, *Viola odorata*. *V. odorata* blooms during the same time period, has the same incredible fragrance and boasts a larger and more royal purple bloom. These early flowering violets are my favorite for magical purposes and medicine making, which I will give suggestions on further down.

The later flowering violets begin to bloom in late March and go through about mid April. They are not fragrant, at least not to my nose. Often the violet ground covers sold at garden centers are of this later variety as well, as are some native varieties. These can be used for medicine/magic if the fragrant ones cannot be found.

Harvest the flower first and wait another month for the leaves. The plants will develop larger leaves as the flowers are fading. Both flowers and leaves are edible and are an excellent addition to springtime salads. Many times, the leaves (not flowers) need to be briefly rinsed off to free them from dirt that has splashed up with rainfall. After being submerged in cold water (the best way to rinse any greens, rather than merely letting water run over them), spin them dry by holding a clean towel by the corners and go outside to whip them around. Then dry or use accordingly fresh.

It is worth noting that violets possess a special 'botanical curiosity'. They make two types of flowers. The showy springtime flowers do not actually make the seeds. A hidden inconspicuous flower blooms in the summer or late summer time and produces the self fertilized true seed, often dispersed by ants. What a tricky little plant we have here.

In terms of magical use, violet can be utilized in love magic of all sorts. It can help to sweeten something stale and bring back feelings of amour. It can be employed for seductive purposes byway of scent, taste, powders for sprinkling, and in a drawing amulet. It seems to bring courage and confidence, helpful for the powers of attraction. I include violet in herb combinations for heartbreak and lost love as well along with rose, hawthorn and willow. Its leaf signature suggests it as a heart medicine, and this is one way to use it in that context.

Violet can be used for sleep both magically and medicinally. Include the dried or fresh flowers in pillows, in baths and use the elixir in sleep formulas. It adds something so soothing to help calm the heart and mind. It is a helpful plant for children, in terms of dealing with grief. Violet and rose together are fabulous for this. Violet brings a gentle courage to those in need. Use the physical or amuletic medicaments for this purpose.

All violets can be used interchangeably for medicine. They have edible young leaves and flowers as well, lovely for springtime salads. You can taste subtle differences between the different types. The qualities of violet are demulcent, mildly laxative and nutritive. The flowers and leaves can be harvested and dried for teas, infusions and washes. After flowering the leaves will become much bigger. Harvest the flowers first and then gather leaves to dry after flowering has finished, in the following month.

To capture the perfume of the fragrant violet flower, they can be picked, wilted and then further processed into incredible syrups, infused honey, oxymels (infused vinegar with honey) and elixirs. You can infuse them in red port wine (or any wine) for a special treat – this catches the fragrance as well. For a strong potion, cover them by an inch or so of the wine, shake daily, wait a few weeks and then strain. This infused wine should be used within three months. Crystallized violets are a special addition to springtime desserts. Remember that after drying the flowers will lose their incredible scent, even when rehydrated later.

Dried violet leaves can be used in infusions for stagnant lymph flow and either as a general cleansing tonic or for the lungs. They combine well with red clover blossom, nettles and mullein for the latter. An infused fat can be made with fresh leaves and flowers, for bruising and to rub around the lymph nodes with any sort of sickness. It won't smell like the fragrant flowers however but gives more of a 'green' smell – I have yet to capture violets scent with oil or fat, though I have tried. It needs some sort of water component to come through, alcohol does the trick. Store the dried leaves and flowers whole until you intend to use them, keeping them out of the light.

It is worth mentioning that you can buy sweet violet plants, *Viola odorata* from some garden centers in mid February or early spring. They sell out though, so make sure to go early or make a request. Plant them in a partially shady spot, they do like part shade and regular water. They will spread joyfully and give you plenty of violets every year if you start with around 8 plants or so.

Many thanks to the violets of springtime, the haunting heart medicine of wind, rain and emerald leaf. Sorceress of seduction, bless us with your luminous perfume and ancient poetry. Great fortune is upon those who come upon your unmatched loveliness, exquisite within the dark forest edges.

Violet Infused Honey

In a double boiler cover sweet violets (fragrant ones) that have been wilted for about 5 hours with pure golden honey that is light in flavor. Add just enough honey to cover and stir with a chopstick. Heat the honey via water of the bottom chamber of the double boiler and let it get liquid like. You want it to be warm enough to start to break down and incorporate the violets. Leave it on the heat for 5 minutes or so, then turn it off. Cover with a lid and let this sit for 24 hours. Wipe the inside of the lid down the next day. Repeat this simple process for a total of 3 times. On the last time strain the honey through a fine sieve into a clean glass jar while it is still liquid. It should be fragrant and taste of violets but wait 24 hours for it to 'cure' and taste it again.

Violet Elixir for Grief and Courage

Cover freshly wilted violet flowers completely with brandy and add about a quarter part honey. Make sure your jar is about 2/3 full (not packed) with the flowers. Shake daily for a month, then strain. The honey will take a few days to incorporate. This very simple recipe is so delicious, that it is healing just to take three drops of it – it is almost mind altering with this small of a dose. It can also be sipped in small amounts from a liquor glass or added to other medicines.

DANDELION
Taraxacum offcinalis

Golden light, bumble bees nectar and delight – behold the common dandelion. Yet once the secrets of this plant are known, one will appreciate its persistence and presence in country and cityscapes. The perfume of this flower is similar to honey, with a bitter edge of green. Best get your basket ready for muddy roots, verdant leaves and shining flowers. Every part of dandelion can be utilized for food, medicine and magic.

Dandelion is perhaps the most well known plant in the Northern hemisphere. This plant has been with people since ancient times. It has been food, medicine and a dye plant for many of our ancestors, being a native to the temperate regions of the world. Dandelion is in the aster *Asteraceae* family, the genus *Taraxacum* has around 35 species followed by many subspecies within that number. Although despised by many gardeners because of its tenacity and deep tap roots, in times past dandelion was a very well utilized plant. It is thought that dandelions ancient symbolism is that of the sun. Its disk shaped golden flowers are very sensitive to the sun and light, opening and closing accordingly. And what a fiery golden rich color, an unmistakable sign of spring in April when lawns are just covered in large golden heads, opened between rain showers.

Dandelion was associated with the Irish spring goddess Brigid. In the Scottish Highlands the plant was called 'the plant of Bride', Bride being short for Brigid. The three emblems associated with Brigid were the dandelion flower, the lamb and the oyster catcher. Some of the Gaelic names for dandelion translate to Bearnon Bride, The Little Notched Flower of Bride and The Little Flame of God. St.

Bride wore dandelion at her breast so that sunlight followed. Other common names include Priest's Crown and Swine's Snout. The French Dent de Lion reveals the association with lion's teeth, as the sharply toothed leaf margins on the plant show. The Latin name *Dens leonis* has the same origins, both names bearing resemblance to the English 'Dandelion'.

The historical magical use of dandelion is less prominent than the medicinal uses, but there is some lore to be found. One use is that of an oracle, that it had the ability to prophesize. Possibly this is because often it was looked upon as a weather indicator. If the flowers were open, it meant fair weather could be expected and if they were closed, one could expect rain. Weather Clock was another name for dandelion in Somerset. Other common names such as Time Teller and Clock-flower also speak to dandelions ability to indicate the time of day in accordance to the suns light.

There were divination charms that follow this belief, such as that the dandelion flower would tell children at what age they would marry, how long they had to live and how many children that they would have. One way to use the plant for this purpose in order to find out the letter of the last name of the person that you will marry; blow on a dandelion seed head and with each puff recite the alphabet. The last letter to be spoken when all of the seeds have dispersed indicates the letter for one's future mates last name. How sad for people that have last names late on the list! If you followed the direction of the way the seeds dispersed after blowing, you would find your fortune. Another dandelion charm for one who was separated from their lover was to carefully pluck a seed head and whisper a message into it. Then face the direction of the loved one and blow as hard as one can. If all of the seeds flew away at once, the message was received. A French belief was to sleep with a dandelion leaf under one's pillow to dream of one's true love. Another bit of lore tells that if a dandelion flower blows in one's face, an important letter relating to business will soon be received.

Dandelion

In Scandinavian lore, there is one Danish name that translates to 'Magic Wand'. The roots were used in love magic. One could string them on a necklace and wear them to attract the affections of another. Thank you to Johannes Björn Gårdbäck for this specific information. According to one piece of Scottish Highland lore, a hoop could be made from dandelion, milkwort, marigold and butterwort (not sure of the genus species here) bound with a triple cord of lint, to be placed under the milk vessels to protect them from being bewitched.

To dream of dandelions was a bad omen. It could mean the deceit of a loved one and that one had enemies. Though to keep the very first dandelion flower of the year, one would have an abundant garden that season, a fertility amulet of sorts. One German spell to obtain justice in court tells to gather the herb Suntull (skunk cabbage, but I am unsure of the German species) during the month of August while the sun was in Leo on a Sunday. This was wrapped in a Bay leaf *Laurus nobilis* with some dandelion (part unspecified) and carried as a lucky talisman for the aforesaid purposes. Though it seems somewhat contradictory given all of the solar associations, dandelion is ruled by Jupiter according to astrologers of old.

Folk Medicine

Dandelion was and still is used as a strong diuretic. Old names included 'Piss-in-the-Bed' and still today 'Pissenlit' in France. Other uses were as a kidney and liver medicine, good for a spring tonic, jaundice, gallstones and kidney stones. The flower wine was taken as a kidney tonic specifically. A cure for jaundice used dandelion leaves boiled in buttermilk. Dandelion leaves were used for anemia, from Ireland and the leaf tea was used for asthma. Also from Irish lore it was thought that to be effective as a tonic, that men should use the plants with the white veins and women should use the plants with red veins. A cough syrup was made from the flowers by the Pennsylvanian Dutch, using the flowers, lemon and sugar.

A wise woman from Donegal, Ireland, suggested that eating three leaves of dandelion in the morning for three mornings would help with dyspepsia or heart burn. She called dandelion '*Heart Fever Grass*'. The details of the cure are both magical and medicinal in nature. The wise woman would measure the person suffering with a ribbon three times round the waist and tie a green thread to the outside of the ribbon. This was to find out if the patient suffered from the condition. If the patient was mistaken on what was causing the pain and it was not heart fever, the thread would remain in place. If it was caused by heart fever the thread would leave the edge of the ribbon and bunch up in the center. If this was the case, she would hand the patient nine dandelion leaves to be eaten three each, three mornings in a row.

The leaves eaten in a bread and butter sandwich were an older cure for ulcers in Glencoe, Scotland. A use from Roy Vickery Dictionary of Plant Lore, 1995 gives a firsthand account for 'Dandelion Tea: *First they put a knife under it and lifted it from the roots. They saved it in the sun until it got quite hard. They boiled the kettle and poured boiling water on it, strained it, and put it into bottles. Then they drank it and it was very good for the nerves.*'. It was thought that if one could dig up the entire dandelion root without breaking it at the tip, that it would cure anything. If it did break, the Devil was to blame – naturally as he was responsible for biting the root off. A glass of dandelion wine every day was helpful for longevity according to some lore from Worcestershire.

Dandelion sap placed on the tip of the tongue was a cure for indigestion in Essex, UK. Midwives from Fenland used to give a 'pain killing cake' to women in labor. A recipe says that this cake was made from wholemeal flour, hemp seed crushed with a rolling pin, crushed rhubarb root and grated dandelion root. These were mixed into a batter with egg yolk, milk and gin and then poured into a tin and baked. Dandelion leaves were used for insomnia from fever and for fertility. One recipe combines dandelion roots, plantain leaves *Plantago lanceolata* and ground ivy *Glechoma hederacea* for fever in a tea.

Topically, a cure from the 17th century states that dandelion had the ability to join and knit wounds. The juice of the leaf was put on a wound in order to stop bleeding. The leaves were used in both Ireland and Scotland to treat stings, I assume as a fresh poultice. There was an East Anglian remedy using dandelion juice for skin cancer. The white sticky sap from the stem was a wart remedy, applied numerous times per day during the waning moon.

Plants that exuded a milky juice such as dandelion, were thought to be good for lactating animals in the spring time to help with milk supply. I know herbalists who include the leaves in tea in formulas for bringing in a woman's milk as well. Poultry keepers and rabbit keepers were known to give their lot dandelion leaves to eat to keep them healthy, full of minerals as they are.

Personal Practices

In terms of magical use, dandelion is helpful included in any sort of divination blend, the dried leaf goes well in teas/washes, incense and powders for sprinkling with this specific intention. Blend with yarrow *Achillea millefolium* and rose for matters of love. Use in dream amulets for enhancing prophetic dreams.

The dried flower which will turn into a yellow fluff, can be used in solar amulets along with other plants of the sun, such as sunflower *Helianthus spp.*, marigold *calendula officinalis*, oak *Quercus spp.* and St. johns wort *Hypericum perforatum*. Make this amulet on a Sunday, and also add amber and gold for the mineral portion. Materia magica from the vulture being a bird who is connected to the sun, can also be added. This kind of an amulet is protective in nature and can be worn by those suffering from seasonal affective disorder during the winter months, also bringing power back to those whom have suffered from a depressing trauma of sorts.

Being a plant of whimsy and enchantment, I believe that dandelion is specific ally to children. The dried leaf and flower can be incorporated into any charm for bringing strength back to a child who has been sick or under stress, also include willow Salix spp. and rose Rosa spp. for grief. The infused oil of the flower (see below) can be used as an anointing oil to lift the spirits and restore joy, applied in an equal armed cross on a child's (or adults) chest, back of the neck, forehead and wrists.

Dandelion is one of the most useful remedies in the home medicine chest. Both the dried root and leaf can be gathered and stored. This is one plant to never be without and truly can keep a family healthy and strong with regular use. The greens can be eaten in the springtime and dried for teas throughout the year as a gentle nutrient rich cleanse. Harvest the leaves from early February on into May for food use. They will be small but less bitter earlier in the season. Patches that are in the shade and the leaves before the plant has flowered are thought to be less bitter.

Certainly, many country people have had a popular pastime gathering dandelion greens in the springtime while the plants are at their least bitter stage and cooking them down as a potherb or incorporating them into salads. Many rustic recipes pair dandelion greens with bacon or pork. It is excellent, add a dash of balsamic vinegar and plenty of black pepper. The small roots can also be eaten, chopped into soups or stews. The greens mixed with equal parts stinging nettles make a palatable and nutritious blend, served in a quiche with salty feta cheese and herbs. To prepare the greens, the crowns must be washed very thoroughly, and separated while submerged in water individually to clean out the sand, dirt and little slugs. A big batch can be prepared this way and then the leaves spun dry in a towel and stored wrapped in a damp towel for a few days in the fridge. If they are too bitter for your liking, boil them briefly and discard the water. I usually do this a few times in a row to remedy the bitterness, especially after April arrives and they

The Author in Autumn Garden

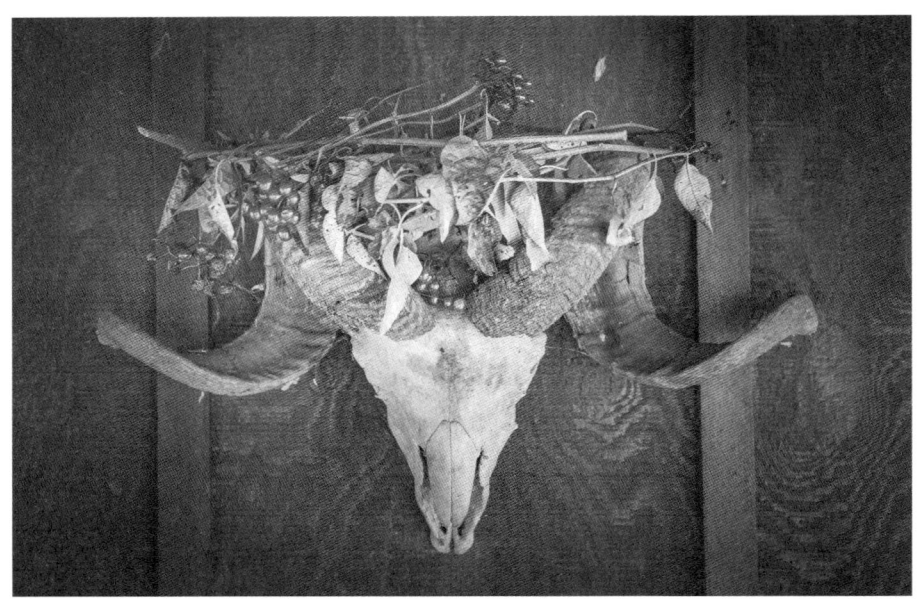

Top: Bittersweet on Ram Skull
Above: Blackberry in Flower

Top: Blackberry Medicines
Above: Broadleaf Plantain

Broom and Birch Sweeping Tools

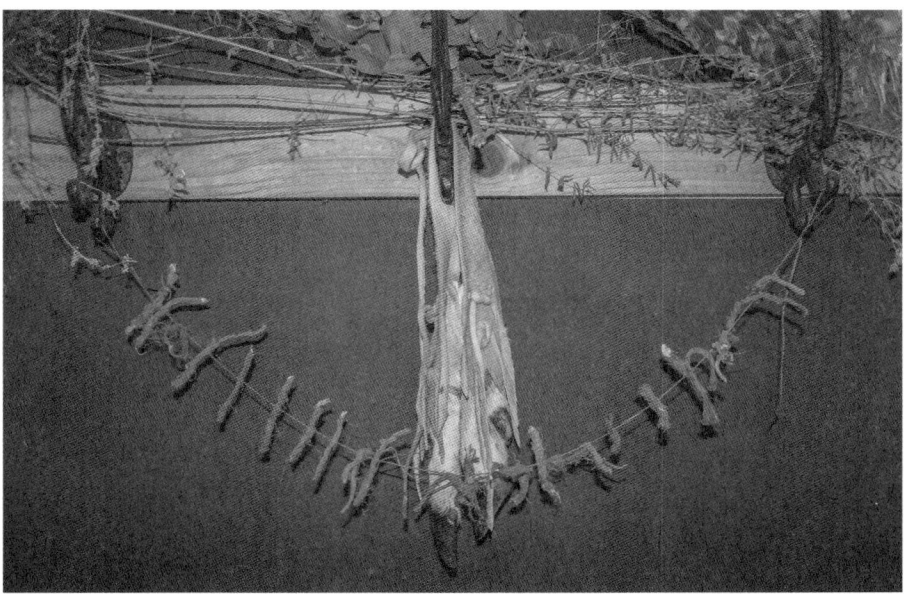

Top: Burdock Bouquet
Above: Dandelion Root Love Charm

Top: Dock Root Medicine
Above: Dock Seeds with Spider's Web

Above: Four Leaf Clover in Locket

Right: Graveyard Ivy Charms

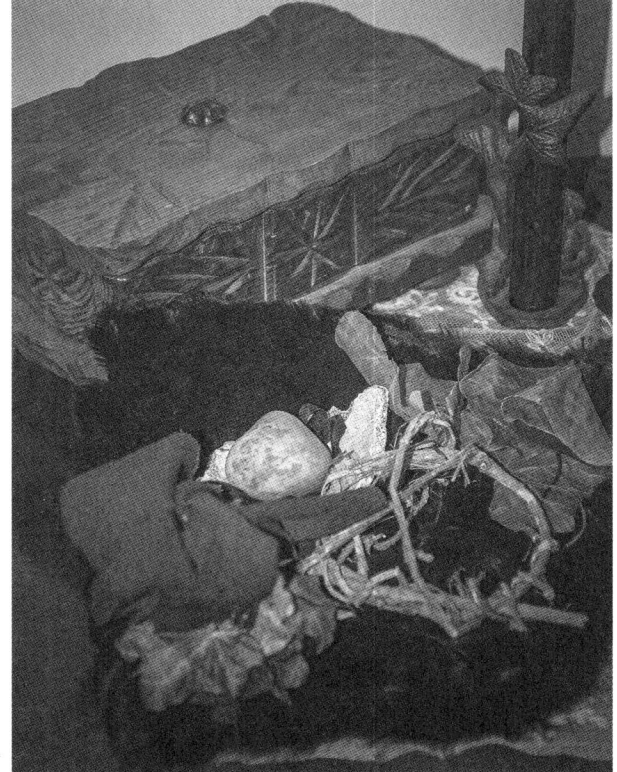

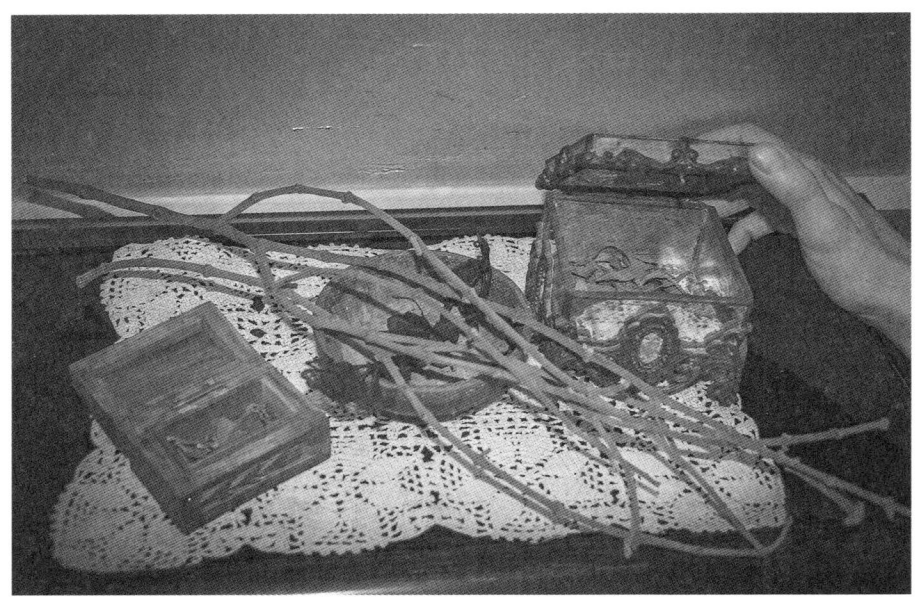

Above: Graveyard Mistletoe Altar

Left: Graveyard Mistletoe in Berry

Hag Tapper

Top: Love Powder
Above: Making Rose Infused Honey

Midsummer Oracle Garland

Mullien in Flower

Above: Nettle
Banishing Box

Right: Purple Violet

Rose Beads

Above: Rose Ink

Right: Scrying in the Mugwort Well

Self Heal

St Johns Wort Oil and Iron

Above: Stinging Nettles Hanging

Opposite: Sweeping the Besom

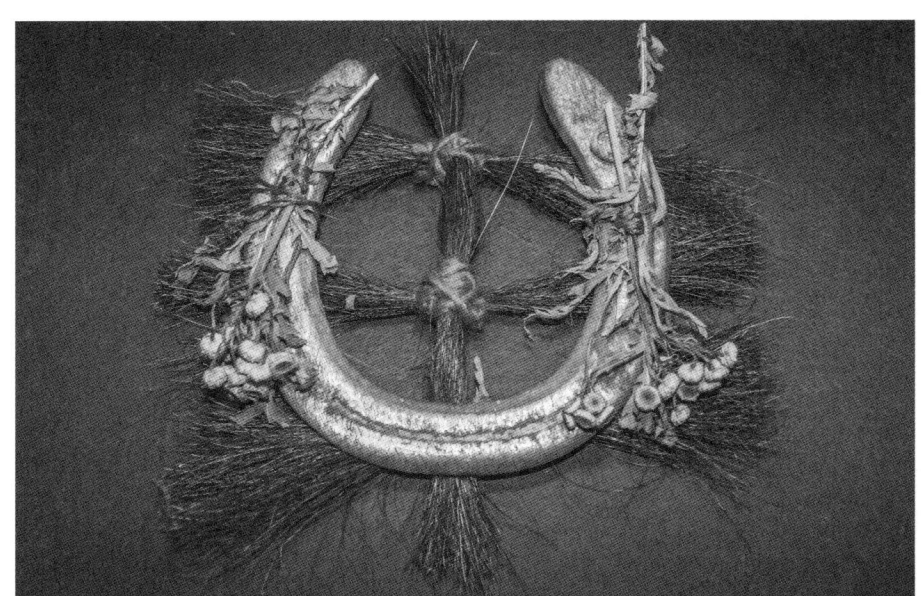

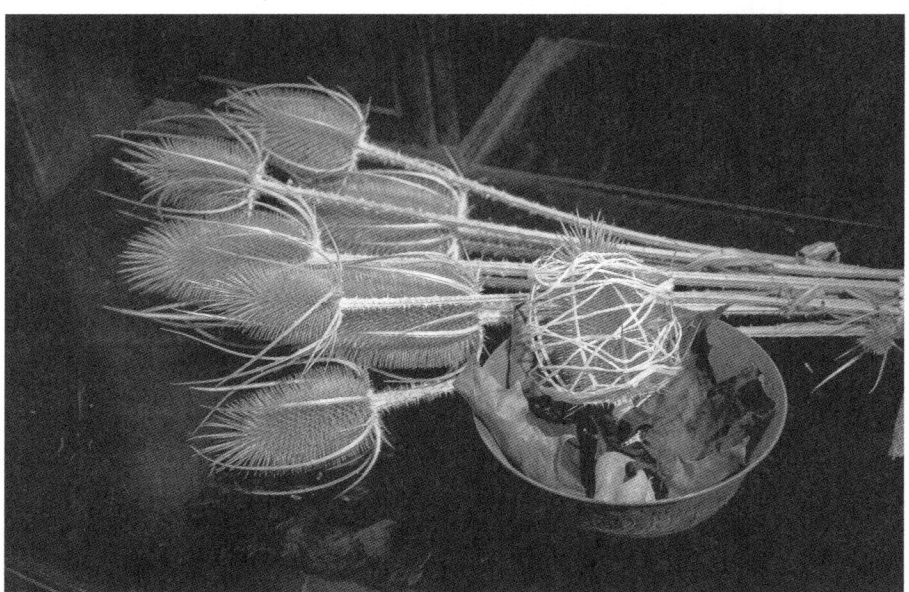

Top: Tansy Horseshoe Charm
Above: Teasel Spindle

Thistle Garland

Top: St. Johns Wort in Mortar
Above: White Violets

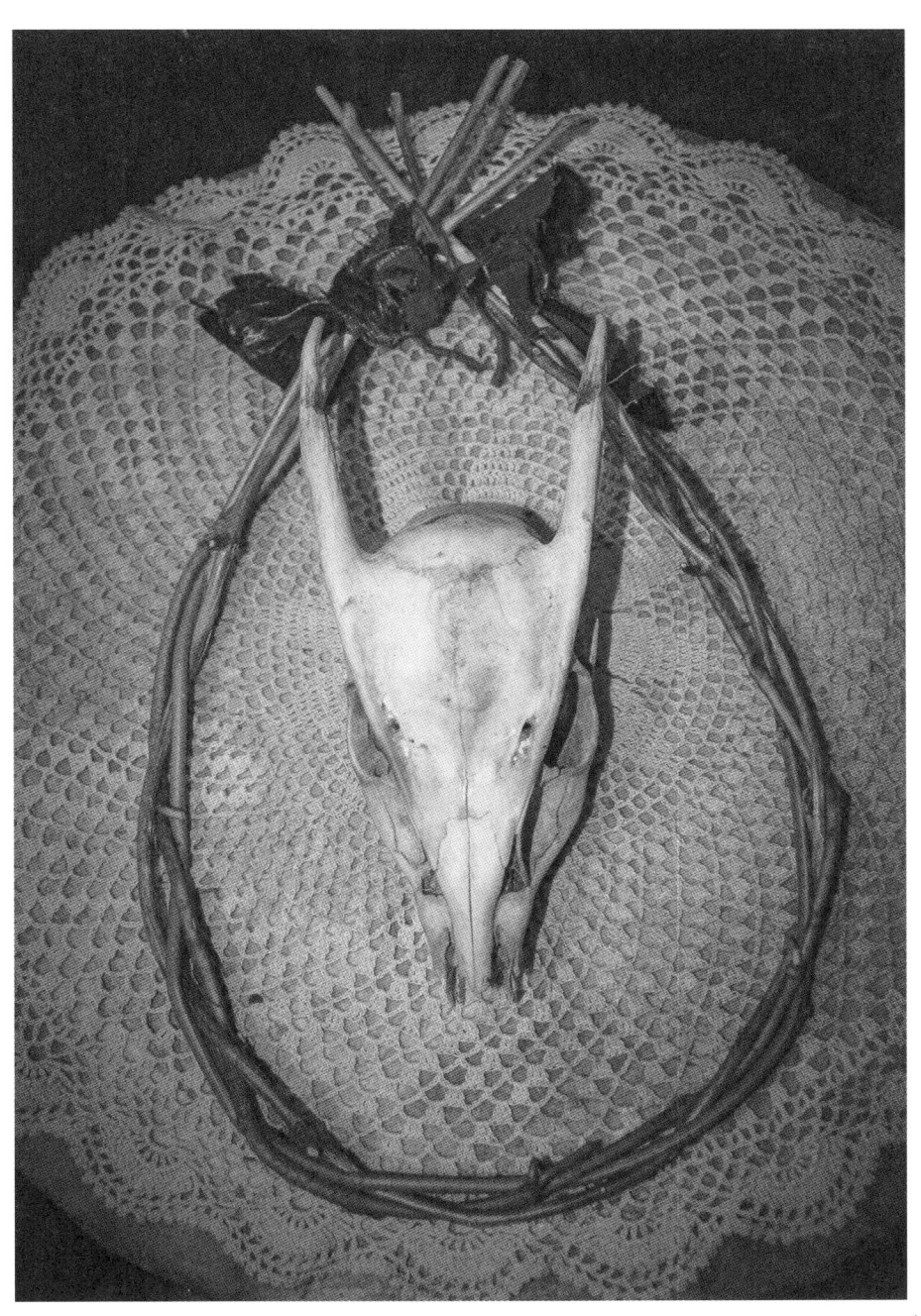

Witches' Rope

Yarrow Infused Wine

are bitter in large amounts. Though some of the water-soluble vitamins are lost in the water changes, the minerals still remain. After a few rounds of this, the greens can be squeezed out and then used as any cooked green. They are incredible tossed with melted butter, fresh garlic and any spices that you may desire.

After they become too bitter to eat, the leaves can be dried for medicinal use. The leaf tea is high in vitamins and minerals, being helpful in women's blends and as a tonic for liver and kidney support in general. The strong diuretic effect of dandelion helps with water retention and iron deficiency.

The roots can be dug and processed for medicine in the spring or fall. They extract well in alcohol for a fresh tincture and also in vinegar for a vinegar extract. The washed and chopped root can be dried for decoctions and tea blends. Dandelion roots make a helpful liver tonic. They are effective for low grade chronic constipation, or even constipation while traveling. They are bitter with a nutritive sweetness. The dried root is excellent in decoctions with only rosehips and cinnamon. Or roast it for a richer flavor, some use this as a coffee substitute. To roast at home, use dried roots spread on a baking sheet at 375 for about 20 minutes, stirring regularly. Watch to make sure they darken fully without burning. The home roasted root is superior in flavor to the store-bought version. When using in decoctions, little is needed to bring out the robust flavor, about ½ teaspoon of the roasted powdered root per 2 cups of water.

The flowers are excellent brewed into a wine (see recipe below), made into an elixir for depression and infused in olive oil for arthritis, pain and sore muscles. The elixir can be made from the fresh flowers; fill a mason jar 2/3 of the way with the opened blooms, including the green calyx and then fill ¾ with brandy, adding honey for the remainder. This needs to be agitated every day for a month and then strained out. It makes a marvelous hot toddy with a slice of lemon during the winter months and during bouts of depression. The oil can be made similarly. Again, fill a mason jar of any size with 2/3 fresh blooms including the green calyx. Add extra virgin olive oil to cover and leave an inch of head space. Shake or stir every day for a month, being sure to keep the oil in a warm (not hot) place, such as near a woodstove or heater but not right next to it. Then strain and bottle for your use. It is a warming massage oil, even by itself. People love this for arthritis pain.

The flowers are also one of my favorite springtime foods for making fritters. I look forward to them every year. On a sunny afternoon, gather 15 large dandelions, keeping the stem on. Use these right away, do not wait more than 20 minutes, or they will change in texture even if placed in water. Remove the green sepals without taking the blossoms apart. Then simply dip the heads in milk, then a savory seasoned flower, then fry in butter face down in a cast iron pan until golden. Eat warm and discard the stem. They are so delicious and make a spectacular meat substitute or can be the perfect side dish to a spring gathered salad and a glass of cleavers lemonade – the ultimate springtime lunch after an afternoon in the garden.

Many thanks to this ancient plant of the suns light, this rustic medicine of the wayside. Common yet enchanted, this flower beckons the return of springtime and the waking up of the natural world after a long winters nap. Bring the bitterness, the sweetness and the earths delight to your table plate, your corked potion, your amulet pouch with this lovely companion. Blessings on the wild bitter herbs that fed our ancestors through Lent and gave them nourishment during the leanest time of the year.

Dandelion Wine 🌼

For one gallon of wine, gather 2 quarts of prepared dandelion flowers. To do this, pick a sunny afternoon and sit in a yard full of open dandelions. Many recipes recommend separating the green calyx from the flower heads, a painfully slow yet enjoyable process. But this is not actually necessary. I find the wine pleasant even with the green calyx included, try it and decide for yourself. There is virtually no difference to me but do make sure that no part of the stem is included. Place the dandelion flowers in a 3-gallon crock/bucket. Add 3 pounds of organic cane sugar and pour a gallon of boiling water over, stirring to dissolve. Add one sliced lemon and orange with the peel to the mixture and 1/2-1 pound of dried chopped apricots. Stir well and when totally cool, after about 8 hours, add ½ teaspoon of wine yeast by sprinkling on top. Let sit 15 minutes and then stir it in. Cover with a linen towel tied on with a string. Stir twice per day for 10 days. Strain into a 1-gallon glass jug with an airlock. Let sit at least 3 months before racking. This wine takes about 9-12 months to mature. Be patient. This is like liquid sunshine on the winter solstice and is well worth the wait.

Dark Hollow Tea

Decoct roasted powered dandelion root, elder berries and nettle leaves for about ten minutes. Use about ½ teaspoon of dandelion and about 1 tablespoon of the other two herbs for 3 cups of water or so. The resulting tea is so dark and beautiful and reminds one of the dark rainy hidden hollows around forested mountain areas. This is lovely plain or with a dash of milk and honey by the woodstove on a cold night.

PLANTAIN
Plantago major/lanceolata

The humble plantain, plant of the wayside and meadow edge, healing wort of green. So common is this plant and often inconspicuous, it would be easy to miss it under ones very nose. When I show students a patch of plantain, they cannot believe that this plant they have barely noticed for their whole life has such remarkable healing abilities. Indeed, it is an important plant to know about, a primary poulticing plant in the harvesting basket.

There are two generally referenced and readily available species, the broadleaf (*P. major*) and the English narrow leaf (*P.lanceolata*), also known as ribwort. These two species originated in Eurasia and plantain has been known to follow the 'English man' around, being called 'White Man's Footsteps'. Common names for plantain included: Rabbits Ears, Waybread, Waybroad, Snakeweed, Devils Shoestring, Rat-tails, Blackheads, Ribbon Leaf, St. Patrick's Leaf and Cuckoo bread. The Latin *Plantago* goes back to *planta*, meaning sole. This refers to the sole of the foot, and plantain has been known to soothe the feet of weary travelers since ancient times. German names for plantain translate into 'Healing Leaf' (*Laekeblad*), or 'Healing Grass'(*Laeknisgras*).

Plantain had remarkable healing powers attributed to it over the past many thousands of years. It is plant of ancient medicine and magic. One tale tells of a toad that helped protect itself with plantain before engaging with a spider and if it was hurt, used the same leaf for healing itself afterwards. An Anglo-Saxon legend tells about the name Waybread, where a maiden was married to a knight whom was greatly revered. After their wedding, he was called away to battle. The day he left, he kissed his new bride by the roadside and bade her to wait for him and watch for his return. She waited faithfully but alas, he never returned. Eventually she turned into the plant Waybread, where she still remains waiting for her long-lost husband to return to her.

In ancient Anglo-Saxon medicine, 'waybread' (broad leaf) plantain was highly valued. A quote from the 10th century from the '*Lay of the Nine Healing Herbs*' goes:

And you, Waybread, mother of Worts,
Open from Eastward, powerful within,
Over you Chariots rode, over you Queens road,
Over you Brides cried, over you Bulls Belled,
All these you withstood, all these you confounded,
So withstand now the venom that flies through the air,
And the loathed thing which through the land roves.

In Irish folklore it was believed that plantain could bring the dead back to life, ribwort plantain specifically. It was a plant that was believed to be put on the Lords wounds in order to heal them after the crucifixion. Another reason why it was a plant associated with the spirits of the dead was that it was one that survived the horse trampling, heavy oxen driven carts and people's footsteps of the funeral parades of old. On the roads that lead to the burial mounds, the plantain grew and survived. Both knotgrass (genus and species not specified) and plantain were dedicated to Persephone from the Greeks because of their tenacity and ability to thrive on the roads of the dead.

Plantain is ruled by Venus according to astrologers of the past and has some love associations as well as divination powers ascribed to it. Divination games were played with narrow leaf plantain in England and Scotland. One Scandinavian tradition to foretell the future was to pick one or two flowering spikes of plantain on St. Johns Eve, pick off the stamens and keep the spike. This was placed under the pillow before bed. If new stamens had developed in the morning, certain wishes would be fulfilled. A similar Scottish custom was for a love divination. One was to pick two flower stalks, with each representing the man and woman in question. The fluffy blossoms were carefully removed and they were then wrapped in a dock leaf and placed under a stone for a night. In the morning, if new flowerets appeared on both heads, there would be great love to come; however if only one of the stalks bore flowers, there would be love not returned. Hildegard von Bingen suggests plantain juice taken with or without water for countering the effects of a love enchantment.

An Irish amulet included plantain roots, colchicum (autumn crocus) and lavender flowers. These were made into a powder and worn in a silken pouch around the neck to prevent cholera and malignant fevers from effecting the wearer. The flower heads were used in children's games. I remember playing with them myself as a child. There is a way to make the head pop off by using the stem to propel it, with the head that traveled furthest being the winner. Children from Cheshire England in times past would recite this rhyme when the first ribwort flowers were in bloom:

Chimney sweeper all in black, Go the brook and wash your back, Wash it clean or wash it none, Chimney sweeper have you done?

This was likely a good luck charm and plantain had the common names of 'Chimney Sweeper' or just 'Sweeper' in those areas. A strange superstition from Iowa tells to pluck a plantain leaf and count the ribs to indicate how many lies will be told that day.

Folk Medicine

Plantains physical uses are mostly external, the leaves being used as a poultice for all sorts of bites and stings, including mad dog bites. It was also used for burns, scalds and wounds. Plantain was thought effective not only for snakebite, but against any venomous bite or sting.

Another older name was 'healing blade', relating to ribwort plantain specifically. Interesting external uses included rubbing the juice of plantain on the temples mixed with oil of roses for 'lunatic persons' and using the roots somehow for headaches. A Saxon headache remedy was to bind plantain leaves to the head with red wool, a protective color used for healing magic in general. A recipe from the *Lacnunga*, an ancient source of Anglo-Saxon medicines gives this recipe for a 'salve for flying venom', which includes plantain (waybread) goes thus:

Take a handful of hammerwort (pellitory) and a handful of maythe (chamomile) and a handful of waybread and roots of water dock, seek those which will float, and one eggshell full of clean honey, then take clean butter, let him who will help to work up the salve, melt it thrice: let one sing a mass over the worts, before they are put together and the salve is wrought up.

Another healing salve recipe that came from an old woman of Exeter for healing burns or raw skin told to combine southernwood leaves, black current leaves, plantain leaves, elder buds, parsley leaf, angelica (part not specified, but I would guess the leaf and stem) with clarified butter and then warmed to extract the medicine. Yet another recipe for healing wounds from the 15th century tells to take a pint of juice from ribwort, a pint of vinegar and a pint of honey and boil them until thick. This sounds like a labor of love indeed, as I know what it takes to extract a small amount of herbal juice without a modern appliance. One would need many plantain leaves, to then smash them and wring them through a muslin cloth. The parts here could be cut in half, and a smaller batch tried.

Plantain had some internal uses as well. In her *Modern Herbal*, Maude Grieve writes that '*A decoction of plantain enters into almost every old remedy, and it was boiled with Docks, Comfrey and a variety of flowers.*' She also writes that it is still used for a diarrhea remedy and for piles, an old word for hemorrhoids. The juice squeezed from plantain could be mixed with wine and drunk for ailments of the chest and liver.

Plantain

Ribwort specifically was used to stop bleeding, for bruises and sores. A tea of the leaf was taken for lung troubles, such as bronchitis and asthma. In Ireland, it was also taken for liver complaints. The seeds if soaked in water for a few hours were used as a mild purgative, much as today's use. Pysllium husk is from a plantain genus seed. Hildegard von Bingen gives helpful uses such as plantain root in honey for healing broken bones, eaten before breakfast. Along with a cooked poultice of plantain and mallow leaves (*Malva spp.* 5:1 ratio of plantain leaf to mallow leaf) the broken bone would be healed quickly.

The Pennsylvania Dutch made use of plantain as well. The seeds were made into a tea in order to expel worms, the fresh leaves were used as a poultice for hemorrhoids and the leaves soaked in milk were employed to aid the irritations of insect bites.

The Tribes of North America used the two species of plantain in similar ways that the Europeans did. There are some native *Plantago* species, but I am not familiar with them. Not only used for all skin complaints, including snakebites, ribwort plantain was generally used as an eyewash, for strengthening children learning to walk, for bowel complaints and for 'bloody urine'. The Cherokee tribe used the leaves as a poultice for headaches to relieve pain. The same tribe use a leaf infusion given to babies to strengthen them while they were learning to walk. The Kawaiisu tribe used the leaves for the pain of earaches as a poultice. Broadleaf plantain was generally used for wounds, swellings, poisonous bites of all sorts, taken for bowel and stomach problems, used for female gynecological medicine and taken as a respiratory aid. The crushed leaves were used by the Delaware tribe for bruises. The Iroquois tribe used the boiled flower heads as a poultice for abscesses. A particularly interesting use from the Navajo tribe was to use a cold infusion of the leaves for 'lightning infection', presumably a disease caused by lightning. The same tribe used the root somehow for a 'life medicine'. The Ponca tribe used hot leaves to draw out splinters and thorns. An important use to remember: the Potawatomi tribe used a leaf infusion to lubricate the throat for helping a bone become dislodged from the throat.

Personal Practices

I have not used plantain for magical purposes, however it is one of the plants that I would never want to be without for medicinal uses. Many years ago I had a dream about a snake biting my leg in a creek and I immediately sought out broadleaf plantain on to heal the venomous wound. That was before I knew of its ancient use as a snake bite remedy, much to my delight of finding out some of its older uses a few years later. It is commonly known to be a readily available bee sting remedy and for good reason. When applied as a fresh poultice, either species will take the pain out of a wasp or bee sting within minutes. To do this, one needs to briefly chew the leaf and keep whatever juices come out of it in the front of the mouth, and then apply the whole green mess to the area in need. It also acts to staunch bleeding, in particular ribwort. Applied as a fresh leaf poultice once again, will help bring to the bleeding to a halt in no time at all.

Plantain grows in full sun, often on edges or parking areas, also in alleyways and yards. Be sure that when harvesting that the plants were not sprayed and try to find places that are not too close to a road. Though the broadleaved plantain makes small flowers on a stalk that are not showy in any noticeable way, the ribwort flowers are always a delight. Either species of plantain is best used in fresh poultices for inflamed, infected or painful slow to heal skin problems. There are many miracle stories that tell of plantain poultices healing skin infections and sores that otherwise did not respond to modern treatment. That being said, one always needs to watch for systemic infection and seek medical response if an area turns into a red streaking inflamed painful situation, along with a fever and dizziness. Hopefully the herbs will have a chance to work before it gets that severe.

The fresh plant is wonderful for making infused fats for use in healing skin salves, it is best extracted in animal fat (see the appendices in my first volume Under the Witching Tree). I have used the infused fat in diaper rash salves and all healing wound salves, often with yarrow and rose (see recipe below).

Internally, the leaves can be dried for use in tea blends for the lungs. They are soothing, demulcent and tonic, helpful for recovering from infections and for dry coughs. They can be incorporated into tea blends for asthma, along with horsetail, nettle and mullein leaf. Harvest these during the month of April or May to avoid bitterness that can come later in the season.

> *Many thanks to this green wayside healer of old, its medicine against venom and pain. A countryside soothsayer in matters of the heart, a child's amulet, a wise person's bandage, plantain brings soothing and wisdom to simple domestic applications. Blessings on the rustic potions, green pulp in fat, and roads of the Dead where this humble beauty grows.*

Emerald Healing Salve

Harvest two handfuls of either species of plantain leaf, as well as two handfuls of chickweed herb *Stellaria media* and two handfuls of stinging nettle leaf. The month of April is best for making this salve, for all the herbs here will be vibrant and green with power. Let them wilt overnight, spread out in an open basket. The following morning, take a glass double boiler and snip the green herbs thus wilted into the top chamber, using heavy kitchen shears. Or chop them fine with a knife. Have ready a clarified animal fat, pig or bear fat works best. Lacking this, unscented coconut oil would suffice. You want to add enough fat to cover all of the herbs, but it will be hard to tell this until the whole mixture heats up. Add water to the lower chamber and a few scoops of fat to the herbs in the top and begin heating, stirring until the fat starts to melt. Add more fat until the herbs swim freely but also remain dense in the mixture. Once heated thoroughly, after about ten minutes, turn the heat off. Cover and let sit for 24 hours. Repeat this for about three-five times total and on the last time, strain out the herbs and keep the green fat in a mason jar.

To make the salve, add one ounce of grated beeswax (the best way to get small chunks is to freeze large pieces and wrap them in layers of cloth. Smash them with a hammer once frozen.) per one cup of the infused fat in a double boiler. Melt them together and pour into jars or tins once done. Let this harden for a day and then try it on your skin to catch the fragrance properly. It will smell like green earth, if infused correctly with enough plant matter to fat. This can be used for any slow to heal wound (as long as there is no sigh of infection and the initial healing process has passed, say a week or so after the injury), for dry or irritated skin, for rashes that are not too inflamed (if that is the case, try a water wash with the same three plants), for healing scars, and for itchy bug bites. It makes a wonderful all-purpose salve.

 # STINGING NETTLE
Urtica dioica

Emerald nettle, plant of the lowland forest and rich earth, you greet the world each spring with your purple tinged mineral leaves. Threat to the skin with a blistering flame, what medicine and magic you hold within. Gracing the abandoned places of human inhabitants, forlorn and haunted are the shaded places where you reside. We remain in deepest respect to your defense and yet seek your counsel for both body and spirit power.

The nettles root name from Latin is Uredo, meaning 'burning itch'. Our common name 'Nettle' comes from the Old English netel, which is derived from the word needle. In Europe there is the U. urens, a small leaved nettle, along with the U. dioica. An old Irish name for nettle was nenaid and translates to mean 'fire heat'. Not only for food and medicine, nettles have been long used for their strong fibers in making rope and materials. Nettles are native to Eurasia and North America and are in the nettle family Urticaceae.

Nettles history in folklore is fascinating. One old quote tells:

This is the herb that is Wergulu,
A seal brought it back over the sea,
As an aid against the wickedness of the other poisons.
It stands against pain, it dashes against poison.
It has power against three and against thirty,
Against the hand of a fiend, against cleaver scheming, against

– The Magic Word (spell) of Evil Creatures – Taken from *The Untold History of Healing,* Wolf D. Storl, 2017, North Atlantic Books.

One ancient tale called *The Six Swans* tells of six kings sons whom a sorceress bewitches into swans. They are only transformed back into human form after their sister makes them shirts with nettle fibers. These pieces of lore give us some indication of the protection that nettle brings. An Irish folktale tells of how nettles were used by a priest to cure an ill woman. A nettle clump grew in the mountains where a fallen church once stood. In times previous, the host had fallen from the lips of the same woman, and into a crack in the floor. The nettles grew up there to protect the host from harm after the church had fallen into disrepair. The priest and a boy located the nettles and found the host still in prime condition. Once the old woman took the host, she was cured of all illness.

Often because of its stinging properties, nettle has been associated with the work of the Devil in European folklore. Common names like Devil's Leaf, Devil's Apron and Naughty Man's Plaything have been used in the past. It was thought that they grew from where the dead bodies of men lay or from the places where innocent blood had been shed, a belief from Denmark. There was also a Lincolnshire belief that nettles came up from spots that had been urinated on. It's of little wonder why such a plant would have associations with the Devil, producing a rash that very logically could have originated in the depths of Hell. It was believed in the Highlands and Islands of Scotland that nettles sprung up from where Satan and his fallen angels landed on the earth, after being expelled from Heaven. From the New Forest in

Stinging Nettle

England it was believed that the Devil gathered nettles on May Day in which to weave his shirts with, so the young shoots were only harvested up until that time. Such advice is well heeded, as it is wise to not gather this incredibly helpful medicinal herb after this date – it develops calcium oxalate crystals that can irritate the kidneys when it clearly is going to flower and putting its vitality into creating tall fibers within the stem.

From County Galway in Ireland came the belief that the nettle was once the finest flower that grew in the Garden of Eden, until the serpent hid underneath it after tempting Eve. Following this, it became envenomed with its stinging poison. In India, nettle was believed to symbolize a demon, and it was held that the Great Serpent poured his venom upon the plant. An interesting parallel, is how the nettle was used by the Iroquois tribe, along with dried snakes blood in a 'witching medicine'. The association with pain and suffering on account of the plants poisonous sting very likely gave it credibility as a cursing or counter-cursing agent, but as we shall see nettle was used for protection as well.

The nettle was associated with the God Thor in Scandinavian mythology. There was an old Tyrolean custom of throwing nettles on the fire during a thunderstorm to protect the house from lightning and carrying the nettle would protect the wearer against lightning as well. Although it was a symbol for evil in some lore, it was also an antidote. Holding nettles in the hand was a safeguard against ghosts, and carrying both nettle and yarrow on one's person would bring luck and drive away fear, a French use. An English belief was that nettles were most powerful if gathered from a spot where the sun never shone on them. In Denmark, nettles growing indicated dwelling places of elves, and the stings from nettles were protection against dark magic.

Nettles have been associated with both the wellbeing of and the ability to bewitch farm animals. In Germany, nettles gathered before sunrise were used to drive evil spirits away from cattle. In some parts of Europe, if a cow ate nettles it was thought that her milk would be bloody, and she would be bewitched. In other lands, if nettles were placed in ewe's milk it was a protective measure so that the flock became like the plant – untouchable. In some beliefs nettles kept a cow's milk from the ill effects of both trolls and witches.

The butter churn could be struck with nettles if the butter did not form properly. A further protective method that comes from the 17th/18th century was that after the butter was made, the buttermilk that was suspected of being bewitched was then poured into a hole in the earth, a stake being driven in the hole and the nettle stalk used to strike the churn buried next to it. To make the witch appear that enchanted the milk, a report comes from 1641 Transylvania. The bewitched milk was poured on a nettle and the plant beaten, in order the bring the witch by contagion. A protective measure used nettle during the twelve days of Christmas. A nettle root was placed in some milk intended for cheesemaking on Christmas night. Then the whole was poured on a dung heap on Epiphany (January 6th) to keep the dairy operation safe from witchcraft.

Nettles were often associated with abandoned places. One saying from Irish mythology was to curse one as being as 'elder and nettle and corncrake', meaning to face ruin, as these plants were found in waste places and fallen settlements where humans had once inhabited. Nettles growing at a crossroads were supposed to witness the meetings of witches that happened there. There was a German custom that used nettles as a sort of scarecrow. Four broomsticks and four nettles were placed at the four corners of the field, while speaking this charm: *There you are crow, that is for you, and what I plant is mine!*

A bunch of nettles could be hung near beehives to drive away frogs and they were also hung in the larder to deter flies. Nettles were used as a vegetarian substitute for curdling milk to make cheese with. Dreaming of nettles was a sign of good health and prosperity, and to dream of gathering them foretold that someone had a favorable opinion of you and that family life would be harmonious. To dream of getting stung by nettle however foretold jealousy and disappointment. In the language of flowers nettles meant 'You are spiteful'.

A few magical cures associated with nettles follow. To cure a fever, one must grasp a nettle and pull it up by the roots, while speaking the sufferers name out loud. The nettles that grow in a shady spot are supposed to be best for this. A very specific cure was used for a child that had poor eye sight. A woman, one who had never seen her father was to blow through a hole in a nettle leaf into the child's eyes. The woman was instructed to do this before she touched anything for the day. A Romany contraception enhancement involved a man placing a thick layer of nettle leaves in his socks 24 hours before intercourse.

Some very interesting magical use of nettles comes from the Kawaiisu tribe of southern California. The local species *U.dioica spp. holosericea* was used by children who would walk through the nettles to toughen their skin or prepare them for the practice of witchcraft. More details are not given (see D. Moerman *Native American Medicinal Plants, Timber Press*) but one piece of information states that walking through nettles would help young people procure dreams.

A divination involving nettles tells that if a girl planted a nettle in wet sand, she would wake to find her fate the next morning. Whatever direction that the plant bent would show her what direction her future suitor would come from. However if its tips bent downward, it was a sign of an early death to come. Here is an interesting custom that involves the curing with 'unspoken nettles'. This comes from *A Dictionary of Plant Lore*, 1995, Roy Vickery:

'Geordie Tamson, who lived near Jollybrands on the south turnpike, not far from the toll-bar, lay sick. After weeks of treatment by the doctor, Geordie lay ill without the least token of improvement. A 'Skeely woman' from the Dounies, a village not far off, was called in. She at once prescribed a supper of 'nettle kail' and added that the dish must be made of 'unspoken nettles', gathered at midnight.

That very night at eleven o'clock, three young men, friends of Geordies, from Cairngrassie, were on their way to the Red Kirkyard of Potlethen, where there was a fine bed of nettles… the nettles were gathered, carefully taken to the sick man, cooked of course and given to him. A complete and speedy recovery followed.'

In Cornwall, May first was known as Stinging Nettle Day and it was a custom to pick a nettle leaf and wrap it in a dock leaf and eat it, with the belief that it would keep one safe until the next years Stinging Nettle day. In Irish lore, southern parts of County Cork named May Eve as 'Nettlemass Night'. On this eve, the boys would parade through town with nettle bundles, stinging those who got too close. Though a show of jest and celebration, this harkens back to nettles protective abilities and it is auspicious in my mind that it was done on May Eve, a historical time for witch and Faerie mischief.

A death divination involved the use of nettles. If one was sick a pot of fresh nettles was placed under the bed. If they stayed green, it was a sign that the person would recover, but if they faded it was a death omen. Nettle is said to be ruled by Mars, according to astrologers of old.

A Scandinavian magical use for nettles was to weave a small mat and then place it in a hidden spot on the porch of a couples who's love you wanted to destroy, essentially as a curse. Another practical way to use the hollow stalks comes from 19th century Sweden. One uses nine nettle stalks to blow away disease or evil from a person. Each one is used one at a time and the words for each stalk are spoken quietly, often in one breath per line. The words translated goes:

I blow in the East,
I blow in the West.
I blow in the South,
I blow in the North,
I blow in the Air,
I blow in the Water,
I blow in the Earth,

Stinging Nettle

I blow in the Light,
I blow for the Night,
I blow forever all diseases away.

— Taken from *Trolldom – Spells and Methods of the Norse Folk Magic Tradition*, Johannes Björn Gårdbäck, YIPPIE, 2015.

Folk Medicine

The sting of the nettle can be mild or intense, depending on what parts of the body get stung and how many nettles are involved. For any of us who know this sting, it can often be felt even 12 or more hours after a nettle encounter. The formic acid in its tiny barbs causes an intense burning and even blistering of the skin when touched. Intentional nettle flogging or urtication has been used by not only Native Americans but also by peoples of Europe. It was believed that by using the nettles sting intentionally and intensely, many inflammatory imbalances could be corrected, by bringing more circulation to the area.

Some plants that were traditionally used to help with the sting of nettles were dock leaves, usually broad-leaved dock *Rumex obtusifolius*, and plantain *Plantago major or lanceolata*, used as a fresh poultice. There was on old rhyme: *Nettle out, dock in, Dock remove the nettle sting'*. This had to be recited as it was applied if it was to work properly. Mallow, *Malva sylvesteris* or *Malva neglecta* was also a remedy in European countries. To use a nettle wash itself was an old cure for the sting, an example of 'like cures like'. A Native American remedy was to place a live slug on the sting, with the enzymes in the slug slime helping the inflammatory reaction. This is probably the best remedy in my book, if you can find a slug in your moment of need. It really does work.

Older (and still in place) medicinal uses for nettles included being used as a blood cleanser, for lung problems such as asthma and bronchitis, for ear infection and mumps, for goiter, for heavy menses, for anemia, jaundice, headaches, heart problems such as high blood pressure and dropsy (edema), stomach upsets, diarrhea, for insomnia, tuberculosis, to prevent nose bleeds, for hoarseness, for gout and rheumatism and used as a gargle for an infected throat. This plant is good for just about everything, as the lore shows. In Welsh lore, it was supposed to be taken to help poor memory and to quicken the senses. In fact, Hildegard von Bingen recommended it for forgetfulness, the juice pounded and blended with olive oil, for anointing the chest and temples before bed. She also advised that it could be used for dispelling internal worms, and as a horse medicine. If a horse has a cough, one should let the steam of nettles and lovage *Levisticum officinale* go into his nose, as well as mixing nettles and lovage into his fodder. One of my favorite remedies – graveyard nettles were boiled down to cure dropsy, an old word for edema – an Irish remedy. A use to make hair grow tells to dip ones comb in nettle juice and then comb the hair in the wrong direction.

An old rhyme attests to its use for health and goes' *If they would drink nettles in March, And eat mugwort in May, So many fine maidens, Would not go to clay*'. Nettles were used topically for stings, rashes, dog bites, infected wounds, bleeding hemorrhoids, boils, pimples, shingles, ringworm and sores. I knew a person who had a firsthand account of nettle infused oil mixed with cayenne that was rubbed on bone spurs for a complete recovery. The person also ate nettles and used the intentional flogging method. An old recipe for an ointment for pain comes from Stockport, Greater Manchester. '*Chop nettles, add a good measure of salt, three tablespoons of vinegar, mix in 2 oz. of pure lard, when well mixed spread a good portion on a piece of brown paper and apply to troubled area, fix with a firm bandage*'. Nettle seeds were a Greek remedy for impotence and they were known to help with sexual dysfunction. To chew bunch of nettles leaves was used as a poultice for toothache. With this long list of use, we can safely say that nettles were considered a 'panacea', a cure all.

Nettles were eaten by some Native tribes, the spring shoots and leaves but mostly used for medicine. Some general uses included nettles taken as blood-cleanser, for colds, for upset stomach, taken to promote labor and birth(fresh juice), as a hair tonic(taken both internally and used externally). The Makah tribe used nettles as a hunting medicine, it was rubbed on whale hunter's bodies to make them strong. The same tribe used the plants to whip the bodies of married persons, to insure faithfulness and affection of their spouses. Different tribes used them for flogging to help with rheumatic pains and arthritis.

As useful as the nettles were to country people of the past, there were a few interesting ways to get rid of them. One piece of advice from Herefordshire is that if nettles are well beaten with sticks on the day of the first new moon in May, they will wither and not return. Another old rhyme says: Cut Nettles in June, they will come up again soon; *Cut them in July, they are sure to die.*

Nettles have a long history of food use in the early spring time. Older sources say that if you eat three meals of only nettles in the springtime, you will remain healthy all year long. Another belief states that eating nettles in spring helps the memory be good and strong. Remember to stop harvesting nettle for internal use as they begin to flower, as they are unfit after that point in the season.

Personal Practices

Magically speaking, nettles are an excellent ingredient in any sort of protective or banishing powder, wash, or amulet. Their irritating properties seems to pass onto the invisible world with helpful effects. When doing any sort of binding magic, one can use nettles along with other plants that boast painful thorns or spines to wrap an effigy in, before the ties are placed upon it. To keep away unwanted suitors, nettle powder mixed with grave earth can be sprinkled around one's bedroom or the perimeter of one's home, this works for hauntings as well. Be sure to complete the spell with an intentional incantation, charming the dust appropriately. A pouch of the same can be worn to keep away unwanted social interactions when on a specific errand.

Nettle medicine comes from its tonic, alterative and nutritive rich leaves. They can be used in any balancing formula in the spring or fall. Because they are so food like, nettles help with almost any disorder, but particularly for issues of the respiratory, urinary, female and skin body systems. Making overnight infusions with dried nettles is an amazing way to enjoy the tea, giving more time for the minerals to come into the water. Place about ¼ cup of crumbled dried nettle leaf in a quart jar and pour boiling water to fill up the jar, making sure to stir them in. Then let it steep overnight, pouring off the deep brown emerald liquid the next morning for a refreshing tonic. A quart of nettle infusion every day during times of fatigue is a simple yet profound remedy, in particular for the few weeks of the seasons most intense shifts. Whenever I am run down or during periods of intense stress, I seek out nettles grounding and nourishing medicine.

There is about a two-month harvesting window in the area that I live in, before nettles start to go to flower. The first month, I use them for food and the second month, I dry them for teas or for use in other medicines/magics. Harvest the leaves for food after the plant is about 8 inches high, leaving the bottom leaves so that the plant can keep growing. Use heavy kitchen shears to clip the plants into a large basket, no gloves are needed. Using tongs, place the whole mass into a kettle filled with fresh cold water in order to sufficiently rinse them. I take the time to then use both tongs and shears to clip off the leaves and tops into a strainer, as the stems are tough. Once this is done, they can be incorporated into any dish and cooked like spinach. Remember, they need to be blended or cooked in order for the sting to be removed. My most beloved springtime dishes are nettles cooked into a cheese sauce and eaten on baked potatoes, nettle quiche, nettles in meat stews, and often just steamed nettles with butter and fresh garlic. I have been blessed to enjoy nettle pesto, nettle lasagna and spanakopita, as well as nettle truffles, thanks to nettle lovers in the Olympia area!

For medicine or drying when the plants get larger but before flowering, use heavy leather gloves to hang them in bundles. They will be dry sufficiently in about three weeks' time, depending on your climate and humidity level. Then the leaves can be stripped from the stems and stored in glass jars, out of the light. While they are drying, they will emit the most exquisite fragrance within the first few days, something like earth, rain and wind. In fact, there is no smell more refreshing and revitalizing as this one. I dare say that it is my most treasured plant aroma in the world, beyond even the sweetness and richness of many flowers which are so intoxicating. There is nothing like a ceiling full of wilting nettles in early April, as the rains fall and the woodstove still crackles.

Many Thanks Verdant Queen, your plant blood brings a quickening to the human body and soul after a long winters nap. Greetings amidst the gray skies of spring, joyful unfurling earthen perfume! The gifts that you bestow to the gathering basket are many. Plant of ill omen and protection, you heal with a cutting edge. Fire under water is the nettles secret, may the folk of the forests and hedges ever seek you out, such a green blessing you bestow!

A Nettle Charm for Safe Passage

For one who is traveling, be it on a short or long endeavor, make this charm in order to avert all harm. Whether wandering graveyards after evening falls, traversing darkened haunted terrain, or going to a place of remote danger, this charm is specific for warding ill intending spirits, rather than humans. That stated, if one is trying to keep safe from people or a person, adding grave earth, red pepper, and a small mirror would be helpful.

The eve before the moon is full, as the hour approaches midnight, gather the ingredients from the apothecary thus.

Stinging nettle leaf dried, Rowan tree leaf dried (*Sorbus acuparia*), Mezeron twigs dried (*Daphne mezereum*) Mugwort leaf and bud dried (*Artemisia vulgaris*) St. Johns wort flower and bud dried (*Hypericum perforatum*). Into a black pouch of leather these five ingredients will be placed once charmed, so have that nearby. A small hagstone as well, which acts as both spirit portal and spirit trap, in this case the latter.

With a single candle of white, speak aloud these words:

By the Hedges Glimmer, I alight the path
To and back again, safe from spirit wrath
Plants of fire, I beg your scarlet power
Of Blood, of Rage, of Passion, at this hour

To tend the traveling body and soul
Safe from evil ghost and troll
Protection as the Eldritch Cloak does bestow
My Footfalls to leave hot cinders aglow.

After speaking, take each herb one by one in a pinch, and walk in a clockwise circle round the table or place where the candle burns, three times. Then place them individually in the selected pouch. Do the same for the hagstone, then breathing on it three times as well, before it is secreted within the pouch. When complete, make prayers to one's personal spirits for protection on your travels, and leave out the appropriate offerings before retiring. Wear the pouch when needed, but do not open it again. Also, this is an excellent formula for nightmares, and can be hung above the bedstead to assist with such.

Nettle Banishing Box

For all things that are once of good use, there may come a time when that which once brought delight and joy, has turned from a sweet wine into a sour one. When such things, people, habits, behaviors, ways of being are no longer serving ones Path, a simple but intentional act may be of great use.

Stinging Nettle

Have a box made of wood that is of a medium size, a shovel, a basket of fresh or dried nettles gathered at any stage of growth. Also bring an iron railroad spike and a hammer sufficient to pound it. Go to a wild spot that you have never visited before and to which you will never return to. Face the north and dig a hole big enough to accompany the box. Within the hollow of it must be placed something that represents that which no longer serves. This could be a detailed letter if nothing else can be used, or an actual item of clothing or gift from a person, a symbol of a specific appetite, whatever feels like a powerful analog to that which will be banished. Once the hole is dug, stay facing to the north and place the item in the box, surrounding it by the nettles. Spit three times into the box speaking three times:

Depart, depart, depart I name you (state here)!
No longer will you haunt me, no longer will you take from my fruiting tree!
I banish you (state here),
I banish you (state here)
I banish you (state here) into the earth, into the Northway, into your next form!
Go in peace and never return to me!

Close and bury the box and pound the railroad spike into the ground to hold fast that which is to be banished. Cover it sufficiently with earth so that no one will notice any trace of your doings. Go without looking back even once, and in total silence, until you are back at your place of dwelling.

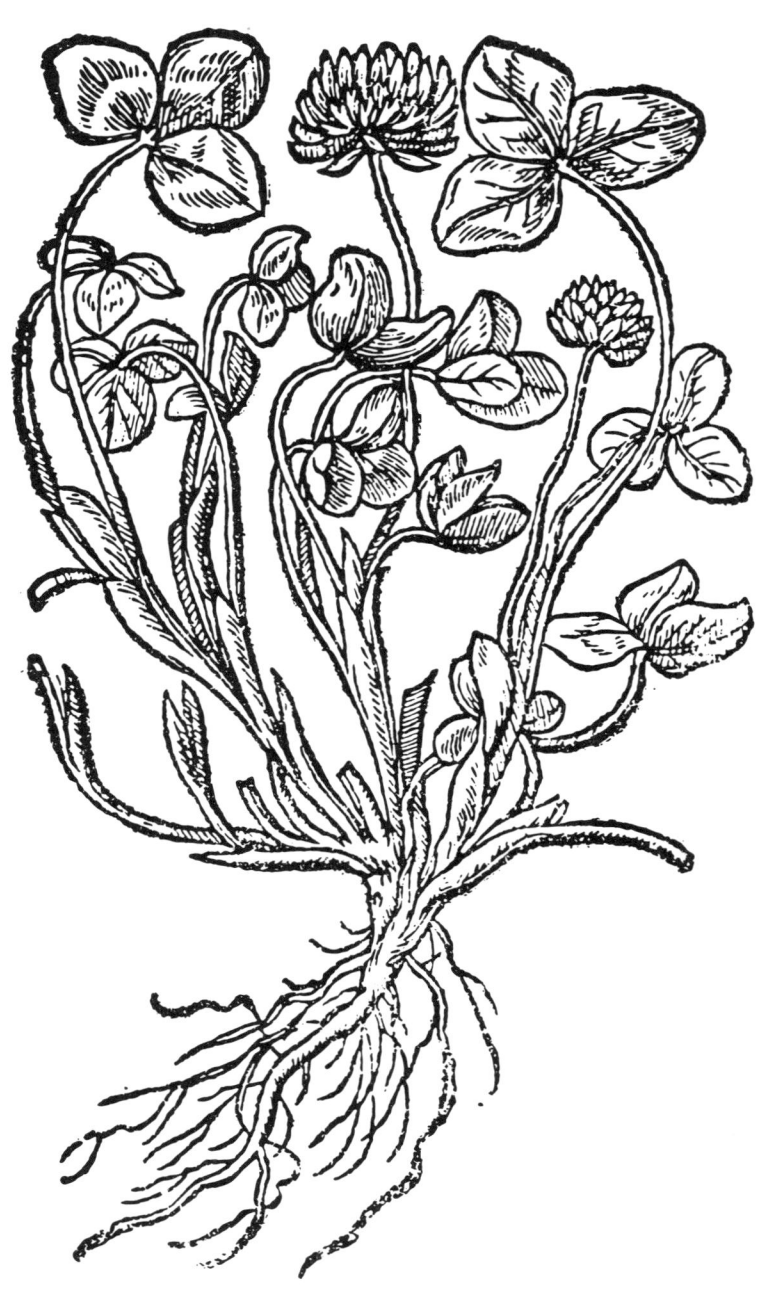

CLOVER, WHITE AND RED

Trifolium repens T. pratense

Abundant clover heads seducing bumble bees in the late springtime are a joy to behold. Though common and often overlooked, clover is one of the few plants that has some of its lore preserved during modern times. Everyone is familiar with the plant itself and its superlative four-leaved version – a lucky charm indeed. If one takes the time to observe the whimsical floral globes of both red and white clover closely, they are absolutely breathtaking when in their full glory and lush byway of the spring rains. Some of the white flowers are tinged with pink or even a deep maroon trace amongst the tiny nectar keepsakes. The red clover is itself like a Faerie Queens jewel, she gleams in the morning sunlight.

Clovers are in the Legume family, *Legumaceae*. Older names for clover included Trefoil, Beebread, Purple Clover, Honeysuckle Rose, Clover Rose, Sugar Plums and Ladies Posy. The Latin *Trifolium* refers to the clovers three leaves. White and red clover are abundant in Britain and most of Europe, to where they are native to. They are found now introduced into America on farm pastures and are a classic meadow flower, flowering in June and onwards throughout the summer. They also grow on the roadsides and on lawns, in city parking lot cracks and alleyways. Such a wayside plant, there is no shortage of clover.

There was an association with the clover and the club of Hercules which had three knobs on it. This is where the club on common playing cards comes from, represented by the clover. The clover also symbolized the Holy Trinity, quite possibly a very old association. The number three is auspicious for different proposed reasons, but this is a significant one. The clover holds quite a bit of lore in its magical uses of old, though the four leaved clover has more accumulated lore by far than the common three leaved one. Most of the lore is for the white clover or is not specified. I will distinguish with the red clover when possible.

There has been some debate about which plant is the real shamrock, the true emblem of Ireland. There have been a few surveys done in Ireland, and from Charles Nelsons study titled *Shamrock: Botany and History of an Irish Myth*, a table of data shows that not much has changed in about 100 years between studies. *Trifolium dubium* or Lesser Trefoil comes in first and *Trifolium repens* or white clover as a relatively close second. Red clover and Wood sorrel or *Oxalis acetosella* are quite low in terms of numbers. Many Americans, including myself think of the shamrock as being wood sorrel. It is helpful to see these surveys, as they come directly from the people of the land of Ireland.

As the 'trefoil' or the three leaved structure of the clovers in general was thought to be both lucky and protective, it was known to keep away both dark witches and snakes. An old charm goes: *Trefoil, Vervain, St Johns wort, Dill, Hinder witches of their will.* Josephine Addison in her book *The Illustrated Plant Lore* writes that clover was 'held in great regard' by the ancient Druids as a charm against evil spirits. She writes *'During the period when witches and fairies seemed to part of everyday life, the clover was considered by both peasant and knight a potent charm against their influences.'*

Four leaved clovers can be from either the white, red or the yellow species. They are somewhat rare to see, though some folks seem to find them more than others and have a knack for noticing them. In times past, people would place a four, five or seven leafed lucky clover in the pages of the bible or prayer book near images of Saints. It is interesting to note that a pressed four-leaf clover looks like an equal armed cross, an old protective symbol in itself. One British belief was that the reason the four leaved clover was lucky was because Eve took one with her when she left Paradise. A few sources tell that wearing a four-leaf clover in one's shoe would bring luck, as the clover faded. This magical plant charm was thought to bring luck to gambling and card games. One German formula included a four-leaf clover and beeswax bound in a pouch made of moleskin to bring gaming luck. However, an Irish belief stated that if the clover is shown to anyone, it loses its luck and also if it is taken into a church the same result would be had.

There were many magical uses for the four leaved clover that went beyond just bringing good fortune. An Irish source states that an ointment made from four leaved clovers could be used to break enchantments, placed by either a Faerie or witch. To allow one to see Faeries, one could place seven grains of wheat upon a four leaved clover. A belief from the Glens in Ireland was that a mixture of clover mixed with whiskey rubbed over the eyes would lift 'fairy blindness' caused by harmful spirits. A Scottish belief was that if one carried the four-leafed clover, then it would be somehow revealed who wanted to cast a spell on them. Four-leaved clovers were also known to prevent madness and could help one from being drafted into the military. A five leaved clover specifically could mean that the finder would have riches come into their life soon, or it could mean misfortune, depending on the location of the lore.

Some superstition relates that a four leaved clover could bring love. There was an old saying that goes: *If you find an even Ash leaf, or a four leaved clover, You'll be bound to see your true love, ere the day be over.* Placing one in the shoe of a person whom was desired was supposed to bring love to the person placing the charm. From West Bohemia, putting a four leaved clover under one's pillow was done to bring dreams of a future mate. Another bit of lore tells that if two people ate a four leaved clover together, that love would grow between them, possibly a good charm to try when love has left a relationship. A two-leaved clover was placed in the shoe to find out the name of one's future spouse, from Cambridge. The spoken charm then goes: *A clover, a clover of two. Put it on your right shoe; The first young man (woman) you meet, In field, street or lane, You'll have him (her) or one of his (her) name.*

French superstition relates that if a woman pins a four leaved clover to her right breast, that she would have good luck in all undertakings, one wonders if this was done on the underclothes so that it would remain hidden. To keep evil away, she would place it in her right shoe and try to forget about it. If the woman had been forsaken in matters of love, she could sew the magic clover into blue silk and pin it near her heart under her dress. If she was seeking love, a four leaved clover was placed in her right shoe and she took her first step with this foot, intending to find the one that she was hoping to meet. And finally, if she happened upon a two leaved clover, this was then twisted with timothy grass and secured in her belt to bring many suitors her way.

There were sometimes specifics that were adhered to in the finding of the magical four-leaved clover. It had to be found by chance, or on the day of St.John's Feast – June 24, Midsummer. A German belief was that it was to be found between a two-wheel track, therefore on the road. A Bohemian practice told to harvest it while reciting the Hail Mary or at midnight. It must then not be touched by the hand but pulled off with the teeth. It was thought best if mass was spoken over a four-leaved clover, so it could be placed under the altar cloth in this case. From Italy, if mass was performed nine times over one, it could be used in love charms. If found in May, it was used as a potent charm against witchcraft, from Wales. In general, if a person found too many in a given time it meant an early death. If one found them frequently, it was taken to mean that the person would always have misfortune.

Here is an old tale that is associated with clover from Cornwall England, thanks to Plant lore, Legends and

Clover White and Red

Lyrics by Richard Folkard: *One evening a maiden set out to milk the cows later than usual: indeed the stars had begun to shine before she completed her task. Daisy, an enchanted cow, was the last to be milked, and the pail was so full that the milk maid could hardly lift it to her head. So to relieve herself, she gathered some handfuls of grass and clover, and spread it on her head in order to carry the milk pail more easily. But no sooner had the clover touched her head, then suddenly hundreds of little people appeared surrounding Daisy, dipping their tiny hands into the milk, and gathering it with clover flowers, which they sucked with gusto. Daisy was standing in the long grass and clover, so some of these little creatures climbed up the stalks, and held out buttercups, convolvuluses (morning glory flower) and foxgloves to catch the milk which dropped from the cows udder. When the astonished milk maid, upon when reaching home, recounted her wonderful experiences to her mistress, the goodwife at once cried out: Ah! You put a four leaved clover on your head!.*

Some general clover lore: from France and Germany, girls would roll and bath in clover dew on May Day, in order to 'become pure'. A May Eve superstition tells that one should take a handful of clover from the four corners of a stranger's field in order to make his/her own farm prosper that year. Sewn into clothing, clover would keep a traveling person safe, a German belief. From Belgium comes the custom of baking a cake shaped like a four-leaved clover to be given to a child before their first communion. This was done to ensure their fertility later in life. Clover gathered from ancient Heathen ruins on Midsummer's Eve was supposed to make exceptionally good wine or beer if put into the mixture. From parts of Britain, red clover leaves were worn against dark witchcraft and to bring good luck.

All clovers seem to be a natural weather forecaster; when the leaves rose up, bad weather was on the way. To dream of clover was thought to be a good omen, indicating strength and prosperity specifically. To dream of seeing a field full of clovers in bloom meant much happiness, abundance, health and good fortune to come. It was a symbol for hope. A story from the Shetland Islands tells that if the breeze came off from the lands at twilight, that fishermen were called back to shore by the strong scent of the red clover coming from the fields. Clover is ruled under the dominion of Venus according to astrologers of the past.

Folk Medicine 🌺

Most medicinal use of clover is for red clover specifically. Uses include using it for the lungs and coughs, taken internally. Red clover syrup is mentioned for whooping cough from Pennsylvanian Dutch folks, a recipe follows below.

Red clover was a folk remedy for cancer, particularly an infusion of the flowers taken for stomach cancer, as it was known as a 'blood purifier'. A recipe from an older herbal specifies taking three quarts per day of red clover blossom tea for breast cancer as a folk remedy. A wash from the blossom tea was used to bath cancerous sores with.

Other uses tell that red clover was used to 'clear the eyes' in particular for bloodshot and red eyes. The infusion was applied to rashes and the leaves were chewed on the Isle of Man for a toothache. Red clover has been used to check heavy menstrual flow and help with cramps in times past. Herbalists used red clover for nerve pain, headaches, insomnia, and stomach distress, for edema and for hypertension. It was folk heart remedy. Externally the leaves and flowers were boiled in lard to make a soothing ointment for cuts, burns, scrapes and bites.

The Native Americans used red clover for a lung medicine, a 'blood medicine' and for cancers. They also used it for 'the change', at woman's menopause time. Modern research shows that this plant is indeed high in plant estrogens and some modern herbalists use it for menopause as well.

The blossoms of either species can be made into wine and one older recipe tells to use white clover flowers on buttered bread with a sprinkle of sugar in making a rustic sandwich. It sounds like a lovely Faerie offering to me. Children certainly love to suck nectar out of the tiny flowers, as the name 'honeysuckle rose' implies.

Personal Practices

Magically speaking, I work with clover as a protection ingredient in pouches, amulets, washes and the like. The leaves harvested on May Eve or Midsummer's Eve are best. I personally look for ones that have the chevron marking clearly imprinted on the leaf. I feel that even if one does not have the four leaved variety, which is of course preferred, that they make a great enchantment breaking or truth telling plant when used magically. I also think this plant has a special affinity for babies and children, a good thing to remember something that is both powerful yet gentle.

Red clover blossoms can be harvested throughout the summer. Continue to pick them, there is a long window, especially if the plants get watered. The leaves just under the blossom can be included. Attempt to gather the blossom when it is perfectly opened, not showing any sign of turning brown. Dry them thoroughly and enjoy in the winter months. Farm animals love this plant as well and I have used it along with oatstraw, nettle and alfalfa as a post birth tea mixed with bran and molasses in a bucket for cows specially. Very important served lukewarm on a cold frosty spring evening, as it nourishes and warms up the mama during the recovery period. Two buckets a day for a few days seems sufficient. The same would be a great formula for human mothers as well, however strained out with a much smaller dosage!

Red clover blossoms can be used in teas and elixirs, primarily for lung support and for cleansing of any sort. Red clover specifically is known as a lymphatic stimulator, helping to move stagnant lymph flow. Red clover and Burdock root combined in a daily tea help immensely with skin issues, specifically acne. A few cups of the tea daily for about six weeks is a good timeframe and dosage to follow. I have recommended it in a tea form for skin troubles including acne, eczema, psoriasis and rashes as well, with good results.

This herb is a nourishing tonic included women's blends. It does provide some cleansing hormonal support, with the green leaves used in mineral formulas for PMS and menopause. For promoting fertility, take a daily tea of the blossom and leaf, along with red raspberry leaf and rosehips. Dandelion leaf can be added as well. The delicious taste of the infusion of the dried blossoms is unlike any other flavor. It is sweet, earthy and yet deeply familiar and comforting. For self-care in general when one has suffered from stress and debilitation, make and take a quart of the blossom tea daily for a few weeks. Also, the same is wonderful for one who is recovering from lung troubles and frequent sickness. Self-heal flowers can be added in this case.

Many thanks to this sweet jewel of the sun, offering abundant joy, protection and good fortune to those who seek it. May it bring truth and clear seeing during dark times. A farmstead dweller, seek out the clovers white and red in meadows, fence lines and garden edges. Blessings upon your threshold as you continue the old traditions forward!

Red Clover Syrup

To make a pleasant and helpful syrup for the lungs and lymph, make a strong infusion of red clover blossom by steeping the dried flower heads in boiling water for a few hours. Make it much stronger than you would for a sipping tea. After straining out, measure the liquid in a glass Pyrex measuring cup. Pour this into a pot and add twice the amount of organic cane sugar, for example one cup of liquid to two cups of sugar. You may add a little less than two parts of sugar, but the less you add the more likely it will spoil. Do not try to substitute honey for this recipe, that requires a different method. Heat both in the pot to just dissolve the sugar, then pour into a warmed glass bottle (using hot water from the tap) and cork. This can be then stored in the refrigerator and will last 6 weeks or more. It is a wonderful cough medicine for children and those folks who do not like bitter herbs or alcohol elixirs. This syrup can also be added to hot water to make an instant sweetened herbal beverage.

Trinity Protection Charm

Gather three good sized and perfectly shaped clover leaflets on the eve before a full moon. Also gather three red roses, and three vervain leaves *Verbena officinalis*. It is best if the harvesting can be done closest to Midsummer's Eve, if possible. Dry these for a few weeks. Also, respectfully gather a bit of grave soil from three related family members, with permission upon asking the spirits. Offer silver coins to each and explain the reason for your purposes. Give gratitude and a blessing to the Dead. The soil must also be dried out and sifted through a small sieve over the coming weeks.

Once dry, on the eve before the dark moon hand sew a small pouch of soft blue wool or silk. Do this as evening falls, before the light of a candle that has been blessed by a priest. Once finished with the pouch, hold the dried herbs and grave soil in the left hand, or if one is left handed, then in the right hand. Speak these words before the flame in a low voice so that none will hear what is uttered, three times total, each verse spoken in one breath:

> *Thrice leaf and petal,*
> *Thrice silver and gold,*
> *Thrice the songs of the Dead,*
> *Breathe upon this charm of Old.*
>
> *As solar light abrades the night,*
> *Thrice the Watchers stance,*
> *From within a circle of angels,*
> *Protected is the serpents Dance.*

Under the Bramble Arch

Blessed be the wearer,
By the Lady and the Host,
In the names of the fallen,
Father, Son and Holy Ghost.

When the invocation is complete, pass the charm bag through the sacred candle flame three times. This can then be worn beneath the clothing on one whom is to be protected, be it a gift to another or for the self. It can also be hung above the bedstead to help ease suffering during the small hours.

Midsummer's Eve Offerings

Down the sun goes, golden hedge
A whisper to bemoan the threads
Of life and death,
Of stifled breath
Mysteries of the earth year's told

The stories that we know of old
To starlit smoke, to blackened earth
The womb flays open at the birth
Darkness is the mother to
The Saints, the Kings, the Olden Oak

And she is the keeper of the cloak
That waits the turn
That heeds the burn
Until this magical Eve,
At last a breath of chill reprieve

For tinkling chimes from winters call
And Icy fingers down darkened hall
Still grasp the golden night
Offerings I have lovingly prepared
For the death of the light

Clover White and Red

Ivy leaf, primrose, amber seed
Oak wand, horsehair, mistletoe bead
Black hen, earth claw, shining vine
Elk horn, gold blood, bay wine
To be buried in the wood dark
At dusk, a grave to dig the mark
The earthen scar to test the fates
The wizened eyes watch at the gates
The wishing cup from Northern well
Will wind a road to darkling hell

The Fairy smoke, pearlescent pipes
The deadened bough of spirit lights
Will follow and in dreamland dwell
The voice to sing,
The tale to tell

A mask unearthed from hidden stone
The resting place of Mother Crone
The threads emerge tangled and black
To give the night, the shadow back
To tree root and velvet moth wing

To flower seed and fruit offering
At once the light will cease to burn
And to shade, smoke and ice
Will all things living return

ROSE
Rosa spp.

There is no joy that compares to being within or near a hedge of fragrant roses. The mystery and history of this plant is beyond comparison to any other flower. She is graceful, she is gentle, yet she is dangerous and holds a wildness that penetrates the heart and soul of the bereft human. While her beauty is apparent in her blooms, her darkness lingers close to her thorns. From the enchanted hedge in the springtime, leaves grow blessed with pink coloring on new shoots, thorns, and leaf petioles. Summer brings her intoxicating flowers forth to touch sunshine and wind. In the autumn months, she is generously adorned by red fruit ornaments. And with the cold winter, her wood of thorns act as a barrier and a shelter, her skeleton exposed to ice and rain. The rose offers medicine and magic in all seasons of the year.

Since ancient times, people have loved and praised roses. Her association with love and joy is still known even in modern culture. It is one of the flower symbols that has survived the industrial and technological age, if now commercialized. Rose is the most recognized of all flowers, they have been on this planet long before humans arrived. Some sources state that the fossilized remains of roses have been traced to be 35 million years old, found in parts of Montana, Oregon and Colorado. They are extremely tough and hardy plants, especially the wild ones. Roses are universal to all temperate climates. There are more than 100 species and around 10,000 cultivated varieties. One of the oldest plants in Germany is a dog rose, thought to have been planted over 1200 years ago. Wild roses generally grow in open sunny meadows or hedgerows often near water, a few grow in the forest shade.

> *'Old garden rose tree hedged it in; Bedroft with roses waxen white; Well satisfied with dew and light, And careless to be seen.'*
> Elizabeth Barrett Browning

The name 'Rose' comes from the Greek word *rodon* which meant red, suggesting that ancient roses were red. Another source writes that the word may come from the Celtic word rhos, which also means red. Something to keep in mind is that most wild roses are generally pink and that there was not a word for the color 'pink' until around the 1700s. Pink and red were not always distinguished. Sometimes something pink was called 'light red'.

The folklore and stories associated with rose are vast. Indeed, a whole book could be written about this plant, so I will attempt to present both some common and not so common lore here. There are many stories about the origin of roses. In the East roses were generated from the sweat or tears of Mohammad. Muslims do not allow roses to touch the ground or this reason. A Greek story tells that when Venus was born from the sea, at the very same moment a rose sprang from the earth and it was considered sacred to her as she is the Goddess of love. Another Greek story tells that the first roses were without thorns until Cupid, Aphrodite's young son was stung by a bee while smelling a newly opened rose. To pacify her upset son, Aphrodite strung a bow with bees, first removing their stingers and placing them upon the rose stems. Another belief tells that Cupid was dancing among the Gods and overturned a cup of their wine, which spilled on the roses turning them red and giving them fragrance as well. Yet another Greek legend tells that the rose was originally a beautiful woman from Corinth named Rhodanthe. She was constantly followed by kings and warriors eager to win her love. To escape her suitors she fled to the temple of Artemis, to the Goddess of purity. The people followed her there, breaking down the gates. Artemis was outraged by this and transformed Rhodanthe into a red rose bush, the color used to symbolize the blush of her beautiful face when looked upon by her followers.

A Roman tale tells that roses were originally white until Venus ran through a rose patch and a thorn tore her foot which bled on the white roses, causing them to turn red. An English legend says that the blood of Christ has made roses red. This plant was and is considered Holy and Sacred in different cultures. It was said that the rose originally had no thorns but as man's wickedness increased, so did the thorns on the plant. Other beliefs say that thorns appeared after the coming of Adam and Eve. Rose is deeply tied to religion from early times, symbolizing specifically the resurrection. It is associated with the Virgin Mary whose one title of many is 'Mystical Rose'. Often times when the Divine Feminine Presence is near, one will smell roses suddenly. A Mediterranean origin legend tells about the red and white roses being the prayers of a maiden falsely accused and sentenced to burning; her prayers quenched the flames of the fires, with her unburned brands becoming white roses and her charred brands becoming red. This is rose symbolizing justice no doubt.

There is an incredible tale by Hans Christian Anderson called 'The Rose Elf'. It is an amazing story about a little elf that lives within the petals of the rose and witnesses a murder; a woman's jealous brother murders her lover who is leaving to go off to sea. The rose elf stays with the woman and avenges her lover's death, by help of the faeries and bees. Again rose and her helpers symbolize justice and right action in the midst of tragedy.

Rose was a symbol of silence since early times. This is supposed to have come from the story of Cupid (or Eros from other sources) receiving a rose from his mother Venus (Aphrodite). He gave the rose to the god of silence,

Harpocrates, to 'induce him to conceal the weakness of the gods.' Some old buildings in Europe with plaster ceilings have a rose imprinted in the middle for a reminder that what was spoken of in the room could not be repeated, hence the term 'Sub Rosa' meaning 'Under the Rose'. An old symbol above a garden gate was that of a rose in full bloom with two buds above it. This signified secrecy of an herbalist's powers that were kept within the garden. Because of its connection with secrecy, the wild rose was sometimes used to represent illicit love. A rose is often over confessionals in a church for its secrecy association, used as such since 1562.

As rose has been connected to true love since early times, it was not surprisingly used in divination rites surrounding such matters. One rite was that by placing a red rose under one's pillow on Midsummer's night eve, it would provoke a dream of one's true love. Another divination was to take rose leaves and name each one of them after a selection of suitors. The leaves were then placed in a bucket of water and whichever one remained floating the longest would represent a woman's suitor. In older recipe books, rose 'leaves' often meant the petals. If a rose was picked on Midsummer's eve and had not faded a month after, it meant that a lover was faithful. To dream of roses in general meant good luck and success in love. One older custom from Devon tells if a young woman on her way to church picked a fully opened rose on Midsummer blindfolded while walking backwards, she would then fold it in white paper and keep it hidden away until Christmas time. Then she would take it out and pin it to her dress; it should be nearly as perfect as when she first picked it. The man at church to come and take the rose from her would be her future husband.

A lover could be returned by this spell to be done on Midsummers Eve, June 23rd. Three roses had to be gathered on this magical eve. One was buried during the small hours of Midsummer morning under a yew tree, another in a newly made grave and the last one placed under the practitioners pillow. If it was left for three nights and then burned, the person performing the spell would haunt the runaway lover's dreams and they would not know peace until they returned. A divination to foretell whether one's sweetheart was true was to be performed on All Hallow's Eve in Wales. Two long stem roses were taken into a woman's chamber in silence. She would then weave them together as she spoke this rhyme:

Twine, twine and intertwine
Let his love be wholly mine.
If his heart be kind and true,
Deeper grow his roses hue.

The woman could then watch to see if the rose named after her love grew darker to indicate or not, his love for her.

An interesting divination was used tell whether an unborn baby would be a boy or a girl. One was to take both a lily and a rose to a pregnant woman. If she chose the lily, the unborn child would be a boy and if she chose the rose, the babe would be a girl. Roses have throughout time symbolized love, beauty, elegance, joy, life, pleasure, secrecy, silence, pride, wine, woman and wisdom, just to name a few associations! The rosebud symbolized youthful beauty and hope specifically. Rose thorns have symbolized death, pain and sin. Red roses are under the dominion of Jupiter, damask roses under Venus and white roses under the moons influence, according to astrologers of the past.

Roses also had and have a strong connection with death and were used in funeral customs throughout olden times. People of ancient Greece decorated tombs and graves with them, believing that the dead would be protected by the power of the rose. It was a Welsh custom to plant a white rose on the grave of an unmarried woman and in England a garland of white roses was used to decorate the grave of a virgin. It was said that roses will grow from the graves of two lovers and intertwine. There are old folk ballads that sing of this. In

Switzerland, the custom of planting roses by the graves of the dead led to the cemeteries turning into rose gardens.

There were many specific beliefs that associated death and roses. If a white rose bloomed in Autumn in Scotland, it was a symbol of an early death of a loved one. But if a red rose bloomed then instead, it was a sign of an early marriage. A red rose that had petals falling as it was carried was a death omen. Overall red roses were more connected with love and white ones with death or bad luck. In parts of England and North America, to even smell white roses was considered bad luck. If rose buds were found to have rot within them, it was an omen of immediate deception, a German belief. To scatter rose leaves or petals upon the ground was an evil omen, in both England and Italy. To pluck a rose from a grave was supposed to bring death to the one whom picked it. If a person who was sick dreamt of roses, it was a sure sign that they would soon die.

Prayer beads or rosaries were associated with mystical roses and used ceremonially not only in prayer but associated with rites of with the dead to protect the living left behind. A German belief was to throw a rosary at a ghost in order to banish it. The word 'rosary' has origins from the Latin word *rosarium*, which meant 'rose gardens'. For more information about the history of rosaries, see the *Compendium of Symbolic and Ritual Plants in Europe*, volume one pages 618-20, by De Cleene and Lejeune.

Wild rose is a plant that is commonly referred to as 'Briar', similar to blackberry in the way that it grows in a large thorny arch; in fact they are both in the same family of *Roseaceae*. The wild roses of the British Isles and other parts of norther Europe, specifically eglantine *Rosa rubignosa* and the dog rose *R. canina*, both have extremely sharp and large thorns on larger examples of older plants. The downward pointing thorns hook into the skin, digging deeper as one tries to escape from their grasp. From France, *R.rubignosa* rosehips were called 'Devil's Bread', and sometimes the names 'Rose sorciere' and

Rose

'Rose du diable' were used as well. A folk story tells that eglantine's thorns are pointed downward, because after the Devil was excluded from heaven, he used the plant to make a ladder made of the thorns in order to climb back up. When eglantine would only grow as a bush rather than a tall vine, he placed the thorns in their hooked position out of spite.

Other common names for either of these rose species were 'Witch Briar', and 'Sleep Thorn'. One reason for these particular names was because the roses harbor a growth that looks like a moss-covered excrescence, also known as 'Robins Pincushion'. This growth was cut out and used by witches as a sleep charm, placed under the pillows of their oblivious husbands so that they could attend the nighttime Sabbats to meet the Devil while the husband slept soundly in bed. Only when it was removed from the bed, could the person sleeping be awoken. Perhaps the clandestine sleep inducing qualities of the dog rose account for this piece of Irish lore: An Irish folk tale tells of how three hags enchanted the Fianna (small bands of Irish warriors) by winding a magical coil of yarn around the thorny stem of a dog rose. The warriors were put immediately into a trance when they laid eyes upon the talisman.

Robin's pincushion had a myriad of medicinal uses as well. It was used as a sleep charm in general, an amulet for whooping cough, piles or rheumatism. These strange growths were powdered and sold in European apothecary shops, taken to cure the stone, as a diuretic, and for colic, and to prevent toothache. A Norfolk remedy for the cramp was to place one under one's pillow. Pliny noted that stamped and mixed with honey and ashes, it was used as a lotion to regrow hair that had fallen out from 'the foxes evil', a patchy type of hair loss.

One spell from Scandinavian trolldom that employed wild roses thorny habit for sending back evil in the name of the Devil goes thus. The person working the spell, on a Friday between the times of noon and one o'clock was to walk in silence into the wind, to find a rose bush bearing hips. The top of the bush was to be bent towards the ground with a hook and held there, while the person suffering crawled three times backwards under the briar. Each time passing under the magical arch, this incantation was to be spoken:

'All the evil sent to me by sorcerers or sorceresses, This I now send away from me, And back to the one who sent it, Amen! In the name of the mighty devil Itagiths'.

Another from 18th century Denmark was done to see if a person was cursed or hexed. A fire was to be made of rose or elder wood on a Thursday. The person in question was to catch the first urine of the day and place it into a newly made clay pot between 11 and 12 o'clock. Over the fire, this was heated in the name of the Devil. If it could not boil over, the person was indicated to be cursed.

For magical healing, I have found many examples that utilized the power of the rose. In Romany lore if a woman wanted to bring about her menses, she would pour rose water over herself and then pour the water over a blooming rose bush. If a thorn was taken from the dog rose on Good Friday, it could be used for transference of toothache. The thorn was stuck into the gums until blood was drawn to ensure the pain would disappear. The rose was used to rid of erysipelas, which is a highly red and inflamed skin infection. One charm was to strike a flint and steel in a cross direction and speak this formula:

Red rose and white rose, dark rose and light rose vanish, like the dew before the sun. Another reads: There came a maiden from Engelland, a rose she carried in her hand, when the sun went down, the seventh and seventieth zahnrose disappeared'.

Yet another for the same affliction was to speak this while stoking the infection downwards:

Rose

There were three maidens on the green ways, the first gathered flowers, the second gathered lilies, the third drove away the hilge and the rose.

In this example, the 'hilge' was eruption and the 'rose' was erysipelas.

Being a thorny plant, the rose was understandably used in protective magic. Bewitched milk could be stirred with a branch of the dog rose and animals thought to be cursed were struck by the same for protection from harm, from Austria and Normandy. From Belgium, roses that were consecrated the first Sunday in July by a priest (sprinkled with Holy water) were hung in homes for protection against thunder, lightning and disease for the following year. One folk rite involving the rose comes from Waloon, Belgium. Roses were strewed in the shape of a crown (circle) on a white cloth over which a priest would then lay his communion cloth and place the monstrance upon it. These petals were then burned when a person was ill, in order to protect the space and drive away evil spirits.

A splinter from a coffin wrapped in a shroud was mixed with some feces of a person thought to be suffering from bewitchment. This bundle was buried under a dog rose before sunrise in order to break the enchantment. If a girl wanted red cheeks, she could wash her first menstrual cloth in water and pour this over a rosebush in order to procure this beauty.

Rose hips were also thought protective from dark magic. They could be buried within the stable floor if a cow stopped producing milk in order to help restore it, from Upper Franconia. From Borinage Belgium, rosehips strung onto a rustic necklace were worn by children in order to protect them from harm and drive away evil. Eating three rosehips (the flesh not the seeds I presume) on an empty stomach on Christmas night or New Year's Eve was done to prevent one from having sickness caused by neck pain, lumbar pain, stomach disorders, rashes and gout for the following year. The hips would be passed inside through a window by another family member or friend, in complete silence before being consumed.

Folk Medicine

Medical use of rose is very old indeed. Pliny listed 32 medicines that could be made from roses. Rose conserve was supposed to prevent miscarriage and help the growing fetus. Other older uses for rose included using it for heart troubles, stomach aches, diarrhea, hemorrhage, headaches (rose vinegar applied to the temples), for sore mouths and for the spitting of blood. Red roses were known to cure anemia, which could have been sympathetic magic at work. The rose in Germany was used as a charm against blood hemorrhage. Rose was often included as a main ingredient in an eye wash. One recipe combines rose with chickweed for this. Rose hip syrup was used for sore throats and colds. The juice of rose was a cough cure from Donegal.

Externally rose offered much in the form of an anti-inflammatory medicine in times past, as they do today. Rose and mint heated in a poultice form were applied warm to the abdomen to strengthen a weak stomach. The leaves of rose were used as a poultice for cuts and scrapes and petals were chewed to sweeten the breath. The dew from rose petals was used to remove spots and freckles from the skin. An ointment for chilblains, a severe rash/irritation of the extremities caused by exposure, was made from seven kinds of roses, rosemary and southernwood. Rose root was used for dog bites, including wolf bites, and domestic animal bites. A liniment was made from red roses heated and steeped in wine, then applied to the strained or sprained area with a silk or flannel cloth overnight, from an old recipe.

Native Americans used roses generally for eye pain, sore throats, child labor pains, for muscle pain, to strengthen babies, as a general tonic, for women's medicine and for diarrhea. The Iroquois tribe used R. *acicularis* or the prickly rose in eye drop form for blindness, working with the leaves and the bark. They also used a decoction of the plants along with a doll for unspecified 'black magic'. The Thompson tribe used the hips of this rose to help hasten a woman's labor by having her chew on them. A decoction of the roots was also taken after childbirth to help the healing process. The Chippewa tribe used the prairie rose R. *arkansana* as a root decoction to stop bleeding wounds. The Ojibwa tribe powdered the rose flowers and took it for heartburn. The California rose R. *californica* was used as a pain reliver for infants by the Cahuilla tribe. An infusion of the petals of the same rose was given to babies for fever by the Diegueno tribe. *Rosa gymnocarpa* was used in ceremony as a wash for the sweat lodge by the Okanagan-Colville tribe. The Thompson tribe used a decoction of this rose to pour over hunting equipment in order to restore lost luck.

Personal Practices

For both magic and medicine, I prefer any rose that is fragrant, has thorns and makes a hedge. This includes therefor wild roses, but also older cultivated varieties. Many folks ask about random roses growing in their yards, so these are my personal preferences. Newer varieties of rose are often lacking thorns and grow in gangly stands, even if they have a pleasant perfume. While beautiful, they seem to lack the power of the older roses, at least in my opinion.

The wild rose is a defensive plant that can be used in protective magical work and for keeping things hidden. A classic example comes from the French fairy tale of Sleeping Beauty, where the briar rose *Rosa canina* encircles the enchanted castle and keeps it hidden for one hundred years, while at the same time trapping any intruder in the hedge to the end of a slow painful death. This can be applied magically by laying roses upon spellwork or including them in amulets to keep unwanted energy away.

A plant that contains darkness within it has the power to assist in grim circumstances. Any wild rose is a potential ally for grief, heartbreak and sexual trauma. This can be applied in many ways. The immense beauty and defensive nature both are of great value here. A simple personal practice that goes beyond sipping the delicious elixir made from fragrant petals, involves visioning and meditation. In order to eliminate disturbing imagery and information from the inner altar, one can imagine an old *R.canina* plant that is growing next to a ruined castle, with deep astringent roots that reach far beyond, into the tombs below, touching the dead, feeding on the ancient bones. By gentle pink blossom and vicious thorn, rose protects the inner temple from poison, for those sensitive and thin skinned. The thorns can also be respectfully collected and infused in a small vial of oil, buried upside down in the earth from dark moon to dark moon. This substance can then be used for anointing all that needs protection, from flesh, heart and home.

Rose is important in love magic as well as in sending back applications. Use the flowers for the former and the thorny branches for the later. The wood with thorns can be collected and hung in the home to trap unwanted energy or spirits, or to remove ill influences from a person. Make a ring with the branches and ribbon and have one step into it, moving it then up and down the body to cleanse the afflicted person. Rose is an important funerary plant and can be used for altars made for the beloved dead or ancestors. Make offerings of dried or fresh white roses when working with graveyard magic and visitations. Use roses when helping a dying person cross over, this can be done in a passive or active manner, by having roses in the room or working with the plant spirit for assistance. Rose beads can be made and used for mourning. They are so fragrant and haunting, no doubt a beautiful relic to invoke or soothe the troubled dead for communication purposes.

Harvest leaves and newly opened flowers in early summer, and hips in the autumn time, before they are exposed to the rains and begin to rot. In dryer areas they can be harvested after the first frost, but in rainy climates like my own they need to be collected before the weather turns them into brown mush. They can be dried whole for decoctions or cut in half in order to remove the irritating white seeds and then dried – this is a painstaking process. Do not ingest the seeds. The fresh hips can also be frozen whole to be make into syrups or elixirs later, an easy way to save and use them. As long as straining is involved, the seeds and hairs can be separated from the flesh.

Medicinally speaking the different rose species can be used similarly, to cool heat and inflammation in the body, to ease congestion of the mucous membranes, to tonify the GI tract, to calm the nerves and to bring peace of mind. Rose petals are an incredible nervine and nerve tonic for stress, insomnia, headaches (not migraines), tension, trauma, broken heart, grief and anxiety. Rose can be included in lung blends for their astringent properties, and strong rosehip tea is helpful for sinusitis. Rose is also wonderful in heart formulas to support vein, capillary and heart health. Rose is excellent in digestive blends, helpful for sour stomach, diarrhea, and indigestion. The petals, leaves and hips can be used interchangeably to some degree, but I prefer the flowers for their nervine properties, the leaves for their astringency and the hips for nutritive virtues.

Topically rose makes an antiseptic wound wash, and the leaves and flowers can make a quick astringent poultice in the brush for bites and stings. Rose infused honey is incredible for burns and as a mask for roseacea and inflamed skin. Rose infused vinegar is good for sunburn, diluted with water, also dabbed on the temples for headaches. Rose tea can be used for diaper rash as a wash and also as a douche for female infections. I absolutely love rose petal infused oil as a face oil – it is my favorite for skin care. Rose infused oil can also be made into salves for skin irritations, dryness, inflammation and to ease a rash. Dried fragrant roses can also be powdered and sprinkled on hot coals as a fumigation. They are amazing, and when mixed with half part lavender and quarter part violet flower, make one of the most profound smelling incenses to behold.

The fresh petals can be eaten in salads and confections, added to wines, honeys, elixirs and brandy, brewed as a wine, and made into rose infused vinegar and rose flower syrup. The flowers and leaves can be dried to have on hand in teas and blends. Infuse roses in oil and fat to be added later to salves, balms and creams. The potions to be made from roses are endless. Rose petals themselves can be incorporated into salads, cookies, syrups and candied. Rose essential oil is extremely expensive and termed 'precious'. It is said that 2000 petals make one drop of the oil. Rose oil has been produced since the invention of the still, as has rose water, both being used in cosmetics for hundreds of years. Roses are endlessly useful, helpful, healing and pleasurable.

Many thanks to the Ancient Queen of all flowers, you entice and seduce with your beauty. Held within your enchantment are healing and baneful ribbons of perfume. What protection you offer for death, tragedy, grief and our closest held secrets. Your medicine is gentle enough for babes, yet powerful enough to surpass the veil between this world and the Other. An ally to humans near and far, may your thorns always draw blood, may your scent always allure and may you survive – held in sacred light before the coming of humans and long after our departure.

Rose Elixir

After wilting fresh fragrant roses for about 6 hours, combine the rose petals with brandy. Fill a mason jar almost full, but not packed with the roses and fill 2/3 with brandy. Top with honey, leave an inch for shaking room. Shake daily for 4 weeks and strain. Strain off and bottle, ageing for at least 2 months before drinking. If honey settles on the bottom, shake before using. This is divine, an ally for grief, depression, sleeplessness, heartbreak and trauma.

Rose Wine

Pick 2 quarts of fragrant roses with the calyx. Let them wilt a few hours and put them into a 2 or 3 gallon crock. Add

3 pounds of organic cane sugar. Cover with one gallon of boiling water and stir well to dissolve. Let this sit overnight. The next morning sprinkle 1/3 of a packet of high alcohol wine yeast onto the surface. Let this sit for 15 minutes, then stir in. Cover tightly with a clean towel. Stir this daily for 10 days and then strain out the new wine into a gallon glass jug. Fit with an airlock. It will be the most marvelous color of pink if your roses were pink themselves, sadly this will in time fall out and be a clear amber color eventually. But enjoy it while it lasts. Store in a dark cool (not cold) place for three months and rack. (See appendices in *Under the Witching Tree* for more wine making details) Bottle after 6 months and wait around a year to drink. Enjoy on Midsummers Eve the following year.

Blood of the Rose Magical Ink

Harvest the darkest red rose petals/flowers that can be found. Dry them well and push them through a mortar and pestle to powder them, removing the calyx. Have about 2 table spoons total. Once reduced to a powder, add just enough hot water to moisten and a bit of moon blood, if desired. Let this sit and add a little more water as needed to keep the consistency thick but not dry. Set for 12 hours, ideally during the dark moon time if that works with the menstrual cycle. Push the mixture through a sieve with a pestle to retrieve the liquid portion and boil down briefly in a small pot to reduce it a bit. Then once cool, pour into an ink well. This has an excellent maroon color and writes equally well on wood or paper for any magical purpose. Keep it in the fridge when not in use. The shelf life is around a month or so, so make in small batches.

MUGWORT
Artemisia vulgaris

Mugwort for the cauldron, mugwort for the fire; The witches scrying potion, the herb of night and dreams, a keeper of the mysterious feminine – what a numinous plant of the wayside we have here. A plant of the moonlight with tall fragrant branches, mugwort leaves are green on top and dusted with silver underneath. Once the fragrance is inhaled, there will be no mistaking mugwort for another. It smells hot, aromatic, bitter, sweet and menthol all at once. In the heat of the sun, tiny inconspicuous flowers form a large bush of silver green fading then to rust as winter approaches.

The genus Artemisia comes from the Goddess Artemis, mistress of the wilderness, of animals, of the hunt, childbirth and women's health. There are roughly 300 species in the genus and they are in the aster family, Asteraceae. Other potentially familiar herbs in the same genus are Wormwood, Sagebush, Southern Wood, Sweet Annie and Tarragon.

D.C Watts writes in his *Dictionary of Plant Lore* that mugwort is one of the most important plants in the folklore of Britain. Allen and Hatfield in their book *Medicinal Plants in Folk Tradition – An Ethnobotany of Britain and Ireland* write *"The medico-magical potency with which this visually unprepossessing plant has been credited through much of Eurasia and the strikingly similar beliefs associated with it in different regions of that landmass indeed suggest that it may be one of the oldest herbs known to mankind."* A significant statement indeed.

Common names included Muggons, Felon Herb, Springwort, Sailors Tobacco, Maidenswort, Moderwort, Johns Feast Day Wort and St. Johns Plant/Herb. It was part of the Midsummer Herbs or St. Johns worts, herbs of St. John. The name mugwort implies that the plant helped to keep away flies, which it was used for in the past. 'Mug' is a German base word meaning 'fly' or 'gnat'. An old meaning of the original Latin name was translated 'Mothers Herb', as this plant historically had an affinity for women. A Pennsylvanian Dutch name for mugwort translated to mean 'Old Woman.' Some sources state that the name mugwort has its root word in the Norse *muggi* meaning 'marsh'. Common mugwort is native to Europe, Asia, North Africa, Alaska and is now naturalized in the US. It is considered an invasive weed in many places.

As mugwort had associations with the summer solstice or Midsummer, there is some lore surrounding it specifically relating to that time of year. It was worn as a 'girdle'(something that encircles like a belt) on St. Johns Eve for protection from ghosts or dark magic. The girdle of mugwort could then be thrown into the fires of Midsummer to burn any misfortune of the wearer, in particular disease an example of transference magic. If the flames of the fires were looked at through a branch of mugwort, it would bring good vision to the beholder. Another Midsummer custom was to hang mugwort over doorways to purify the house from evil spirits. From Scotland it was traditional to protect cows from witches and faeries by placing mugwort in the animal sheds on Midsummer's Eve.

Yet another belief related to Midsummer was that if a 'coal' was found and dug at the roots of mugwort on Midsummer's Eve at midnight, this 'coal' could be kept as an amulet throughout the year to protect a family from a number of diseases, such as ague, plague, falling sickness and from lightning. One finds this tradition with plantain and burdock as well, having magical coals that even glow at midnight when being sought out for magical purposes. Nowadays it is supposed that the 'coals' were older rotten roots under the plant.

Mugwort

Mugwort was a symbol of happiness and tranquility. It had the ability to open locks ascribed to it. A charm for the traveler, he or she who carried mugwort in their shoe would never feel weary. It also protected a traveler from wild animals, fatigue, evil spirits and sunstroke if it was carried with on a journey. In China mugwort was hung during the Dragon festivals to protect from the influences of evil. Prophetic powers were attributed to mugwort, crystal gazers found that by drinking mugwort tea their powers were enhanced. It was a practice to rub oneself with mugwort after handling a corpse so that the handler would not be haunted by the ghost of the deceased. Mugwort was supposed to have life protective and longevity qualities. An old Scottish adage that came from a mermaid watching a funeral procession went: *If they eat Nettles in March and drink Mugwort in May, so many fine maidens would not go to clay.*

Mugwort had the power to keep one from being affected from the Evil Eye, keep away 'devil sickness' and help keep evil leechcrafts from happening in a dwelling – lore from early English receipts. In German magic it was used to treat illness caused by spellcraft and to protect from the Devil as well. A potion could be made of mugwort to give to one whom had been bewitched from Belgium lore, and a cross could be made by the plant and worn as a protective amulet. It was also used to keep milk and eggs safe from bewitchment. From France and Belgium, there are records of mugwort keeping away devils, witches and lightning. A mugwort root worn around the neck was supposed to keep one safe from poisonous animals and creatures. If mugwort was gathered on St. Johns Eve, it could be saved for making a decoction to un-witch cows from giving scanty milk if it was applied as an anointing substance. A German belief tells that if a person whom is sick sleeps on a pillow underneath which mugwort had been placed, he would be cured. However, the plant must have been placed there without his/her knowing and if the person could not sleep, it was a death omen.

With all of this protective lore, we find a small amount of love magic with mugwort. From a Greek papyrus comes the mention of using *Artemisia* (which could also be wormwood or Southern wood) to gain love and friendship. Widows from Poland would wear a sprig of mugwort to attract new love and bring another marriage prospect. A Belgium practice was for women to place a mugwort sprig between their breasts to attract a suitor to them. Mugwort was protective over newly married couples, one wonders about its ability to protect from the Evil Eye helping here.

I will end the folklore section here with a story about mugwort, it is worth recording in full. From the book *A City Herbal*, by Maida Silverman: "*There is a Russian Folktale about how mugwort, called Zabytko, got its name: one day a young girl went into the forest to gather mushrooms. She stumbled and fell into a deep pit, which turned out to be the abode of serpents. They did her no harm and actually took care of her, even showing her a certain stone that glowed in the dark and magically provided the snakes(and the girl herself) with nourishment. She stayed with them throughout the winter and when spring came, the creatures formed a ladder with their intertwined bodies, and the girl was able to climb out of the pit. As a parting gift, the Queen of the Serpents gave her the power to understand the language of the plants, but warned her never to name mugwort, for if she did, her magic gift would immediately be lost forever. One day, long afterward, as she was walking with her lover, he asked suddenly 'What is the name of the plant that grows in the fields, beside the little footpaths?' Taken by surprise she answered 'Mugwort'. From that time on, the maiden forgot the speech of the plants, and the Russians have called the mugwort Zabytko, the herb of forgetfulness.*"

Folk Medicine

Older medicinal uses of mugwort are many. In China, it was and is used in Moxa, a treatment which helps to clear meridians of the body used often in conjunction with acupuncture. Mugwort was known as a vermifuge, taken to kill worms. It was used for rheumatism and fevers, for epilepsy and shaking. Mugwort was known for easing coughs and cold symptoms, including the dreaded consumption. It is a very bitter herb and has use as a digestive bitter after fatty meals, according to Culpepper. The fresh juice of mugwort was supposedly an old cure for the overdose of opium. The mystical Welsh Physicians of Myddfai recommended an eggshell of mugwort juice for weariness, one wonders at the strength of that dose – I would personally start with less. A sweet Korean woman once relayed to me that drinking some mugwort juice was the only thing that helped her horrible stomach cramps and diarrhea. Drinking a little mugwort in gin was a remedy for living into old age, according to a Belgium woman who lived to be over 100 years old.

The whole plant was a strewing herb, used to repel insects. In old cottages, the floors were made of earth and rushes were often strewn on the floors, as a sort of covering. Aromatic plants were also used to repel fleas, rodents and whatnot. Mugwort was smoked as a tobacco substitute in Berkshire. It has been used to flavor ales, along with other bitter herbs such as yarrow. Pounded with lard it was used on sore feet. Or mixed with Oxe-Eye daisy *Chrysanthemum leucanthemum* in lard, it was used as a topical for a sore neck from an old recipe.

This plant was once highly valued as a women's herb for bringing on menstrual flow, easing in birth and delivery and is still mentioned as an emmenagouge and abortifacient in modern herbals. Old lore tells that to cut the plant downwards stimulates menstrual flow and that by cutting it in an upwards direction, one could keep bleeding in check. There is an old charm for helping a woman with a difficult delivery by tying mugwort to her left thigh, then instantly removing it when she had delivered to prevent a hemorrhage. A rustic recipe comes from Gabrielle Hatfield's Hatfields Herbal; *"For a Poor Country Woman in Labor to Hasten their Birth – Take three handfuls of mugwort, 12 cloves whole and boyle them in a pint of white wine half an hour, then strein it and let the party drink it blood warm at a draught, you may gather mugwort and dry it in a chamber and soe keep it all year which is as useful as the green is."* Another old recipe states that a steam can be made by infusing the freshly chopped herb with boiling water, with a woman then squatting over this healing steam to help with uterine troubles. A tea made from mugwort was said to calm the nerves and help with hysteria, a term generally used for women's 'episodes' or emotional outbursts.

There are many Native American uses for the many species of *Artemisia*. The *A. vulgaris* that was possibly introduced was generally used for pains after birth, for headaches, for colds and for rheumatism. The Miwok tribe used it as a ceremonial medicine as leaves worn up the nostrils for mourners when crying to help clear the head, leaves were rubbed on the body to keep ghosts away and it was worn as a necklace to prevent dreaming of the dead; 'poisoned' leaves were carried to prevent personal injury. The Paiute tribe made a poultice of crushed leaves to clear congestion in a chest cold and for sore muscles. The Pomo tribe heated the leaves and applied them to a newborns navel and used the plant for venereal sores, to name some specific uses.

Personal Practices

Mugwort is an incredible ritual and dream herb. It is powerful and helps induce trance in a safe way in reasonable or even small amounts. I enjoy a dropperful of the elixir, see recipe below. This can be done upon retiring as well but be mindful that there are about 10% of folks who have a negative reaction to this plant, in that it causes intensely unpleasant dreams. Usually those folks cannot even have this plant in the room or house. The smoke is a valuable fumigant in the magical apothecary. It is cleansing and helpful to protect space and it should always be included in divination blends. Making a smudge wand out of the flowering tops and leaves is an easy way to enjoy the smoke as a fumigation. Let the material on the stems wilt for about 3 days and then wrap them tightly with a strong woolen thread. Let the bundles dry for about 3 weeks. Store by wrapping in cloth and placing in a drawer. These wands can be burned as needed or the loose dried herb can be placed on hot coals alone or in a combination. I harvest when the plant is in flower, in late summer for the best fragrance.

Because of its connection to ghosts and protecting the living left behind, mugwort qualifies as a funerary herb. As the lore tells, using it for cleansing the space after one has passed or to help the ones in grief is helpful, along with other evergreens. But mugwort is a specific standalone for protection against the unquiet dead, along perhaps with St. Johns wort. Include it in any formulas for hauntings, for a person or a place. Mugwort along with tansy can be used for sending back magic, that is sending back a curse to the one who gave it. This herb is perfect for mirror magic in this way.

Use this plant for scrying, divination and for enhancing clear 'seeing'. And ointment may be made and used for anointing the third eye, behind the ears and the chest. Sleep with a sprig of this plant under one's pillow for prophetic dreams on the high nights of the year or on the full moon. The connection between mugwort and the moon is powerful, as trance and visions will reveal if one takes the time for them.

My preference is to harvest the European mugwort from the garden when it is most aromatic, usually in August during its flowering time. Hang the large plant to dry and use the aerial parts, specifically the leaves and flowers dried and stripped from their stems. Growing mugwort in the garden is easy, in fact she will take over if allowed. This plant will get very tall, a good one to plant next to motherwort or marshmallow behind smaller plants. It takes average soil and water and does best in full to part sun.

Medicinally, mugwort is excellent in a bath or footbath as 'bath tea'. It is helpful for inducing sleep and dreaming. Think of mugwort tea made into a compress for menstrual cramps to bring on the flow of stagnant blood. Make an infused wine with mugwort combined with roses, lemon balm and vervain for anxiety and stress relief. It also blends well with chamomile, hops, linden, lemon balm and lavender in a tea for the same. Mugwort can be used in a dream pillow, by itself or in combination with other dream plants. Mugwort is a wonderful digestive bitter, helpful for sour stomach and bloating after large meals. It helps stimulate appetite and can be used in any bitters formula. Use less instead of more, it is surprising how little is needed to be effective medicinally.

Infused in oil/fat for a soothing rub, mugwort is helpful for stimulating stagnant energy, such as with sluggish menstrual flow, swollen lymph nodes, digestion and for headaches. It can be incorporated into chest rubs as well. Use this oil for sore muscles and pain topically. A rehydrated mugwort poultice held warm on the outside of the ear is helpful for ear pain and infection. Mugwort moves stagnant energy, it is a strong stimulator in that way. Rub fresh mugwort leaves on the skin (though not the face) as an insect repellant, it works wonders as the sun is going down and the bugs are biting. Strew the whole plant in places where rodents or insect infestations are occurring and replace regularly for best results.

Many thanks to the Green Lady between the Ways, through mirror and smoke, She who haunts the veil with her dream medicines. Bitter brew, Matron of the Womb, warding smoke – enjoy and immerse oneself in the shadow of the Moon's daughter.

Mugwort Orange Elixir

This elixir is absolutely delicious and the orange flavor really compliments and masks some of the intense hot bitterness that mugwort has. For a pint mason jar, fill 1/2 part with cut and dried European mugwort, recently dried if possible, meaning within a month or so. Pour in good quality brandy to about ¾ of the way up, stirring the herbs in with a chopstick. Top off the rest of the jar with honey and leave room for about half an orange worth of fresh chopped fine peel only. Cap and shake every day for a month. Strain and let mellow for a few months in a dark place – though you can drink it right away, it will taste better if you wait. I use it for anxiety (5-10 drops every 15-30 minutes for a few doses only), to help with cramping (a dropperful or two every 30 minutes for a few doses, then easing off) and for before or after meal bitters (a dropperful). It is also helpful for depression, one dropperful three times a day.

Scrying in the Mugwort Cauldron

On the eves of the year that one wishes to see into the future or the past, make a strong tea from dried mugwort. After steeping for at least one hour, strain it into a black cauldron and dim the lights down to a few candles. It is helpful when scrying in liquid to get the light just right – not too direct onto the surface, yet not too dim. I mention this under the Mistletoe Spirit Powder for Scrying section as well.

It is best to have layers of texture within the water and this can be further achieved by using a witch ball or a medium/small glass float. These can be found for a reasonable price at most any antique store. Place the ball within the cooled down tea and allow for at least 20 minutes of uninterrupted time for peering into the pool. Alternatively, with mugwort as the scrying liquid place a silver dollar in the bottom of the cauldron. Another option when outside and a full moon is visible, is to catch the moons light in the tea rather than use a candle. Burn a wand of mugwort before invoking any assisting spirits. Enjoy and pay heed to the reflections that come from the beyond, captured in the toad colored liquid. When finished pour the tea somewhere outside, ideally back into the mugwort plant from which it came. Failing this, roots of a guardian tree will be sufficient.

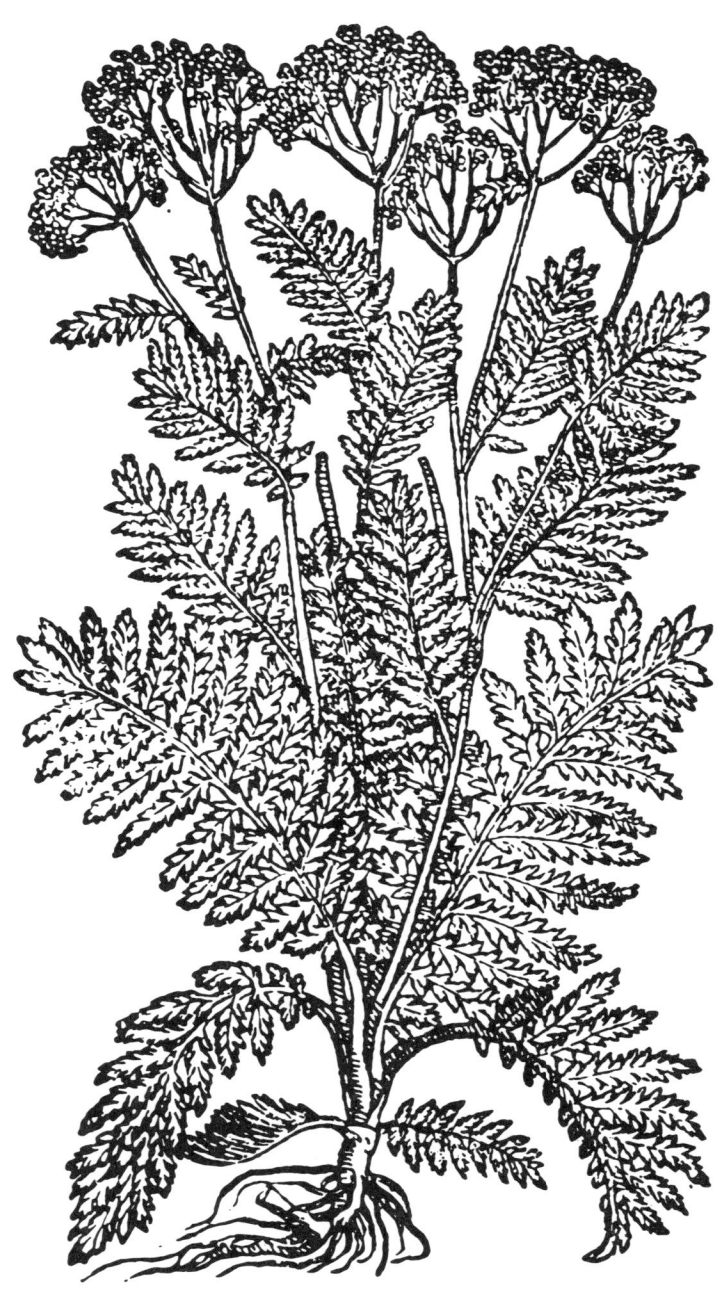

YARROW
Achillea millefolium

Bone colored yarrow, such a precious wildflower within the pestle or upon the coals, a companion to the human path for so very long. All of the medicine and magic within this aromatic plant can be felt when spending time with this haunted flower of Midsummer. Hot and dry in the blazing sunshine, yarrow survives and gains strength with the rising of the light. As the year turns, one can hope to keep bundles of leaves and flowers hanging in the cottage for nearly every physical malady, not to mention as a premiere divinatory and protective herb.

Yarrow is in the *Asteraceae* family and believed to have been here on earth for at least 60,000 years according to fossilized pollen found in Neanderthal burial caves from the Iraq area. It is native to Northern hemispheres in general including Europe, Asia and North America. There are around 80 species in the genus and yarrow is a perennial plant. The Latin name of yarrow, *Achillea* comes from Achilles, a Greek hero who stopped the bleeding wounds of his soldiers with this plant. *Millfolium* means "thousand leaves" because of the way the leaves are dissected. Common names for yarrow included Old Man's Pepper, Carpenter's Herb, Milfoil, Thousand Weed, Dog Daisy, Angel Flower, Herb-of-the-Seven-Cures, Soldier's Woundwort, Bloodwort, Nosebleed, Devil's Nettle, Devil's Plaything, Sneezeweed and Yarroway. The Dutch name for yarrow is *Yerw* and the German name is *Garbe*. The old Anglo-Saxon name was *Gearwe*.

Yarrow has been used as a magical and protective plant by those who have walked before us. It was one of the seven herbs in Ireland that were thought most protective, the other six being eyebright, mallow, self-heal, St. Johns wort, speedwell and vervain. Yarrow was one of the herbs of St. John's Eve in different parts of Europe. In Ireland an old custom was to hang up the plant in the house during Midsummer to ward off illness. Boiling yarrow in combination with other herbs was given to cows in order to keep them safe from Faeries mischief and ill-luck, also from Ireland. Putting yarrow in one's pocket when going to sell cattle at the local fair would help guarantee success in the sale. Sewing yarrow into clothing was used to prevent the wearer from disease. Yarrow tied to a babe's cradle would protect both the mother and little one from harm, while bringing long life to the growing baby as well.

Strewing Yarrow on the doorstep in Fen country in England would allow no witch to enter. A charm for going on a journey told to pick ten stalks of yarrow, leave one behind as an offering to the spirits and put the nine under the right heel. By working this charm, no evil would come to pass on the trip. A magical formula used to restore bewitched milk was to place three sprigs of yarrow, three leaves of plantain and a bit of well water into the churn. From the Highlands of Scotland, yarrow was used to counter the ill effects of the Evil Eye. One piece of lore tells that wearing yarrow was used to attract distant relations and bring the attentions of those that one wished to see most. Placing a yarrow leaf over the eyes was believed to help with the second sight from Hebrides and wearing it in one's shoe was thought to help with speech fluency.

Yarrow was used for divinations in particular for matters of love at the auspicious times of the year. Some sources suggest that yarrow had to be picked on the new moon or on Midsummers Eve to be effective. One method that called upon both the plant and the power of the dead was for a young maiden to gather yarrow from a young man's grave on the night of Midsummer's Eve and sleep with it under her pillow. This was sure to bring prophetic dreams of her future husband. A young man could do the same by picking the yarrow from the grave of a young woman in turn. More information about this method comes from South Devon. If this was done in the graveyard while the clock struck midnight, a charm was spoken: *Yarra, yarra, I seeks thee yarra, and now I have thee found. I prays to the gude Lord Jesus as I plucked 'ee from the ground.* When the maiden returned home, she was to place the yarrow in her right stocking, tie it around her left thigh and get into bed backwards. Before falling asleep she was to speak: *Good night to thee yarra, Good night to thee yarra, Good night to thee yarra.* Then three times *Good night purty yarra, I pray thee sweet yarra, Tell me by the marra, Who shall me true love be.*

A beautiful formula that is incomplete told to make a posy of grave yarrow, rue, and various colored flowers; this was bound into a posy with hair from the maiden's head and sprinkled with a few drops of oil of amber. The left hand was used to secure the posy around the maiden's head before she retired for the evening in a bed of clean linen in order to dream of her future mate. Yet another example of using yarrow for a love divination was to sew a flannel pillow full of yarrow and fall asleep with it under one's pillow in order to dream of the one that you will marry. The proper rhyme to recite during the sewing of the pillow was: *Thou pretty herb of Venus' tree, Thy true name is Yarrow. Now whom my bosom friend must be, Pray tell now me tomorrow.* There are quite a few variations on this rhyme and the details vary a bit as well. One version tells that on May Eve yarrow should be found and nine leaves plucked from the plant. As it was harvested, this charm was spoken: *Yarrow for yarrow, if yarrow you be By this time tomorrow my true love to see, The colour of his hair, The clothes he does wear, The first words he will speak when he comes to court me.* Then the leaves were placed under the girls pillow to bring an informative dream.

As flowers were used in Victorian times to communicate based on their given meanings, yarrow was used by Fenland girls to declare their love to a man by pinning it on their dresses. If a man showed little interest despite the clue, the girl would wait until the next full moon and go to a yarrow patch. Walking barefoot she would pick a bunch of yarrow with closed eyes. If dew remained on the yarrow the following morning, then hope remained. If not, then a new suitor was sought. A custom from Donegal introduced from Scottish settlers was to cut a piece of sod that had yarrow growing in it in order to sleep with it under one's pillow for dreams of one's true love. The cutting of the sod and transporting it home had to be done in strict silence.

Another yarrow love association: In some parts of Europe, yarrow was put in the bridal wreath. It blessed the newly married couple with seven years of love. In Gloucestershire, the name "Seven Years Love" has been recorded for yarrow because of this custom.

One divination that foretold the health of a patient with a fever was to place a sprig of yarrow in their right hand while they slept. If it withered and faded overnight, it was a sign that the patient would soon die. From Icelandic magic comes the use of yarrow for detecting a thief. A magical sigil was carved in the bottom of a wooden box (See *Norse Magical and Herbal Healing – A Medical Book from Medieval Iceland* translated by Ben Waggoner page 4 for the sigil) And water was added, as well as ground up yarrow. The words to be spoken over the water before scrying were: *I desire, by the nature of the herb and the power of the sign, that I may see the shadow of the one who has stolen from me and others*. If yarrow was harvested on St. Johns Eve roots and all, without letting the sun shine upon it when the sun was in the center of the southeast, it could be used against theft as well. The words to be spoken upon it in Latin were: '*Qui te creauit qui perte latronem vel furenntem*'. Yarrow stalks were used for the I Ching, an old Chinese divination system. Such a plant of foretelling we have here!

Yarrow harvested on May Eve could be used for both blessing and baneful purposes. If the Holy Trinity was invoked while collecting, then the herb was used for healing and helping, but if Satan was invoked instead the same plant was used for malevolent magic. This is a beautiful example of the duality of a plant's powers based on intention. In some parts of Ireland yarrow was referred to as being the Father of all Herbs and was harvested using only a black handled knife. Yarrow was called death flower in Glamorganshire, Wales. It was unlucky to bring into the home, as it was believed to bring death to one or even three within the family. It is under the dominion of Mars, according to astrologers of the past.

Folk Medicine

As a medicinal plant, yarrow also has a long history of use. Traditional European uses for yarrow included taking it for fevers and colds, for respiratory troubles (including asthma and bronchitis), as a digestive bitter often included in older beer recipes, for melancholy, for jaundice, for rheumatism, for pain, to cleanse the system and as a poultice for toothache. It was used to stop bleeding, as the name common name Carpenters Herb gives a clue about this particular use.

In British and Irish folk medicine, there are some records of yarrow being used for uterine hemorrhage, for the cramp (by wearing a leaf inside the shoes) and for lowering blood pressure. From England the plant was put in boiling water and put on the nose for nose bleeds. It was also kept on the back of the stove in a brew for aches and pains. The tea was used for people who suffered from consumption and when infused in wine or ale, was taken for heartburn. From Essex yarrow was taken for depression with a little gin added. In Germany yarrow steeped in wine was prescribed for failing apatite and for listlessness.

Hildegard von Bingen had an interesting use for yarrow, besides using it for bleeding and for healing ulcers. From *Hildegard von Bingen's Physica* translated by Priscilla Throop: '*A persons whose vision is darkened from flowing tears should pound yarrow a moderate amount and place it over his eyes at night, not letting it touch the inside of his eyes. He should take it off when it is almost midnight. Then he should rub the best and purest wine around his eye lashes, and his eyes will be healed.'* One wonders about the connection with yarrow and melancholy here, though it sounds as if it helps the inflammation caused by intense crying which makes sense, as it is astringent.

Yarrow was used topically in ointments for healing the skin and one recipe from the early 1900s Norfolk calls for using the entire plant, roots and all in cooked and sieved into a green mash that was incorporated into lard, one imagines with heat added to help it all emulsify. This was used for cuts, scrapes and general injuries. Anglo-Saxon medicine indicated that yarrow be used for wounds afflicted by iron specifically, *ad vulnera ferrofacta*. An old recipe from the early seventeenth century mixed yarrow with southernwood *Artemisia abrotanum*, fenugreek, cumin seed, dittany *Origanum dictamnus* bruised all with black soap as a drawing poultice for removing iron, splinters, and/or thorns.

Culpepper wrote to pound yarrow with toadflax *Linaria vulgaris* and a perfumed unguent applied outwardly in order to lessen pain and promote sleep. Norwegian folks used the leaves topically for rheumatic pains. The tea brewed strong and made into an herbal bath was used in Europe for muscle aches and pains. A poultice of meal boiled with yarrow was laid on the stomach to help the bowels move, from Alabama. Yarrow combined with mistletoe in a bag or pouch was worn next to the stomach to prevent one from getting chilblains and ague, amulet medicine from Scotland. From the Isles of Scilly comes the use of making a decoction of the flowers to give to cattle as a drench for when they had stomach problems.

The Native Americans made much use of yarrow, as there are subspecies native to North America. To describe all of the uses would take many pages, but it is not surprising that folks from North America and Europe used the plant similarly. The general uses were for colds, fevers, headaches, respiratory problems, stomach pains, hemorrhages, as a women's herb, for toothache, for wounds, as a steam in the

Yarrow

sweat lodge, to purify the blood, as a wash for sore eyes – it was essentially a panacea.

Some specifics follow. The Bella Coola tribe pounded yarrow in candlefish (eulachon) grease and applied it to the chest for bronchitis. The Blackfoot tribe used the crushed leaves applied to swellings and as a diuretic to pass sickness with urine. The same tribe used an infusion of the leaves to ease delivery pain and expel the afterbirth. An infusion was drunk for sore throats. The Chehalis tribe used a leaf decoction for blood in diarrhea. Women in the Shoalwater Bay tribe from the Pacific Northwest coast would eat yarrow leaves when they desired to have a male child. The Cherokee tribe smoked the leaves to help relieve coughing and would take an infusion of the leaves for promoting sleep. The Cheyenne tribe took an infusion of the leaves and flowers as a heart medicine and for chest pain. The Delaware and Oklahoma tribes used the plant for kidney troubles. The Iroquois used yarrow for babies with any kind of sickness and for fevers. The Lummi tribe used the flower decoction for aches and pains. The Potawatomi tribe used the flowers as a smudge in order to expel evil spirits.

Personal Practices

Magically yarrow is not only used in divinations for love but can be used for love formulas in general. Think of using it in powders along with ivy leaf, sugar, pink hawthorn bloom and periwinkle flower for attracting the one desired, this can be worn or sprinkled near the home. One must be careful with such magic, but when used with less specificity the outcome is quite well favored. Yarrow is also an important dreaming herb, beyond love prophecy. A pillow stuffed with dried yarrow flowers alone will impact the dreamers experience and bring more clarity and recall to the one seeking. When working with communicating with the dead, it is a highly valuable plant. Use it as a smoke, a smudge, or an oil for anointing the ears and eyes, or as a wash for helping with all matters of such desires.

As an herb of Midsummer, it is best to harvest it for magical purposes as close to Midsummer as possible. The potency will be greater and if upon Midsummer's Eve, so the better. Use it before fire scrying as an offering, or to ensorcell ones scrying mirror with a strong tea of the plant. The tea also makes a wonderful cleanser for a home to protect from dark energy or to remove it once the source has been identified. Combined with salt, it can be used to mop floors and neutralize and restore a toxic space. A bath can be used similarly for one's body, as a restorative and to rid of evil influences.

Medicinally, there is no herb with such power as yarrow. It works with just about every body system and is indeed one plant for so many ailments. Harvest in full flower near Midsummer and include some leaves yet be careful to leave some on the plant. Use a knife or hand pruners, otherwise you will uproot the plant, it is fibrous to pick without metal. When visiting a patch, harvest in a way where no one would be able to see the impact with the passing eye. It likes to grow in open fields and on the seaside, as well as desert terrain. Hang the bundles to dry and then strip the leaves and cut off the flowers once dry, discarding the heavy stems unless one is inclined to use the I-Ching.

The dried leaf and flower then can be used for many applications. Powdered it can be placed directly on bleeding wounds and carried in the first aid kit for emergencies where the fresh plant is not found. The fresh leaves work as well, both methods not only stop the bleeding within about one minute but also take away pain effectively. I have remedied deep cuts with this plant many times with great success, though obviously it is important to use common sense and get medical help if needed. Pack the powder on after allowing some blood to cleanse the wound naturally. Then carefully wash the wound as soon as facilities are handy. If the bleeding starts again, reapply the yarrow and a bandage. Allow it to be washed out naturally over the next few days. The infused oil or fat can be incorporated into salves for wounds when they begin to heal, as a natural antibiotic. Use also in chest rubs alone or in combination with other decongestant herbs. The salve or powder mixed into a salve is famous for its use in painful hemorrhoids, and suppositories made with yarrow for this are claimed highly effective by many.

A tincture of the flower and leaf can be diluted and used for a bug repellant and also used as a diluted mouthwash or as a tooth liquid to assist in brushing and helping to tighten gums and prevent infection. This application is also used for lung troubles and for asthma. I once was in a situation where a family friend was on the ground having an asthma attack and was without her inhaler. I grabbed yarrow leaves growing on the edge of the driveway and had her chew them. It helped her breathe normally again within seconds. Since that happened many years ago, I never underestimate this plant, and I carry the tincture in my purse.

The tea made from the dried plant is excellent for fevers and colds. It is bitter to taste but add some honey for better palatability. For fevers, make a strong tea and let it steep at least 30 minutes before straining. Rewarm and drink as hot as can be tolerated. Then cover with blankets and retire for the day to sleep. A yarrow and mugwort steam helps with congestion that is unrelenting and feels stuck, excellent for sinus pain. A yarrow steam is also really helpful for acne, I recommend drinking a cup of tea every day in addition to assist the liver and digestion.

For women's ailments, there is no better plant. The tincture can be taken for menopausal flooding, and for postpartum hemorrhage. It is also used as an emmenagogue when combined with common sage *Salvia officinalis* and blue cohosh *Caulophyllum thalictroides* to help bring on sluggish menses. It is a normalizer for the blood. It can be taken to help with cramps and used as a douche for yeast infections when prepared as a tea, along with rose petals. Use twice a day for a few days and it will generally subside. Use the tea for premenstrual depression and for weariness associated with those times. Yarrow is an excellent urinary tract diuretic. It can be taken for UTI's as a tea, along with soothing marshmallow *Althaea officinalis* and plantain leaf. Yarrow is astringent, styptic, antibacterial, anti-inflammatory, diuretic, vulnerary, diaphoretic and is good for circulation and capillary health. It can be included in heart formulas along with hawthorn and rose for a delicious blend in tea or as an elixir.

> *Many thanks to the warrior's fire that is yarrow, lace under glass, in steam and smoke. By solar light bring your blessings and medicine to the wounded and sick. Great healer of supernatural repute, there is no more comforting perfume that fills the home as yours — menthol scorched bitter earth. In the cauldron, bring both Sight and Grace to those who seek you. Within the veil between this world and that one, may you always stay close.*

Dreaming Salve

During the time of Midsummer, harvest Yarrow, Corn Poppy flower *Papaver rhoeas*, St. Johns wort, Mugwort, Roses, Elder flower, and English Walnut Leaf *Juglans regia*. Dry them all for a spell and then break them down with a mortar and pestle until quite fine. In a double boiler, have ready enough clarified pig fat to saturate them once melted down. Heat the mixture for around 20 minutes each day for five days. On the last day, push the herbs through a sieve. Take the fragrant and green tinted fat and for each cup of fat, add one ounce of beeswax to make a salve, again done in the double boiler. A pinch of grave earth can be added to each tin before pouring in the finished salve. (See the appendices in *Under the Witching Tree* for more details about animal fat rendering and infusing fat)

This can then be used to anoint ones third eye and brow before retiring in order to aid with dreaming. Also, the same mixture dried can be enclosed into a small pillow and set next to one's pillow for a similar effect. Some people find herbal pillows too strong and place them on a nightstand

Yarrow

rather than on one's pillow. This same salve can also be used to protect one on outings, when anointed as a cross on the chest, back of the neck, wrists and forehead. Do the same before and after taking a ritual bath for a lovely effect.

Witches Winter Brandy

This was first inspired by my dear teacher Carol Trasatto many years ago, with her winter solstice yarrow brandy. It is nice with a few additions as well. Combine fresh yarrow leaf and flower, fresh common sage leaves and fresh German chamomile in brandy. If fresh herbs cannot be had, dried ones will do. For fresh herbs, chop the plants and fill a mason jar 2/3 then add brandy to fill leaving an inch of shaking room. For dried herbs, fill the jar half way and add brandy to fill. Shake daily for a moon cycle and strain out. This can be sipped during the winter months while taking a hot bath or enjoy it as a hot toddy with hot water, honey and lemon during a bout of sickness. It is invigorating and comforting, so very fragrant and wonderful for whatever ails you. The same could be infused in apple cider vinegar for an alcohol free variation and used in the same way.

SELF-HEAL
Prunella vulgaris

Self-heal is a humble summer beauty, a common yet breathtaking wildflower commonly found in many landscapes. There is something so gentle and soothing about this little purple blossom, beloved of bees, spreading joyfully under the waxing sunlight. While not as dominating in magical use or lore, the medicinal value of self-heal is worth including here, for she is a lovely plant of the wayside to gather in ones harvesting basket for the rustic apothecary. There are quite a few magical healing applications.

Common names included Self-Heal, Heal All, All Heal, Prunella, Brunella, Carpenters' Herb, Blue Curls, Heart of the Earth, Touch-and-Heal, Hearts-Ease, Pickpocket and Poverty Pink. From Scotland, names such as Cailleach's Tea and The Veiled Ones Tea were given to self-heal. It is in the mint family, *Lamaiceae*. It is native to all temperate zones and found widely in the British Isles and North America on disturbed ground. It amazes by growing in shade and sun, lawn and mead, wood and ocean side.

'*The wayside blue and innocent heal-all…*' – Robert Frost

Self-heal was considered to be one of the Herbs of St. John or Midsummer. In Ireland in particular, this little herb was valued and considered one of the most protective of seven herbs, the others being St. Johns wort, mallow, speedwell, eyebright, vervain and yarrow. Self-heal was used in Ireland for sudden blows or a 'stroke' which could affect one, possibly being applied magically for the Faerie Stroke – an affliction of the Good Folk that caused illness. A magical cure from Roy Vickery's *A Dictionary of Plant Lore* states

'The minerac herb (self-heal) cures the minerac, a mysterious wasting disease.... Nine pieces are got(saying the name of the person you require for it), washed clean and rubbed until a froth is produced from it. The froth is mixed with water and it turns it green. The person that needs it drinks it three mornings in succession and blesses himself each time. He is not allowed meat, eggs or much butter while taking it.'

An interesting quote from Culpepper reveals another magical healing use from The English Physician:

The Root, Crollius says, that being dryed, and rubbed upon an aking Tooth till it fetch blood, and then put into a pierced Willow, and the hole stop with a peg of the same Willow, it will ease the pain of the teeth by a magnetick power.' Here we see transference magic being used, as well as the willow tree and its sympathetic pain-relieving properties.

To tell if a person had a fever type illness, one test was to rub self-heal in the persons hand and see if froth developed. Specifically for fevers in children from Ireland, the leaves were rubbed on the palms of the hands and soles of the feet, three times. One piece of lore of self-heal from the late 1800s in Hampshire tells that nursemaids warned their children 'not to pick black-man flowers', and that the plant belonged to the Devil. If the flowers were picked, He would be greatly angered and carry off the child whom committed the act in the night. Self-heal is ruled by Venus according to astrologers of old.

Folk Medicine

An old French proverb states: *No one wants a surgeon who keeps Prunelle.* In folk medicine, self-heal had three primary uses; for treating respiratory troubles in particular coughing, heart troubles and to stanch bleeding. It was also included in an old drink called a 'Posset' for fevers. A posset is a British drink of hot milk curdled with wine or ale and spiced. This drink was popular from Medieval times until the 1800s or so, thought to have nutritive and medicinal qualities. Not only for coughs and taken as a lung tonic, self-heal was used for tuberculosis as well.

Other less common folk uses included using self-heal for eczema, to help dispel of worms in children, as a treatment for piles(an older term for hemorrhoids), for toothache, as a gargle for sore throat and taken for weak blood. The tea was taken for heart troubles and for those recovering from a stroke, from Scotland and Ireland. From County Mayo, a tea from self-heal was made and taken for weak hearts and heart palpitations.

An old remedy specific for the lungs recorded in 1910 from Colonsay, a Scottish island, taken from A Dictionary of Plant Lore – Roy Vickery:

…a popular remedy for chest ailments, self-heal was collected in the summer, tied in bundles, and hung up to the kitchen roof to dry for winter use. The plants were boiled in milk and strained before using, butter was added.'

Self-heal was known to be one of the best wound herbs used for both inward and outward wounds, ulcers, boils and bruises. Poultices and washes of the plants were used. Common names such as Carpenters Herb (also given to Yarrow), Hook-weed and Sickle-wort tell about its ability to staunch bleeding and heal wounds. A recipe from Culpepper tells that self-heal juice mixed with the oil of roses could be rubbed on the temples to relieve a headache. The same preparation mixed with honey would help to heal ulcers in the mouth and throat.

Native Americans used the plant in similar ways to European folk. The whole plant was used generally as a decoction for a heart medicine, for diarrhea and stomach complaints, as a blood purifier, as an eye wash, for fevers, for coughs, to help burst a boil and applied for sores. The Bella Coola tribe boiled the entire plant, flowers, roots and leaves for a heart tonic. The

Cherokee tribe used a cold infusion as a burn dressing. The Iroquois tribe took an infusion of the plant for back pains and for stomach cramps. From the same tribe, a decoction of the plant was taken to strengthen the womb and an infusion of the plant was given to babies that cried too much. The same infusion was taken for sickness caused by grieving. The Ojibwa tribe used a compound with the root for a female remedy and used the root as a hunting medicine, to sharpen powers of observation taken as a tea before going hunting.

Recent information from China has shown that self-heal is a natural antibiotic, that it has a strong antimicrobial action against a wide range of pathogens.

Personal Practices

Self-heal is helpful medicinally as a lung and lymphatic tonic. Even though the plant is not aromatic, it has a strong and pleasant mineral rich taste in infusions. It has a long harvest window and can be gathered while in bloom, taking the stems and leaves as well. The size of the plant varies greatly – I have seen very small versions in lawns that get continual mowing and plants up to two feet tall growing in sand in full sun near the ocean. Harvest the top few sets of leaves when gathering the flowers and do not strip from the stems – include all of the aerial parts in teas, poultices and oils. The flower 'cobs' bloom tiny purple hoods (rarely light pink or white if one is lucky) sporadically, which means some of them will be open, but some will not when harvesting. Dry the plants in baskets and store in jars when finished for use in teas or use freshly wilted and bruised plants in an infused oil.

Besides its use as a lung tonic, self-heal combines well with *oatstraw Avena sativa* and hawthorn *Cratagus spp.* for a heart tonic to help lower high blood pressure. Think of using self-heal along with rose and red clover *Trifolium pratense* in a tea for grief and loss. This is gentle yet delicious and can be given to children as well. Use in a strengthening combination tea (recipe below) for chronic colds and general malaise.

Self-Heal

Topically, self-heal can be included in any wound healing salve, alone or in a combination formula. It is helpful for diaper rash, along with roses, calendula flowers *Calendula officinalis* and plantain leaves. This same formula can be used for dry skin, irritations, inflammations and eczema. It can also be used alone or in a combination for lymphatic massage.

Many Thanks to the wayside self-heal, to the homespun medicine and magic that it provides those wandering the forgotten and yet timeless countryside. By green oil and steaming winter infusion, may She bless the sick and weak ones with her assistance and soothe those in need with her humble beauty.

Forest Tonic Tea
For a helpful tonic, gather these plants, dry them well and combine:

1 cup Stinging Nettle leaf
1 cup Self-Heal flower/leaf/stem
1 cup Violet leaf
½ cup de-seeded chopped Rosehips
½ cup Reishi mushroom slices broken up, Ganoderma lucidum
½ cup chopped alder buds/young twigs *Alnus rubra/ glutinosa*

Mix together and store in a glass jar. Use about ¼ cup decocted in a quart of water daily for a few weeks, helpful for getting over a sluggish cold or for seasonal fatigue. Also this formula can be used as a preventative for colds/flus taken in the beginning of both September and February for a few weeks.

Soothing Flowers Ointment
During the time of Midsummer, gather Self-heal flowers/ leaves, fragrant Roses, Calendula flowers and Yarrow flowers/leaves. Wilt them over night and chop lightly with

a knife. With equal parts of each by volume, add them to either olive oil for a solar infusion or to pig fat in a double boiler (my strong preference for this preparation is to use animal fat) Follow instructions for the infusion process (See *Under the Witching Tree*, Appendix D, Infusing Fats/Oils with Plants, page 255) When the oil/fat is ready and strained out, add 1 ounce of beeswax for every cup of oil/fat to a double boiler. Melt together and pour the ointment into tins. This makes an excellent general all-purpose salve used for inflammations, irritations, bug bites, scratches, healing up wounds/scars and rashes. The same formula with dried plants used in a wash or a steam works well for skin problems, acne, eczema and psoriasis.

 # ST. JOHN'S WORT
Hypericum perforatum

The golden spray of flowers that comes forth from the earth during the height of the suns light is magical indeed – St. John's wort is a very special herb, a plant full of grace and mystery. Look closely at the golden buds and opened flowers, dotted with tiny dark red pin pricks. If you rub a ripe bud that is ready to open between your fingers, a dark maroon stain will appear full of a sweet balsam perfume unlike any other. This plant carries the blood of the sun, a beautiful red sap that exudes from the buds around the time of the summer solstice. St. John's wort is fairy gold, being a primary protective ally that brings light into dark places, illuminating all through black shadow and heavy mist.

This perennial plant of the wayside comes up with small rounded green leaves with reddish stems, growing in full sun on edges and garden borders. It seems to prefer gravelly spots and stony pastures. St. John's wort is in the *Hypericaceae* family and has roughly 350 species within the genus. Older common names for the plant included: Balm of the Warriors Wound, Amber, Devil's Scourge, Rosin Rose, Penny John, Touch and Heal, Bloodwort, Hundred Holes, Witches Herb, *Sol Terrestris* (which means 'Sun and Earth' in Latin), Scaredevil, Chase Devil and Exorcist. One name *Sanguis Hominis* translates to 'human blood'. Such telling names! The Latin Hypericum roughly means 'over an apparition' in Greek. The leaves can be identified if held up to the light, they are full of tiny 'holes' or perforations, hence the Latin species name *perforatum*. Some beliefs state that these holes were made by the Devil himself, pricking them with a needle in anger, as this plant was used to keep evil spirits at bay.

In times past, St. John's wort was thought to represent the blood of St. John the Baptist, of whom this plant was named after. Originally it was dedicated to Baldur from Norse Mythology, who was Odin's second son and the God of summer light and radiance. This plant was later Christianized as St. John's wort, the plant named after St. John who was supposed to be born on June 24 at midnight. St. Johns day is June 24 and often called Midsummer, with Midsummer's Eve being the night before on June 23.

In pagan mythology, the summer solstice or Midsummer was a day dedicated to the sun and it was believed that witches held festivals at this time of year. St. John's wort was the symbolic plant of this day though interestingly Mugwort *Artemisia vulgaris* had the name Herb of St. John also ascribed to it and was associated with this time of year as well. St. John's wort was gathered before sunrise on Midsummer before dawn, with dew still on it as a talisman against evil powers. It was burned in the Midsummer fires for extra protection against ill influence. A bit of information from *A Dictionary of Plant Lore* by Roy Vickery about its use on Midsummer's Eve from Cornwall: "*At St. Cleer the fire is crowned with a witch's broom and hat, a sickle with the handle of newly cut oak is thrown into the flames and wreathes of St. John's wort are hung around the village – all this was traditionally said to banish witches.*" In Aberdeenshire,

Scotland it was believed that by sleeping with St. John's wort under one's pillow on Midsummer's Eve a Saint would appear in a dream and give a blessing, preventing one from death within the following year.

There is an old English folk tale called 'Crooker' that tells of a late-night traveler going to visit his sick mother. He is warned to not take the way by the river at night, for the water spirits are hungry for weary travelers during this time. He could not delay the journey however and ventured onward. On the road he met an elderly woman dressed in green linen, who gave him a posy of primroses. She reappeared two more times, giving a posy of both daisy and St. John's wort as well. The river roared and raged at him, with gurgling noises and the ominous ash tree reached out its branches towards him. Each time he felt threatened, he would throw a posy over his shoulder and run faster. At last, he threw the St. John's wort posy at the ancient ash tree that seemed to be following him and made it across the river, safe from the Crooker and the river spirits seeking his soul on that dark night. These plants were all known for their protection, with St' Johns being the most so. Yellow flowers were supposed to keep one safe from dark witches and spirits.

In Ireland, St John's wort was one of seven herbs that nothing supernatural or natural could injure along with vervain, speedwell, eyebright, mallow, yarrow and self heal. In Scotland, it was often carried as a charm against harmful fairies and witches, if tucked in an armpit or sewn in clothing. From the Eastern US, Pennsylvanian Dutch have been known to hang it over windows to keep evil spirits out. In parts of the United Kingdom it was hung in windows to prevent witches from looking inside.

St. John's wort was also supposed to ensure abundance and peace in the house. In London during Elizabethan times at Midsummer, doors were decorated with green birch, fennel, St. John's wort, white lilies and orpine *Sedum telephium* for protection. From 1900, the Scottish *Carmina Gadelica* states: *St. John's wort is one of the few plants still cherished by the people to ward away the second sight, enchantment, witchcraft, evil eye and death, and to ensure peace and plenty in the house, increase and prosperity in the fold, and growth and fruition in the field.'*

Apparently to be effective as an amulet, St. John's wort had to be found accidentally and not sought out. Also it was said to move away from anyone about to pick it. If one stepped on it while looking for it, a fairy horse would rise out of the earth and gallop away with the unlucky soul, taking him/her on a wild ride for the night. Though some of the lore holds this same information for Tansy Ragwort *Senecio jacobea*, so one wonders at the possible confusion of the yellow flowers. Ragwort was a Faerie plant in times past, so who can say which magical plant this bit of lore arose from.

St. John's wort was known to have supernatural powers. As one old saying goes: *St. John's wort, scaring from the midnight heath The witch and goblin with its spicy breath*. It was used to rid homes of unwanted spirits or ghosts. It could be placed underneath one's pillow to banish the dead, from as far back as the early 1600s. It was also used to protect homes from wicked spirits entering at will. The British Isles held St. John's wort in high repute, as an herb that could protect one from demons. It was used presumably for its protective powers to bring back the ghost of a suicide, specifically a man who had hung himself in some lonely place. A hazel wand was crowned with the head of an owl and a bundle of St. John's wort, this powerful staff being used in the conjuration process.

In England it was believed that by carrying the plant as an amulet, one could not be approached within nine paces by the Devil. If it was gathered on a Friday, and worn around the neck, it would keep away evil spirits. In one instance from the 14th century, a woman was tormented by a demon in the shape of a young man and Christian prayers were not effective. Another male spirit who was helpful by nature relayed to the woman to take St. John's wort and wear it in her bosom, while also strewing it within her home in order to banish him. It was successful, and after being shown to a

St. Johns Wort

monk by the woman, it was employed in another situation for a couple troubled with demons, in which it was also an effective antidote for. A strange bit of lore tells that a potion of thistle seed and St.Johns wort was given to suspected witches during the early witch trials on the continent, in order to break the pact with the Devil. This way the tortured 'witches' would speak the truth, a sad state of affairs indeed. But the fact that this plant was used to force people to admit their pact with the Devil in confessions speaks to its power, even in such dire circumstances.

A Gaelic incantation against evil using the plant from the nineteenth century translates:

St. Johns wort, St. Johns wort,
My envy whosoever has thee
I will pluck thee with my right hand
I will preserve thee with my left hand,
Whoso findeth thee in the cattlefold,
Shall never be without kine' –

It could be planted at the four corners of a house or field to protect property from evil influences. From Germany, an extract of St. John's wort was placed in the babies very first bath for protective purposes. It was also a plant that protected farms and people from lightning, storms and destructive weather, in particular from central and southern Europe, France, Belgium and England. In this way, it was burned during a thunder storm or used as an apotropaic charm hung in the home or hung on the roof during the time of Midsummer for that specific purpose. One name from Belgium translates to 'Yellow Thunder Flower'.

St. John's wort was used in divinations for both love and death, especially if gathered around Midsummer's eve. When plucked by a maiden on Midsummer's eve and laid out all night, if the plant still appeared fresh in the morning, marriage prospects were good. A quote from Richard Folkards *Plant Lore, Legends and Lyrics* tells: *The young maid stole through the cottage door, And blushed as she sought the plant of power; 'Thou silver glow worm, O lend me they light! I must gather the mystic St. Johns wort tonight, the wonderful herb whose leaf will decide, If the coming year will make me a bride.'* This tells of one variant when gathering the St. Johns wort for prophetic powers, which was to do so by the light of a glow worm to illuminate the harvest.

The pigment marks in the leaves would bleed if your love was faithful, otherwise the pigment would be colorless, suggesting that it was not a good match. From Orkney northern Scottish islands, girls removed 'Johnsmas' flowers as they were known, gathering both one long and one short floret. These were wrapped in a dock leaf and buried overnight. In the morning, if florets had reappeared on the plant, it was taken as a good omen of future events. From Wales, there was an old custom of taking a piece of the plant and naming it after each person in the household. The pieces were hung in the rafters and in the morning the most faded pieces foretold disaster for the names attached to them.

A magical use included using this plant to promote fertility. If a 'barren' woman walked into a garden naked and in silence at midnight on Midsummer's Eve to pick the plant, she would be able to conceive within twelve months. In southern Slavia, a potion of St. John's wort that was blessed by a priest was drank by an infertile woman to increase her chances of conception. From Italy, the plant was known as an aphrodisiac. Anointing a girdle of a maiden with St. John's wort oil was supposed to improve sex, interestingly. When used specifically for 'heart melancholy' (a broken heart), it was to be gathered in the hour of Jupiter on a Friday, while the moon was full. In an old healing charm for working against dark witchcraft, three leaves of both sage and St. John's wort were steeped in ale and were to be taken both morning and night.

St Johns wort was hung up in animal sheds and barns to protect the flocks and herds from becoming enchanted. It was dried and incorporated with flowering thyme to stuff pillows and help against nightmares. It was thought that if a traveler wore St. John's wort leaf in his/her shoe, that they would never get tired, no matter how long the journey lasted. One magical cure of interest from 1696 was to use an unguent made from the red oil against an evil tongue. One was to take a red hot poker of iron and place it into the salve. Then this resulting fire charged substance was used to anoint the human or animal that was thus afflicted, on the breast or the backbone.

In Ireland, a tea of Marsh St. Johns wort (not sure of the specific species here) was drank to expel the Evil Eye. From parts of Germany, the red sap from the plant that seeped out on Midsummers day was rubbed onto one's gun barrel to improve accuracy of the shots fired during the coming year. From Mecklenburg, St. Johns 'blood' was smeared on one's shirt in the heart area to protect one from the bite of a mad dog. It could also bring good luck in gambling, using the same application – the sap rubbed onto one's clothing. In the language of flowers, dating from Victorian times, St.John's wort meant '*You are a prophet.*' It is under the dominion of the sun and of the astrological sign of Leo according to astrologers of old.

Folk Medicine

Some older medical uses of St. John's wort included treating mania and hysteria, lung complaints, urinary tract issues, fevers, using it as a wound healer of all sorts, in particular for burns and to staunch bleeding.

A poultice of the plant could be used for sprains and compresses were used to help dissolve tumors. It was used as a painkiller in England. It was known as a tonic for low spirits on the Isle of Man, UK. Even wearing a sprig around the neck would keep one in good spirits. An interesting use was that it helped children/elders that wet the bed at night, and modern herbalists still use the plant for this reason. It was used for pain, a nervous tonic, for melancholy, to stimulate hair growth, for snakebite and in Russia for hydrophobia. It was thought to have an affinity for the liver and was used for jaundice. From Belgium, the boiled pulp was taken to stimulate menstruation.

An infusion of the leaves was used for excess mucus or catarrh and for stomach problems. A tincture of the seeds taken for 40 days is an old remedy for sciatica. Juliette de Bairacli Levy writes in her book *Common Herbs for Natural Health* about using St. John's wort for ulcers, both internal and external. She also mentions its use for both toothache and earache, along with rashes, blisters, inflammations and skin infections. An old Romany use for St. John's wort oil was to stimulate hair growth and as a hair dressing.

Personal Practices

Without question St. Johns wort is one of the most protective plants in folklore. Magically it can be applied in many ways to this end. Harvested on or near Midsummer, the plant can be hung in the home for protection for the following year. I like to burn the previous year's chaplet in the Midsummer fire and then harvest anew each year. The dried buds and flowers along with some leaves, can be incorporated into fumigations for protection in any circumstance. I find this plant more protective against supernatural powers than maligned humans. For hauntings it is essential, both for person, place or beast. A mixture of the red infused oil of St.John combined with equal parts dragons blood tincture makes a supreme anointing potion for making equal armed crosses on thresholds, bedsteads, hearthsides as well as on ones chest, back of the neck and forehead. It can be used for candle dressing during ritual work as well. A powder made of St. Johns wort is a good sprinkle for around the perimeter of a home or animal shed for protection on the auspicious eves of the year.

I had a powerful dream once about hanging flowering St. Johns wort, rowan in berry and a hagstone above the

St. Johns Wort

bed or in a room where hauntings were occurring or where bad energy was lingering. This plant is the great illuminator, catching the high sun of midsummer like no other plant. Think of it also in situations where truth telling is needed, where light may be flooded into hidden depths in order to restore sanity. Also, carry this plant when visiting graveyards, if one is in a weakened or vulnerable state.

It is useful to hold up a leaf in the sunlight to observe the tiny perforations before the plant flowers, one way to identify it in the spring. The stems are reddish near the base of the plant. St. Johns wort grows in full sun, in gravel and poor soil, but also will thrive in a garden happily growing quite tall. When the yellow buds are ready to open, if one squeezes them between the fingers, a maroon stain will be noticeable. The smell of this plant blood is quite aromatic and pleasant, unlike any fragrance that I know of. It smells bitter, hot and almost fermented to my senses, with a slight vanilla tinge.

Generally, harvest the top 4 inches or so of this plant in early July or whenever the plant is in both ripe bud and full bloom at the same time. Use hand pruners, as to not uproot the plant with excessive pulling on the stems.

It makes sense that modern herbalists use St Johns wort for depression, remembering in times past melancholy was thought to be caused by evil spirits or witchcraft. It is an excellent nerve tonic. It can be used for nervous exhaustion and impending sorrow. It is often only needed for a week or two, with the feeling of being restored and newly energized after that time. It is excellent during the depths of winter when the sunlight is but a ghost. Enjoy it in an elixir or an infused honey, but an infusion (tea) made from hand harvested and home dried plants is also very effective.

St Johns wort can be included in formulas for sleep, mild anxiety, stress and for chronic low-grade infections. It is known to be an anti-viral, hepatic, nervine, vulnerary and a tonic. There are warnings about taking it while on anti-depressants and/or birth control pills. I recommend some thorough research if you are drawn to this plant but dealing with either of those scenarios. A flower essence would be a good way to use it in those cases, free from any unwanted side effects. Also, there are warnings about fair skinned folks taking this plant internally and becoming sun sensitive. According to my knowledge this has only ever happened with cattle that have grazed on the plant and then had a reaction from being exposed to the sun. However it is something to consider if one is taking concentrated amounts, has fair skin and is out in the high sun. Take necessary precautions if so.

The plant can be used topically for almost everything, including burns, pain – nerve pain specially, general scars and wounds, inflammation and soreness. Make an infusion to use as a wound wash, or simply use the infused oil (if there is an infection, use a wash made from the dried plant, as oil traps heat in) there is a simple recipe below. Equal parts of the infused oil and the tincture can be shaken together to make a sort of liniment for nerve pain, massaged externally. Use the infused oil incorporated into healing salves, helpful in particular for scarring. It can be helpful for healing burned skin, after the initial skin recovery has begun and the risk for infection has passed.

Use the dried plant for infusions – when dried at home in small batches, an infusion of the herb is extremely fragrant and flavorful, becoming deeply amber colored. There are rumors about the tea of St.Johns wort being ineffective, but I strongly disagree, if it is not the store bought herb. The quality difference is significant. Make an incredible blood colored folk tincture from mashing the fresh buds, leaves and flowers together (with more buds than anything else though) and steeping them covered in 80 proof vodka for a month, remembering to shake the mixture every day. An infused honey can also be made (see appendices for specifics on making infused honey) by using the fresh buds, flowers and some leaves and results in a blood red honey. It is spectacular and catches the plant perfectly.

St. Johns Wort

Many thanks to the Blood of Midsummer, to the ghost chaser, to the lifter of spirits. St. John's wort sparkles in the dark, with an old magic. Blessed be this plant of high solar repute, its bitter garnet sap a healer to wounds inside and out. May the magic of Midsummer be exalted by a fire of golden and aromatic plants!

St. John's Wort Infused Oil

A truly gorgeous oil can be made with fresh St. John's wort by infusing it in the sun for roughly four weeks. Wilt the freshly picked buds, along with a few flowers and leaves. Simply mash the buds with a pestle in a jar after they have wilted for 12 hours. Cover with good quality olive oil and stir, making sure that the plant material is covered. Place in a place that gets moderate sun exposure and stir every day with a chopstick and wipe the condensation from the lid with a dry towel. Strain when it becomes a deep blood red, or in 3-4 weeks. Be careful not to overheat. This oil is excellent when incorporated into skin salves.

Midsummer Oracle Garland

With the sun's light at its peak, much can be gleaned between worlds. Midsummer much like Midwinter, is a potent time for divination work of any sort. Here is an oracular garland made from both dark and light powers for encircling your work.

Take nine crow feathers and nine sprigs of the solar St.John's wort. Have thin black twine and a knife at the ready. By a single candle on the Eve of St. John begin your work in earnest. As the sun falls behind the trees, darken the room, draw the curtains and dress the candle with St. Johns oil. Cut three cords of black and tie them into a knot together. Make sure they are longer rather than shorter, three feet or so for each piece. Place the first knot in your teeth and begin to braid. Count as you go, for each nine twinings, add a crow feather or a sprig of the plant, alternating as you braid. It is quite engrossing if one keeps to the work at hand. When finished, tie a final knot, then tie the two opposing knots to make a circlet. Cut any extra twine.

This circlet can be used to enwreath any spell work in which the truth begs to be revealed. It can be hung in the place of working divinations. It can be used on a dreaming altar to bring forth prophetic dreams or hung above the bed on certain eves of the year for the same. Each time before using, speak these words all in one breath between the teeth:

Crow and fire, crow and fire,
Illuminate by St. Johns blood, the blackness of the mire
Gold and Soot will stand to show
That which in shadow I seek to know

Appendix A

 # The Home Apothecary

Creating a space for one's apothecary that continually evolves, changes and is re-created over time is a very satisfying aspect of working with plants for both medicine and magic that is rarely addressed in books about herbalism. I recommend finding a space in your home for a dedicated apothecary cupboard, rather than having bits and pieces throughout your kitchen and closets. The apothecary itself becomes like a vessel for one's creations and having an organized area helps inspiration and application – bringing herbal work into day to day life.

Find an old dish cupboard, writing desk with a drop-down table and small drawers, or even a discarded entertainment cabinet that can be utilized as an apothecary space. With all of the thrift and antique stores, one can find a wooden piece to suits ones needs for a reasonable price. Things to consider when shopping for your perfect apothecary space: the aesthetic should be pleasing to you, let yourself be led to the right piece of furniture, Fate will dictate and line up if one is patient! There needs to be varying sizes of shelves and drawers. Larger shelves for mason jars of dried herbs, and smaller shelves for potion bottles. Small drawers for *materia magica* and a place for empty bottle and tin storage. Also doors that close to protect the contents from being degraded by light, whether natural or artificial, is important to consider.

I have personally seen so many shapes and sizes of potential herb cupboards, it is possible to find smaller versions to fit in a hallway or corner as well. One thing that is nice to find is one with a working space, like a drop-down shelf for mixing and formulating. Keeping things organized is important – many folks hold on to herbcraft that they don't use for years because they feel guilty for throwing it out. I recommend composting all older material that does not serve, in order to make way for new creations!

I enjoy keeping animal and mineral *materia* in my apothecary and find specific smaller wooden boxes and ornate glass containers for them. Labeling is essential – for all jars. Design your own labels if you have the time and know-how. Especially important is to label poisonous plants and things designed for external use only appropriately. It is very helpful to have a small journal for recording preparations and notes about them. Then there are somethings that do not fit into containers but are more like the guardians of the apothecary. The coyote skull and the obsidian scrying mirror for example. It is indeed satisfying to put charms on the outside of one's magical cupboard in order to protect the sacred medicines and magics within.

The apothecary is meant to be used and worked with regularly. Make it easy and assessable, as well as beautiful. It is helpful to go through it twice a year and re-arrange things, dust (even in a closed cupboard dust will accumulate), and discard what is ruined or past its prime. There is nothing more satisfying than working in the apothecary by candlelight in solitude, with an unstructured agenda.

Appendix B

 Water Extracts – Teas, Infusions & Decoctions

The art of brewing teas and working with water as a medium for plants is ancient, one of the oldest ways to take the medicine of plants into the human body. Water our universal solvent infuses the herbs and draws out their healing properties, with assistance from fire. Transformation occurs as the plants that are so perfectly preserved in dried form are brought back to life. They give their healing essence up to the water that holds them.

Water extracts offer versatility that other medicinal preparations do not. With water and fresh or dried herbs you can make infusions(hot/cold), decoctions, compresses, steams, washes and baths. The creation of formulas for these preparations are endless. Here I will go over the basics of making 'tea' which is a blanket term for herbal infusions and decoctions. These are some things to keep in mind and information that I find valuable when working the art of making water extracts or medicinal herb teas. The following information is a general guide and NOT for low dose botanicals or laxative herbs.

Infusion – The method of making a water extract/tea by steeping the aerial plant parts (flowers, leaves, stems) in boiling water. Infusions can be made with fresh herbs or dried herbs. They can be made hot, with boiling water or 'cold', with room temperature water. The ratio of herb to water can vary, depending on the purpose and the plant. The time to steep the herbs in the water also varies. Do not use tea bags, let the herbs be in full contact in the water – a mason jar works well for this.

I generally use dried plants for teas, as they are more concentrated and available to the water. Fresh teas are very good as well, but take more material and preparation when you need them. <u>For hot dried herbal infusions</u>, use 1 teaspoon to 1 tablespoon per 1 cup of water. Steep 20-30 minutes for 'tea' and overnight for a very strong extract. This is especially important for mineral infusions. Remember, the longer you let the herbs mingle with the water, the stronger your tea will be. <u>For cold infusions</u>, using dried herbs, use the same ratio as above, use room temperature water. Steep at least a few hours or overnight.

Decoction – The method of making a water extract/tea by simmering the more fibrous plant parts (roots, barks, berries, woody stems, thick leaves) in water. Decoctions are generally made with dried herbs but can be made with fresh as well. The general ratio of dried plant material used is 1 teaspoon – per cup of water. Because the plants are simmered for a time on the stove top they will expand quite a bit, particularly roots if dried.

The water is brought to a boil, then turned down to a simmer with the lid on. The time simmered varies, depending on the size of the plant material used and the desired strength of the extract. With smaller pieces simmering for 20 minutes or so, then letting the brew steep an additional 20 minutes will do. A good rule of thumb is to let the brew steep after it is pulled off of the heat for the same amount of time that it was decocted for. If you simmer herbs for an hour, let them steep for an additional hour off of the heat. This step is actually crucial in the process and much medicine is lost if the brew is strained to early. Remember water extracts take time...the longer you wait, the better the extract will be.

Equipment – <u>Teapot and Pot</u>-I use glass for making teas. Watching the colors change and the plants expand is very enjoyable. A clear glass Pyrex teapot and double boiler bottom pot are perfect, as they are made for heat and can withstand boiling. However, you will crack the glass by exposing it to temperature extremes. When it is hot, never

Appendix B

add cool water or set it in a cold sink. If you don't have glass handy, stainless steel or enamel works fine. No aluminum, copper or cast iron as these add unwanted minerals to your brew and alter color/flavor. Decorative tea pots are nice for company, but I find them tiresome to clean out when making medicinal teas. I prefer to steep my teas in quart mason jars or in glass liquid measuring cups (2-4 cup) or in the Pyrex teapot itself. This way there is enough for the day (the therapeutic dose for tea is 2-5 cups per day depending) and it is easy to clean up.

Strainers/Sieves – A few sizes of nice stainless-steel sieves are helpful. These work great as a filter, catching the spent herbs to be discarded into the compost. Tea balls, muslin bags and small tea strainers are not helpful for making herbal teas. It is best to keep the equipment minimal buy using simple and durable utensils. Watch out for older second-hand sieves, as the metals on these can be questionable.

Storage of Water Extracts – Infusions/decoctions can be kept in the fridge for up to 5 days. I prefer to make fresh tea daily instead of storing them. It seems that the vitality of the extract changes once it has gone into cold storage. However, sometimes it is necessary to store them. Concentrated teas can also be frozen for later use. Teas will start to ferment within about 24-36 hours or so, if left out at room temperature. Leaving them out to steep for 12 hours or overnight is fine.

Tea Blending – Blending delicious and effective teas is an art, one that takes time and practice to learn. Something that I suggest is to try herbs by themselves in tea. Then you will have a chance to really taste them and feel them in your body. These were called 'Simples' in times past, working with one plant at a time.

For blending, the way I 'measure' is by volume and not by weight. What I find helpful is using a large wooden bowl and making piles of herbs in 'parts', a sort of herbal mandala. For example, make a pile and call it 'one-part peppermint' and all other parts will be compared to that pile. Then there may be an ingredient that is 'half part' compared to the peppermint and also one that is 'quarter part' and so on. This way recipes can be created and recorded for future use in parts and results are repeatable, without being measured in a standard way.

As far as ingredients go, there is a learned nuance to making a tea blend taste good, be balanced and yet effective for what one is seeking it for. It helps to the pick the title first to give the tea blend a focus, for example 'Women's Health Tonic Tea' or 'Sinus Trouble Tea'. Those are some basic examples, but of course you can get creative with names like 'Divination Dreams Tea' and so forth.

Then choosing from ingredients, it is helpful to look at the flavors and qualities of each plant. There are a few rules of thumb, such as not combining too many bitter or menthol plants in one blend, same with overly floral plants. Also, if there are too many 'green' and bland herbs, the tea may be not be terribly exciting, so be sure to include some good flavor herbs. Not too much spice either. Tea blends with 5-8 ingredients tend to work well. Theses make wonderful gifts and are beautiful to behold in a clear glass jar.

Appendix C

 # Poultices & Compresses

Applying herbs to the skin is a lost art in modern herbalism it seems. Many folks use a plantain poultice for a bee sting or something similar in the brush, but in comparison to people in the past, the use seems quite limited these days. In reading old recipe books centered around historical medicine, poulticing in particular was a large part of herbal treatment. Poultices were used for every ailment imaginable, from headaches, stomach maladies, broken bones, sprains, cramps, lung troubles… far beyond wounds and injuries to the skin. As they take more time to be reapplied throughout the day, are messy and require sitting for a time, it makes sense that modern folks would not prioritize this kind of application. However, there is old wisdom to be had with poulticing and it is effective, if one has the time and patience to enjoy the benefits of this timeless treatment. Here are some basic definitions and pointers for using poultices and compresses.

Poultice – A treatment in which a fresh plant or a dried plant (that has been rehydrated) is applied to the skin on a certain area of the body that is inflicted with an imbalance. Contact with the plant and the skin is made. Often times heat is used, in order to help with the healing process. Depending on the plant, it can be used fresh or dried. Many plants are most effective when used fresh, but this is not always possible.

When making a fresh plant poultice, heated whole leaves can be used or plants can be mashed up/macerated. To heat whole leaves, simply place them in boiling water for about 30 seconds. A mortar and pestle can be used to crush the plant material, with attention to keeping the juices with the poultice. Depending on the plant, our teeth can also be used to mash the plants, keeping the material close to our front teeth while grinding along with the juices. To rehydrate a plant for a poultice, add boiling water just enough to moisten, waiting then until the plant expands.

A poultice usually needs to be held in place and the body needs be still for a time in order for the plants to stay put and have an effect. A clean bandanna is helpful for this purpose, this can be tied in place on a limb or laid in place. Layers can be used, especially when heat is involved. It is important to change the poultice as needed and replace the herb with new material. Anywhere from 2-4 times a day seems reasonable, depending on the situation. Some plants may be irritating to the skin, so the poultice can be spread between layers of cotton and then applied, with one layer protecting the skin, an example being an old fashioned mustard 'plaster', which will burn the skin if left on for too long. A plaster is a form of a poultice, usually involving powdered plants mixed with liquid to make a spreadable paste that can be applied.

Compress – The method of using a strained infusion/decoction applied to a clean cloth for a poultice. This way, all of the plant material is strained out before the application, and there is no mess to deal with. This is similar to using a wash, except a compress is often applied hot and changed regularly throughout the day/night with new cloths. The compress is kept on the skin for 10-30 minutes, depending. Sometimes a compress is reapplied when cooled, 4-5 times in row, then covered for a time. A formentation is an older term used for a compress.

Old Recipes – Here are a few old poultice recipes that I include for their inspiration, it always amazes how people used plants long ago. Taken from '*Seventeenth Century English Recipe Books: Cooking, Physic and Chirurgery in the Works of Elizabeth Talbot Grey and Aletheia Talbot Howard*' Ashgate Publishers, edited by Betty S. Travitsky and Anne Lake Prescott, 2008.

Appendix C

'**For A Bruise** – *Take six spoonfuls of honey, a great handful of linseed, bruise these in a mortar, and boyle them in a pint of milk an hour, then strain it very hard and anoint your breast and stomach with it every morning and evening, and lay a red hose upon it.*'

'**A Very Good Medicine to Stay the Vomitting** – *Take of spare mince wormwood and red rose leaves dried, of each half a handful, of rye bread grated a good handful, boyle all these in red rose water and vinegar, till they be somewhat tender, then put it in a linen cloth, and lay it to the stomach as hot as you can endure it, heating it two or three times a day with such as it was boyled with.*'

'**For One that hath a Great Heat in his Temples or Cannot Sleep** – *Take the juice of houseleek, and of lettuce, of each spoonful, of womans milk six spoonfuls, put them together and set them upon a chaffing dish of coals and put thereto a piece of rosecake and lay it to your temples.*'

'**Against all Aches, and especially of a Womans Breast** – *Take milk and rose leaves, and set them on the fire, put thereto oatmeal and the oyle of roses, boyle them till they be thick, and lay it hot under the sore and renew it so till it be always hot.*'

'**For a Felon in the Joynts** – *Take rue, featherfew, boars grease, leaven, salt, honey, six leaves of sage, shred them altogether small, then beat them together, and lay it to the sore place.*'

'**For a Boil** – *Take the yolk of a new laid egg, a little English honey, put it into the shell to the yolk, put in as much wheat meal as to make it to spread, take one branch of rue, and one of featherfew, shred them very fine, and put it to the same medicine, stir them very well together, spread it upon a piece of leather, and lay it to the place grieved.*'

Appendix D

 Folk Tinctures

In herbal medicine, a solvent is a particular liquid that has the ability to extract certain phytochemicals from plants. Solvents commonly used to extract medicine from herbs are: water, wine, vinegar, milk, distilled alcohol (brandy, vodka, rum), vegetable glycerin, honey, oil, fat (butter, lard), pure grain alcohol (everclear). There are advantages and disadvantages of using each one. Taking into account the preservation properties of each solvent, the range of extracting ability for the particular herb, the overall expense of the solvent and the convenience of taking the extract are some of the things to consider when choosing your optimal solvent. Another important factor to consider is taste and personal preference.

Here I will describe the simple process of making folk style tinctures with alcohol. First, I will give a small preface to give a basic education surrounding tincture making nowadays. Tinctures are very popular in Western herbalism; they are convenient in that they require no preparation to ingest, they last for years on the shelf and they are a cost-effective way to make a small amount of plant material available in a concentrated form. They also present an application that makes dosage easier to control. For those interested in making 'scientific tinctures' with specific ratios and measurements, please see the book *Making Plant Medicine* by Richo Cech.

In plant medicine, a tincture can be simply defined as an herbal extract that has a variable ratio of both distilled alcohol and water. As both water and alcohol act as extracting solvents, they are used in tinctures in different combinations depending on what plant is being used. Usually the extract is at least 40% pure alcohol, with a minimum of 30% to preserve it. Many people use Everclear alcohol that is 95% pure grain alcohol as a base and add varying amounts of water to the menstruum in order to control the alcohol to water ratio. I stopped worrying about this many years ago, and find that Everclear is more of an industrial product that has no place in the human body. This is after some horrible experiences with Everclear based tinctures, not to mention the taste is ghastly! One can make perfectly therapeutic and good quality tinctures from 80 proof or 40 % alcohol. Modern culture often treats plants like drugs, and there is a belief that the more constituents we can extract from a plant, the better – I highly disagree. Just because something is 'natural', does not make it healthy.

Tincture Making – The Folk Method

When making 'folk tinctures' using vodka, a standard proof such as 80 proof (40% alcohol, 60% water) is used. I personally prefer to use vodka no stronger than 80 proof, as I am no longer interested in extracting all of the 'active constituents'. 80 proof brandy can also be used if desired, or any spirit for that matter. The simplest way to make a folk tincture is to take the appropriately sized glass canning jar, (pint or quart) depending on how to much material you have. Pack it mostly full of fresh crushed/chopped herbs (not to tightly) and then cover with the alcohol, shaking every day, letting the mixture steep for one month. For dried plants, fill any sized jar **half way** with cut and sifted (broken down and garbled) herbs, as they will expand, and add alcohol to fill. Simple! It's helpful to use the French canning jars for this, as their lids are mostly glass – mason jar lids can corrode and leave unwanted metals in the tincture. However if you use newer mason jar lids, this isn't too much of a problem.

A blender can be utilized with fresh plant material, once it's all measured out, but it's not necessary as long as you can chop well. Make sure to label and date the jar. Keep the tincture out of direct sunlight, shake daily and strain at the end of 4 weeks. If you are working with dried dense material, such as roots or berries, give the tincture 6 weeks. Store the finished tincture in a dark bottle out of the light, in a cupboard is ideal.

    Some important terms to know: The solvent is referred to as the **menstruum** and the process of steeping the herbs is known as **maceration**. When the tincture is ready to be strained, it can be done by using a sieve and a pressing cloth, (a clean white linen dishcloth). Use a glass measuring cup with a spout as the receptacle and set the strainer on it. Lay the open cloth over the strainer and pour it through. Squeeze the remainder of the mass through the cloth by pulling all the corners together and twisting to get the liquid out. This is a little disappointing with roots that were tinctured dry, as little gets expressed. Tinctures presses are available for an expense if you are a tincture maker in production. The dried out remainder in the cloth is known as the **marc**, and is generally discarded.

    Most fresh or dried plants tincture beautifully in 80 proof alcohol. Some plants make better water extracts/teas, such as demulcents like marshmallow root and comfrey, as well as nutritive herbs like nettles or red raspberry leaf. A general dose for a tincture that is not a low dose botanical or a laxative plant, is 1-2 dropperfuls, 3-5 times a day. I recommend starting with less instead of more. There are many herbalists who dose much lower and see results, as with using 3-5 drops a few times per day. Often our bodies are more sensitive than we give them credit for. Tinctures can be taken with a small mouthful of water or without dilution, I prefer the former. The shelf life for most tinctures is around 10 years, however some with a higher water content will only last 2 years.

Appendix E

 # Infused Honey

When infusing a honey with a plant, the intention is that the honey acts as a carrier for the effects of the herb. The honey takes on the flavor and the medicine from the herb chosen. Aromatic plants are preferred, plants that have a strong smell and flavor to them. It's important here to consider the quality of your honey before beginning the process. Buy the best you can afford for medicine. Local honey is amazing, a medium colored and flavored honey works well such as 'wildflower'. Darker honey can overpower the flavor of your herbs, but it is one's personal choice. Crystallized honey can be harder to work with but will melt down with some heat.

The Double Boiler Method

This method captures the plant essence without too much heat and still seems to preserve it enough without having to refrigerator it. This has only been true when using fresh flowers and/or leaves, roots require a slightly different approach, see below.

Simple Instructions for Fresh Flowers/Leaves/Conifer Tips –

Let the fresh plant wilt for 6-8 hours, laid out on a basket/screen/paper bag. Do not wash the plant. It will become more fragrant during this time. Depending on what part of the plant you use, it can be chopped lightly after wilting and before adding to a double boiler. I do not usually do this with flowers or leaves, only conifer fir tips. I prefer to use one plant at a time, not mixing them to enjoy each onto their own in the honey.

Using a glass double boiler, place the wilted plant material in the second chamber, with water in the bottom one. Cover the plant with honey, use less then you think at first. Only add enough to cover and hold the plant, not to drown it. Use a chop stick to stir it up. Heat the bottom chamber to a boil and then stir regularly for 3-5 minutes to help distribute the heat to the top chamber. Take the pots off the heat and set on a hot pad. Continue to stir every few minutes, as the water in the bottom chamber is still hot. The honey should liquefy and feel warm to your touch. Cover the pot with a lid and let sit overnight.

The next morning take off the lid and wipe off the condensation. Repeat this process three times total, on the third day when the honey is warm, strain through a fine strainer into jars. The marc (leftover honey and herbs) can be covered with a quart of boiling water and steeped for an amazing drink to enjoyed later that day. Or use it in a bath as bath tea. The infused honey itself will have its full flavor when totally cool, the next day is the best time to try the honey. Depending on the plants you use, the honey will be more or less liquid like because of introduced moisture.

Some favorites include: rose, sage flower, thyme, fragrant violet, fir or pine tips, peppermint leaf, vanilla bean, St. Johns wort bud/flower, cottonwood bud, alder bud, and lavender.

Fresh roots can be used as well, but they take a different method than above. The honey requires more cooking time to reduce the water content. A double boiler can be used but instead of heating just to warm the honey for five minutes, heat it on medium low for a few hours watching the water to make sure it doesn't run out. Remember never add cold water to a hot pan that is glass – it will break. Add boiling water carefully, or let it cool between adding water and heating again.

Another way to infuse honey in the summer time is by solar infusion. Wilt your herbs as previously mentioned and pour honey over the plant material to cover in a glass jar. Cap the jar and place it in a sunny spot. Everyday open the lid, wipe away any moisture that has accumulated and stir the plants in the honey with a chopstick. After a few weeks of hot weather, the honey should be well infused with the plant's qualities, take care to not overheat them. On a warm afternoon, strain through a fine sieve and store in clean jars. The cold honey will not strain well.

Herbal honeys can be used topically in skin preparations; rose and lavender infused honeys are helpful for burns and inflammation or irritation. Generally, they are best eaten by the spoonful or added to teas, though the flavor is easily lost. They make a lovely way to take plant medicine for those who cannot tolerate alcohol, also they are easy and require no preparation to ingest. They have a shelf life at room temperature for about 3 years. If fermentation or discoloration/mold ever occurs, discard.

Appendix F

Infused Vinegars & Oxymels

Making infused vinegars consists of choosing a type of vinegar and infusing it with fresh herbs and/or fruit and spices. These home infused vinegars can be used in cooking and make marvelous salad dressings and marinades for vegetables and meats. They can be used topically and cosmetically in diluted form, depending on the choice of herbs. They can be incorporated into other medicines, such as elixirs, honeys or syrups, and taken as tonics. Many people take vinegar straight or diluted in water or sparkling water.

For infused vinegars that are culinary in nature, choose vinegar that is clear. Apple cider vinegar results are muddy looking. White wine and red wine vinegar work well as does brown rice vinegar. If you are after purely medicinal effects, use apple cider vinegar.

The Simple Process

Choose a clear glass container, such as a mason or French canning jar. A French canning jar is preferred, because the lid is glass and will not corrode like a mason jar lid will. If all you have is a mason jar, use the newest lid available because if it is older and even slightly corroded, it will get much worse with the daily shaking of the vinegar and taint your batch. Fill the jar about 2/3 full with fresh fruit and/or chopped fresh herbs. Pour vinegar over the contents and stir with a chop stick. Close the lid and shake daily for a month to admire. If you want a strongly medicinal extract with just herbs, fill your jar mostly full with chopped plant material, fresh material is preferred.

Strain the mixture out in 4 weeks and bottle. Store your vinegars in a dark cupboard.

Making an Oxymel

Oxymels are a great way catch a plants medicine without using alcohol. They consist of apple cider vinegar and honey as a base. Many elixir recipes can be made into oxymels instead, with satisfying results. I find that oxymels are best made with fresh plant material. However, dried berries, such as elder or rosehips seem to work well. Experiment with dried if you like, but if you use fresh plant materials, make sure that it is wilted beforehand, or just chop the plant up well to break down the plants and let the flavors become more available to the solution.

Fill any sized mason jar ¾ full with the wilted/chopped plants. Then fill 2/3 full of vinegar and the last 1/3 full of honey. Leave an inch on top for shaking. Shake well every day and strain after 4 weeks. The honey may take a week or so to incorporate. Strain through a sieve, bottle and store in a dark place. Oxymels are intense with a vinegar flavor so dilute as needed or desired. Children will likely be found of this sweet and sour medicine. You can also incorporate fresh citrus peel, berries or fruit into them, which is like making an infused vinegar and adding honey.

Bibliography

Addison, Josephine. *The Illustrated Plant Lore*, Sidgwick and Jackson, 1985

Bairacli Levy, Juliette de. *Common Herbs for Natural Health*, Ash Tree Publishing, 1996

Baker, Margaret. *Discovering the Folklore of Plants*, Shire Publications LTD, 1969

Baker, Margaret. *Folklore and Customs of Rural England*, David and Charles Ltd, 1974

Baker, Margaret. *Gardeners Magic and Folklore*, Universe Books, 1978

Bevan-Jones, Robert. *Poisonous Plants – A Cultural and Social History*, Windgather Press, 2009

Boland, Bridget, *Gardeners Magic and Other Old Wives Lore*, Michael Omara, 1977

Boyer, Corinne *Under the Witching Tree*, Troy Books, 2017

Chamberlain, Mary. *Old Wives Tales*, The History Press, 1985

Culpeper, Nicholas. Culpeper's *Complete Herbal*, W. Foulsham and Co. Ltd. 1977, (1653)

Daniels, Cora and Paul Stevens. *Encyclopedia of Superstitions and Folklore, Volume 2*, W.H. Yewdale and Sons co., 1903

De Cleene, Marcel and Marie Claire Lejeune, *Compendium of Symbolic and Ritual Plants in Europe*, Volume one and two, Man and Culture Publishers, Belgium, 1999, 2000, 2003.

Ellacomb, Henry Nicholson. *The Plant-Lore and Garden-Craft of Shakespeare*, Bibliolife, (1884)

Folkard, Richard. *Plant Lore, Legends and Lyrics*, Forgotten Books, 2012 (1892)

Friend, Hilderic. *Flower Lore*, 1981 (1884)

Gårdbäck, Johannes Björn. *Trolldom – Spells and Methods of the Norse Folk Magic Tradition*, YIPPIE, 2015

Gordon, Lesley. *Green Magic*, Viking Press, 1977

Grieve, Maude. *A Modern Herbal – Volumes 1 and 2*, Dover, 1971 (1931)

Bibliography

Hatfield, Gabrielle and David Allen. *Medicinal Plants in Folk Tradition – The Ethnobotany of Britain and Ireland*, Timber Press, 2004

Hatfield, Gabrielle. *Encyclopedia of Folk Medicine*, ABC-CLIO Inc. 2004

Hatfield, Gabrielle. *Hatfield's Herbal*, Penguin Books, 2009

Hatfield, Gabrielle, *Country Remedies – The Survival Of East Anglia's Traditional Plant Medicines*, The Boydell Press, 2009(1994)

Jacob, Dorothy. *A Witch's Guide to Gardening*, Taplinger Publishing CO. 1964

Jones, Kelvin. *The Wise Woman*, Oakmagic Publications, 2012

Jones, Pamela. *Just Weeds – History, Myths and Uses*, Chapters Publishing, 1994.

Leland, Charles Godfrey. *Gypsy Sorcery and Fortune Telling*, Castle Books, 1995 (1891)

Maple, Eric. *The Secret Lore of Plants and Flowers*, Robert Hale Limited, 1980

Moerman, Daniel. *Native American Medicinal Plants*, Timber Press, 2009

Moss, Kay K, *Southern Folk Medicine* 1750-1820, University of South Carolina Press, 1999

Muller-Ebeling, Ratsch, Dieter Strol, *Witchcraft Medicine*, Inner Traditions, 1998

Opie and Tatem, *A Dictionary of Superstitions*, Oxford University Press, 1989

Pennick, Nigel. *Secrets of East Anglian Magic*, Capall Bann Publishing, 2004.

Pickering, David. *Cassell Dictionary of Superstitions*, Cassell Wellington House,1995

Pickering, David. *Cassell Dictionary of Witchcraft*, Cassell Wellington House, 1996

Pollington, Stephen. *Leechcraft – Early English Charms*, Plantlore and Healing, Anglo-Saxon Books, 2000

Radford, E. and M.A. *The Encyclopedia of Superstitions*, Metro Books, 1961

Ristic, Radomir. *Balkan Traditional Witchcraft*, Pendraig Publishing, 2009

Ryan, W.F. *The Bathhouse at Midnight*, The Pennsylvania State University Press, 1999

Silverman, Maida. *A City Herbal*, Random House, 1977.

Skinner, Charles M. *Myths and Legends of Flowers, Trees, Fruits and Plants*, Fredonia Books, 2002 (1911)

Thiselton Dyer, T.F. *The Mythic and Magickal Folklore of Plants*, Samhain Song Press, 2008 (1896)

Thompson, C.J.S *Magic and Healing*, Bell Publishing, 1989 (1940)

Thompson, C.J.S. *The Hand of Destiny*, Bell Publishing, 1989 (1932)

Thorpe, Benjamin. *Northern Mythology*, Wordsworth Editions, 2001 (1851)

Throop, Priscilla. *Hidegard von Bingen's Physica*, Healing Arts Press, 1998.

Trevelyan, Marie. *Folklore and Folk Stories of Wales*, EP Publishing Ltd.1973 (1909)

Vickery, Roy. *A Dictionary of Plant Lore*, Oxford University Press, 1995

Von Hausen, Wanja. *Gypsy Folk Medicine*, Sterling Publishing, 1992

Watts, D.C. *Elsevier's Dictionary of Plant Lore*, Academic Press, 2007

Wilde, Lady. *Legends, Charms and Superstitions of Ireland*, Dover, 2006 (1887)

Wright, Elbee. *Book of Legendary Spells*, Marlar Publishing, 1974.

www.wikipedia.com for current botanical nomenclature information

– About the Author –

Corinne Boyer is a folk herbalist, teacher, and writer with a passion for traditions surrounding plants and folk magic. She has been studying and working with plants since 1998. Corinne has taught community herb classes since 2005 and teaches weekly classes out of her home with a focus on wild crafting, medicine making, plant lore, folk medicine and traditional magic. She has been published in various journals with articles about plant lore and history. She created a free quarterly herbal newsletter called The Gathering Basket, which was distributed to her local community from 2012-2017. Her books include Under the Witching Tree and Under the Bramble Arch published by Troy Books and Plants of the Devil published by Three Hands Press. She lives with her family in the forests of the Pacific Northwest. Visit her website for more information at www.maplemistwood.com

Index

A
Abortion 27, 62, 65
Afterbirth 75, 207
Alabama 53, 85, 87, 206
All Hallows Eve 21, 23, 72, 86
American 33, 42, 50-51, 53, 61-62, 70, 81, 84-85, 87, 89-90, 104-105, 125, 153, 155, 196, 249
American folk medicine 89
Amulet 23, 34-35, 38-40, 43-44, 50, 54, 60-61, 64, 82, 87-90, 95, 102, 104, 127, 133, 135, 138, 143, 147, 157, 181, 192-193, 206, 222
Anemia 24, 28, 29, 113, 115-116, 133, 155, 184
Anglo-Saxon 23, 33, 43-44, 61, 76, 89, 110, 141-142, 144, 201, 206, 249
Antimicrobial 55, 216
Ants 64, 127
Appetite 42, 61, 117, 161, 198
Aries 50
Asia 69, 81, 121, 192, 201
Assumption Day 51
Asthma 24, 34, 41, 52, 54, 114, 125, 133, 145, 147, 155, 205, 209
Australia 102
Austria 183

B
Bad omen 103, 133
Balkan 60, 72, 103, 250
Balkans 20, 23, 24, 40, 44, 60, 72, 74, 94, 104
Banishing powders 45
Basil 52
Bear 9, 102, 111, 147
Belgium 167, 183, 193, 194-195, 223, 226, 248
Besom 93-99
Bewitchment 22, 102, 104, 183, 193
Birth 65, 74, 89, 97, 105-106, 157, 169, 172, 195-196, 227
Birthing 26
Blackberry 19-29, 113, 180
Blackthorn 21, 45
Blessing 11, 46, 90, 99, 159, 171, 204, 221
Bohemian 94, 166
Breast milk 41-42
Bridal chamber 22

Brigid 131
British Isles 70, 96, 180, 213, 222
Brittany 20, 88
Bronchitis 24, 52, 61, 76, 114, 125, 145, 155, 205, 207
Bruises 33, 53, 61, 105, 124, 145, 215
Butter churn 50, 152

C
Cancer 34, 41, 115, 124, 135, 168
Canker sores 117
Capricorn 39
Card playing 21
Catholic 51
Celtic 20, 102, 124, 176
Celts 82
Cemetery 54, 123
Ceremony 55, 104, 185
Charm 22-23, 29, 35, 44, 46-47, 51, 60, 63, 65-67, 71-75, 85, 94, 96, 102, 106, 110, 114, 132, 136, 143, 152, 159, 163-166, 171-172, 181-182, 184, 193, 195, 202-203, 221, 223-224
Cheshire 143
Chickens 21
Chilblains 33
Childbirth 24, 185, 191
Chimney 35, 65, 87
Christ 20, 96, 177
Christmas 70-72, 83, 85, 90, 95, 99, 152, 178, 183
Church 70, 72, 74, 83, 84, 96, 150, 165, 178
Cleansing 26, 27, 63, 106, 115, 125, 128, 169-170, 196-197
Coast Salish 25
Coffins 59
Conception 24, 51, 84, 224
Constipation 115, 117, 137
Consumption 52, 75, 195, 205
Convulsions 32, 104, 124
Cornish 98, 102-103, 110
Cornwall 22, 24, 70, 113, 154, 166, 220
Cottonwood 34, 244
Coughs 24, 52, 62, 76, 114, 125, 147, 168, 195, 215
Court 133, 203
Crossroads 152
Culpepper 32, 62, 195, 206, 214-215
Curse 23, 38, 69, 72, 152, 154, 197

252

Index

D
Dairy 73, 152
Dandruff 27, 105-106
Dark moon 34-35, 45, 64, 67, 171, 186, 189
Death omen 154, 180, 193
Defensive magic 26
Depression 41, 45-46, 137-138, 188, 199, 205, 209, 227
Devil 20-21, 23, 40, 43, 50, 70, 86, 102, 134, 150-151, 180-182, 193, 201, 214, 220, 222-223, 251
Devon 21, 24, 76, 87, 112, 178, 203
Dew 74, 110, 121, 167, 176, 182, 184, 204, 220
Diarrhea 24-25, 27, 53, 105, 144, 156, 184, 187, 195, 207, 215
Divination 34, 71-72, 85, 103, 110, 132, 135, 142, 153-154, 178-179, 196-197, 203-204, 229
Divinations 23, 26, 41, 51, 71-72, 202, 207, 223, 230
Dog rose 21, 26, 65, 175, 180-183
Donegal 134, 184, 204
Dorset 25, 113
Dream 11, 21, 41, 47, 70, 72, 98, 122, 132-133, 135, 146, 152-153, 167, 178, 196, 198, 203, 221, 226
Dreaming pillows 34
Druids 82, 164
Dunbartonshire 72
Dysentery 24, 105

E
Earache 52, 226
East Anglian 22, 135, 249
Easter 63, 95, 119, 123
Eczema 75-76, 105, 117, 170, 215, 217-218
Elf 86, 177
Elf shot 111
Elf-shot 39
Enemy 23, 65
England 20, 22, 24, 70-71, 82, 90, 94, 113-114, 123, 125, 142-143, 151, 166, 179, 180, 202, 205, 222-223, 225, 248
Epilepsy 40, 88-89, 195
Epileptic fits 51
Epiphany 71, 152
Equinox 122
Essex 40, 75, 88, 112, 134, 205
Estonian 38
Eve 21-23, 38, 50, 71-72, 77, 83, 85-86, 90, 99, 102, 119, 142, 151, 154, 165, 167, 169, 171-172, 177-179, 183, 189, 192-193, 202-204, 208, 220-221, 224, 229
Evil Eye 65, 193-194, 202, 225
Evil influences 26, 208, 223
Evil spirits 21-22, 38, 82, 87, 95, 151, 164, 183, 192-193, 207, 220-222, 227
Exeter 144

F
Faeries 23, 32, 86, 165, 202
Fenland 59, 134, 203
Fertility 26, 59-60, 62, 66, 81, 84, 86, 90, 96, 109-110, 114, 118, 122, 133-134, 167, 170, 224
Fever 34, 41, 43, 52-53, 55, 105, 134-135, 147, 153, 185, 204, 214
Fire 20, 23, 25, 29, 33, 35, 45, 47, 50-51, 56, 60-61, 63, 65, 67, 72, 77-78, 83, 85, 91, 99-100, 103, 111, 149, 151, 160, 182, 191, 208, 210, 220, 225-226, 229-230, 233, 239
Fishing 24, 52
Fleas 41, 60, 64, 123, 195
Flies 60, 142, 152, 192
Folktale 112, 150
Foxglove 49
France 50, 114, 133, 167, 180, 193, 223
Franconia 183
Frankincense 47
French 25, 74, 107, 115, 132, 151, 166, 185, 214, 241, 246
Frog 23
Full moon 26, 28-29, 35, 45-46, 55, 64, 66, 77-79, 87, 88, 90-91, 171, 197, 199, 204
Fumigations 26, 59, 123, 226

G
Gaelic 131, 223
Gambling 21, 165, 225
Genital sores 26
German 31, 38, 49, 51, 60, 72, 96, 133, 141, 152, 165-167, 180, 192-193, 201, 211
Germany 51, 73, 85, 87, 123, 151, 167, 175, 184, 205, 223, 225
Ghost 23, 96, 172
Ghosts 26
Goats 76
Good fortune 23, 66, 82, 165, 168, 170
Good Friday 94, 182
Gout 33, 53, 61-62, 76, 98, 104-105,

253

107, 156, 183
Grave dust 50
Graves 22, 40, 179-180
Graveyard 34, 70, 77, 91, 123, 156, 186, 203
Greek 25, 37, 43, 50, 59, 69, 87, 101, 121, 156, 176, 194, 201, 220
Grimoire 123
Guernsey 71, 95

H

Hair rinse 27, 53, 64, 106
Harvest 45, 54-55, 78, 99, 106-107, 117, 126-127, 136, 147, 158, 186, 189, 208, 216
Hauntings 63, 157, 197, 226-227
Hawthorn 74, 78, 81, 88, 118, 127, 207, 210, 216
Heartbreak 127, 185, 188
Heartburn 24, 115, 117, 185, 205
Hearth 51, 77, 86, 91, 98-99, 118
Heart trouble 25
Hebrides 202
Hell 20, 173
Hemorrhoids 33, 52, 113, 144-145, 156, 209, 215
Hesquiat tribe 25
Hildegard von Bingen 25, 42, 52, 62, 75, 95, 143, 145-156, 205
Holly 32, 70-71
Holy water 23, 71, 110
Holy Well 23
Honey 20, 24, 29, 44, 46, 54, 61, 85, 99, 107, 111, 115, 125, 127-129, 131, 137, 139, 144-145, 170, 181, 187-188, 198, 209, 211, 215, 227-228, 239, 240, 243-245, 247
Hoodoo 50
horse 32, 111, 118, 123, 142, 156, 222
Horseshoe 16
House doll 26
Hunting 85, 157, 185, 216
Hysterectomy 27

I

Icelandic 204
I-Ching 208
Ill wish 221
Immortality 70, 83
Infections 105, 146-147, 187, 209, 226-227
Invisible 11, 13, 16, 86, 157
Iowa 143
Ireland 12, 20-23, 32, 50, 53, 60-61, 63, 76, 81, 114, 133, 134-135, 145, 151, 164-165, 191, 201-202, 205, 213-215, 221, 225, 249-250
Irish 41, 69, 71, 74-75, 88, 97, 104-105, 109-110, 112, 131, 133, 142, 143, 149-150, 152, 154, 156, 164-165, 181, 205
Iron 28, 46, 60, 65, 73, 115-116, 137-138, 161, 206, 225, 235
Isle of Man 34, 112-113, 168, 225
Italy 60, 94, 166, 180, 224

J

Jaundice 22, 34, 61, 75, 88, 97, 113, 133, 155, 205, 226
Jesus 42, 203
John Gerard 51, 104
Jupiter 112, 121-122, 133, 179, 224

K

Kentucky 85
kidney stones 24, 133
Kittens 21
Kwaliutl tribe 25

L

Lammas Tide 46
Laurel 39
Leechdom 61, 111
Lice 64, 76, 98
Lightning 40, 46-47, 83, 87, 102, 145, 151, 183, 192-193, 223
Lincolnshire 24, 32, 83, 150
Livestock 38, 40, 51
Loki 82
Love magic 26, 39, 50, 72, 74, 77-78, 97, 103, 106, 127, 133, 186, 194

M

Magical cures 21, 74, 153
Magpie 86
Malevolent spirits 22
Mandrake 44, 95
Marigold 34, 133, 135
Marriage 72, 84-85, 99, 180, 194, 223
Mars 41, 96, 154, 205
May Day 103, 151, 167
May Eve 22, 77, 154, 167, 169, 203-204
Mecklenburg 38, 225
Medieval 39, 50, 59, 63, 72, 123-125, 204, 215
Mediterranean 177
Menses 116, 155, 182, 209
Menstruation 24, 27, 44, 51, 62, 64, 88, 226
Mercury 32
Mice 64

Index

Michaelmas day 19
Midsummer 7-8, 50, 102, 166-167, 169, 171-172, 178, 192, 201-202, 208, 210, 213, 217, 220-221, 223-224, 226, 229
Midwife 62
Midwinter 7, 67, 70, 77, 83, 90, 229
Milk 16, 22-23, 34, 39, 41-42, 46, 50, 52-54, 63, 73-74, 77, 87-88, 99, 105, 124, 133-135, 138, 139, 145, 152, 167, 183, 193, 202, 214-215, 239-240
Milking pail 22
Miscarriage 62, 184
Moon 26, 28-29, 34-35, 39-40, 45-47, 50, 55, 64-67, 74, 77-79, 85, 87-88, 90-91, 112, 135, 157, 159, 171, 186, 189, 197, 199, 202, 204, 211, 224
Moonlight 26, 46, 73, 78, 191
Mother Mary 40, 42, 50
Mourning 122-123, 186
Mumps 75, 155
N
Native Americans 25, 53, 155, 168, 184, 206, 215
New Year's Eve 71, 183
Nightmare 8, 46
Normandy 71, 88, 183
Norse Mythology 82, 220
Norway 24, 32
O
Oak 20, 29, 81-83, 86-90, 94, 135, 220
Ointment 25, 33, 61, 98, 113, 115, 156, 165, 168, 184, 197, 218
Ozark 33, 53
P
Pain 33-34, 42, 52-55, 62, 72, 88-89, 104-105, 125, 134, 137-138, 145-147, 150-151, 156, 168, 179, 182-185, 198, 205-209, 214, 225, 228
Painkiller 225
Pennsylvanian Dutch 113, 133, 168, 192, 221
Pennyroyal 44, 110
Pentagram 26
Peppermint 52, 235-236, 244
Persephone 87, 142
Pimples 25, 156
Pine 52, 122, 244
Plague 41, 75, 192
Pliny 24, 74, 82, 181, 184
Pneumonia 52
Poison 26, 40, 67, 113, 150-151, 186
Poisons 14, 39, 44, 84, 88-97, 150

Primroses 25, 221
Prophetic dreams 23, 34, 72, 78, 85, 135, 197, 202, 230
Protection 26, 29, 34, 38, 40, 46-47, 49-50, 60, 63-65, 73, 82, 90, 94, 98, 102, 150-151, 159-160, 169-170, 183, 186, 188, 192, 197, 220-221, 226
Prussia 39, 94
R
Rabbit 135
Rabbits 141
Rain 41, 49, 128, 131-132, 159, 175
Rheumatism 32-34, 53, 61, 97, 104, 156, 181, 194, 196, 205
Rickets 21
Ringworm 53, 75, 105, 156
Ritual 56
Roman 49, 74, 82, 112, 177
Romany 25, 38, 41, 61, 75, 97, 104, 113, 153, 182, 226
Rosaries 180
Rowan 20, 22, 73, 99, 226
Rue 45, 61, 94, 118, 203, 239
Russia 32, 40, 102, 226
S
Sabbat 50, 94
saint 71
Satan 40, 150, 204
Saturn 32, 41, 50, 70
Scandinavia 32
Scandinavian 39, 73, 133, 142, 151, 154, 181
scarecrow 152
Scotland 20, 24, 31, 37, 74, 86-88, 95, 98, 134-135, 142, 150, 180, 192, 202, 206, 213, 215, 221
Scottish Highlands 32, 41, 73, 113, 131
Scrofula 33
Sedative 34, 52
Shakespeare 21, 122, 248
Sheep 63, 76-77, 89, 109, 111
Slavia 224
Sleep 16, 23, 46, 52, 66-67, 72, 96-97, 124, 127, 132, 181, 193, 197, 202, 204, 206-207, 209, 227
Smoking blends 27, 55
Snake 31
Snakebite 105, 143, 226
Snow 35, 51
Somerset 24, 70, 74, 88, 113, 132
Sore throats 24, 184, 207
South Carolina 52, 249

255

Spell 23, 84, 86, 133, 150, 157, 165, 178, 179, 181, 210, 230
Spirit flail 22, 26
Spirits 11, 20-23, 26, 38-40, 46-47, 54, 71, 82, 87, 90-91, 95, 104, 114, 123, 136, 142, 151, 159-160, 164-165, 171, 183, 186, 192-193, 199, 202, 207, 220-222, 225, 227, 229
Spirit trap 22, 46, 160
St. George 38-39
St. john's wort 45
St. Johns Wort 8, 47, 221, 223, 225, 227, 229
St. Michael 20
Stomach troubles 24
Storm 45, 51, 223
Storms 45, 102, 223
Sweden 31-33, 85, 88, 154
Sweeping magic 22

T
Teasel 7, 37, 44-45, 47
Teething 32, 53, 74, 104-105
Teutonic 82
Thistle 37-42, 45-47, 64, 101-102, 110, 223
Thor 40, 70, 82, 102, 151
Thorns 15, 20, 26, 28, 45, 65, 118, 146, 157, 175-177, 179, 180-181, 185-186, 188, 206
Threshold 45, 60, 65, 72-73, 94-95, 170
Tonic 24, 27-29, 34, 54, 61, 97, 106-107, 113-117, 124, 125, 128, 133, 137, 147, 157-158, 170, 184, 187, 215-217, 225, 227
Toothache 24, 50, 61, 76, 89, 156, 168, 181-182, 205-206, 215, 226
Toxic 27, 31, 61-62, 69, 75, 85, 87, 107, 110-111, 208
Transference magic 21, 74-75, 105, 192, 214
Transylvania 152
Troll-shot 39
Tuberculosis 52, 156, 215
Tumors 34, 61, 88, 105, 225

U
Ulcers 24, 33, 134, 205, 215, 226
Unwanted lover 64

V
Vampires 44, 65
Venomous bites 25
Venus 24, 43-44, 60, 78, 82, 103, 122, 142, 168, 176-177, 179, 203, 214

Vertigo 32
Viking 37, 248
Vinegar 24, 28, 41, 52-53, 61, 75-76, 85, 89, 105, 107, 124-125, 127, 136-137, 144, 156, 184, 187-188, 211, 239-240, 246-247
Virgin Mary 177
Virgo 50

W
Wales 20, 44, 85, 96, 166, 179, 205, 224, 250
Waning moon 29, 45, 135
Wart 44, 75, 105, 135
Warts 33, 43, 52, 75, 105, 113
Wash 25, 26-27, 45, 53, 61, 64-65, 76, 89, 97, 107, 113, 143, 148, 155, 157, 168, 183-185, 187, 207-208, 215, 218, 228, 238, 243
Weather 33, 41, 51, 132, 167, 186, 223, 245
Weather oracle 41
Welsh 21, 40, 72-73, 75, 81, 83-84, 87-88, 94, 156, 179, 195
Whitlows 33
Whooping cough 22, 41, 74, 168, 181
Willow 55, 61, 127, 136, 214
Wine 17, 24, 28, 33-34, 44, 61, 74, 76, 85, 89, 98, 104, 113-114, 124, 127-128, 133-134, 137-139, 144, 160, 167-168, 173, 176, 179, 184, 188-189, 195, 197, 205-206, 214, 240, 246
Wise woman 134
Witches 20, 22, 35, 37, 39-40, 44, 49, 50, 55, 72, 77, 83, 94-95, 98-99, 118, 152, 164, 181, 191-193, 220-221, 223
Wizard 40, 69
Womb 29, 62, 64-67, 172, 216
Women's health 27, 191
Women's rites 26
Worcestershire 83, 134
Worms 25, 43-44, 61, 145, 156, 194, 215
Wormwood 191
Wounds 25-26, 37, 41, 53, 96, 105, 111-112, 135, 142-145, 156, 185, 201, 206, 208-209, 215, 218, 228-229, 237